SPY SHIPS

SPY SHIPS

One Hundred Years of Intelligence Collection by Ships and Submarines

Norman Polmar

Lee J. Mathers

Foreword by

Rear Admiral Thomas A. Brooks, U.S. Navy (Ret.)

POTOMAC BOOKS

An imprint of the University of Nebraska Press

Manufactured in the United States of America.

Except where noted, all photographs from author's collection.

Library of Congress Cataloging-in-Publication Data
Names: Polmar, Norman, author. | Mathers, Lee J, author. | Brooks, Thomas A., writer of foreword.
Title: Spy ships: one hundred years of intelligence collection by ships and submarines / Norman Polmar, Lee J Mathers; foreword by Thomas A. Brooks
Other titles: One hundred years of intelligence collection by ships and submarines
Description: [Lincoln]: Potomac Books, an imprint of the University of Nebraska Press, 2023 | Includes bibliographical references and index.
Identifiers: LCCN 2022043570
ISBN 9781640124752 (hardback)
ISBN 9781640125919 (ePub)
ISBN 9781640125926 (pdf)
Subjects: LCSH: Military intelligence—History. | Naval history, Modern—20th century. | Submarines (Ships)—History. | Submarine warfare—History. | Electronic intelligence—History. | Intelligence service. | BISAC: HISTORY / Military / Intelligence & Espionage | HISTORY / Military / Naval
Classification: LCC VB230 .P65 2023 | DDC 359.3/432—dc23/eng/20220927
LC record available at https://lccn.loc.gov/2022043570

CONTENTS

ILLUSTRATIONS

Photographs

Figures

FOREWORD

REAR ADMIRAL THOMAS A. BROOKS, U.S. NAVY (RET.)

Every maritime nation at times has used naval and merchant ships to collect intelligence. Ships often go places that might not be otherwise accessible, and their personnel can observe, obtain ground-level photography, meet with local officials, and conduct collection that even today's most sophisticated satellites could not accomplish. Thus, naval units often have "collateral duty intelligence officers," and selected merchant ships may have vetted crew members who can be called upon for collection. Submarines, which are covert by nature, are obvious candidates for accessing denied areas and making observations. Indeed, it would be a rare nuclear submarine that has never conducted reconnaissance or specific intelligence collection missions.

Surface naval ships and merchant ships periodically are used for collection, with specialized personnel taken on board and equipment sometimes installed, but these ships have limitations in their available space and operating areas. Submarine antenna and periscope heights limit their collection capability, while their space for specialized equipment is limited. Dedicated ships have been required for sophisticated, long-term afloat intelligence collection.

Spy ships at times masquerade as naval auxiliaries, research ships, and even fishing trawlers. During the Cold War, the United States operated more than two dozen such ships, while the Soviet Union operated some 100 units ranging in size from converted trawlers of 500 tons displacement to specially built ships of almost 5,000 tons. Soviet spy ships operated off the coasts of the United States and other countries of the North Atlantic Treaty Organization (NATO), in the approaches to Western strategic submarine bases, and wherever a Western/NATO fleet exercise was taking place. During the Vietnam War, those intelligence collectors operated off the island of Guam, where they could observe U.S. B-52 bomber activity, and in the Tonkin Gulf to intercept tactical communications of U.S. naval ships.

The best-known U.S. spy ships—unfortunately—were the USS *Liberty* and USS *Pueblo*. The authors of this book provide carefully researched, succinct, and objective analyses of the *Liberty* and *Pueblo* incidents, both of which are likely to remain controversial for the foreseeable future.

Because most countries have never openly admitted to operating spy ships, putting together a compendium of such ships and their operations presents a major challenge—thus explaining why there has not previously been a serious book on this subject. With painstaking research, authors Norman Polmar, my longtime friend and associate, and Lee Mathers have made a unique and valuable contribution to the literature of naval operations and to intelligence history.

PERSPECTIVE

Ships have been used for intelligence collection for thousands of years and continue to be employed in that role today. Early in the twentieth century, the development of radio and, subsequently, radar led to the use of ships to intercept those transmissions and eventually to the development of specialized intelligence ships—*spy ships*. Those specialized ships as well as submarines employed for intelligence collection have had a major impact on national policies and on military operations.

Almost from the start of man sailing the seas, he has used ships for spying. For many centuries, ships would sail along enemy coasts and poke into enemy harbors to look for threats and opportunities, and often they would carry spies to land on enemy shores. In the era of Napoleon and Nelson in the late 18th and early 19th centuries—in the age of sail—"the frigate was to be the 'eyes' of the fleet, trying to identify where the enemy was, what they were doing, and then communicating that information to larger fleet units."[1]

In a letter to the First Lord of the Admiralty in 1798, Vice-Admiral Horatio Nelson wrote: "Was I to die this moment, 'Want of Frigates' would be found stamped on my heart. No words of mine can express what I have, and am suffering for want of them."

During that era, those British frigates—and other British sailing craft—also spied on the French coastal semaphore signal towers, especially those along the Mediterranean coasts. Although their semaphore signals were in code, the British often captured code-related documents when seizing French ships. When the towers were no longer useful to the British, the ships would send ashore sailors or marines to blow them up. The British had a similar system of signaling towers in a chain from London to the main fleet anchorage at Portsmouth, but French ships rarely were in a position to observe them.[2] (The subsequent development of the electrical telegraph rendered such mechanical systems almost instantly redundant, and they quickly were discarded.)

In the 18th and early 19th centuries, a method of intelligence collection that was very useful to navies was primarily in the realm of a nation's diplomatic establishment. Intelligence was obtained by making diplomatic contacts, conducting on-scene observations, reading the local press, recruiting local agents, and opening the mails (especially diplomatic, when it could be accessed). Within the fleets—beyond the frigate or sloop observing activities in an enemy harbor—at times an enemy ship could be intercepted and seized before her officers could gather their codes and correspondence, and throw them over the side in a weighted bag.

Spying at sea would change radically in the twentieth century with the advent of radio—initially called wireless—and the efforts to intercept those transmissions. As radios were installed in naval and civilian ships at the start of the century, a major problem arose for navies: A message sent out through the air could be received by almost anyone with a wireless set who was within transmission range. In those early days of radio with the "spark" system and primitive receivers, one could not tune the transmitter to a specific station to the exclusion of all others.[3]

For example, in February 1904, when conflict broke out in the Far East between Russia and Japan, it marked the first time that both opposing fleets employed wireless communications while preparing for battle and in combat. Reportedly, as the Russian fleet was being prepared for that conflict, the British second-class cruiser *Diana*, at the time in the Suez Canal, intercepted the radio signals Russia sent out for the mobilization of the fleet.[4]

The coming conflict introduced the concept of electronic warfare. On the morning of 14 April 1904, the Japanese armored cruisers *Kasuga* and *Nisshin* carried out a long-range bombardment of the Russian base at Port Arthur in Manchuria with 10-inch (255-mm) and 8-inch (203-mm) guns.[5] A Japanese destroyer was sent inshore to spot the fall of shot and to call corrections to the cruisers by radio. A Russian wireless operator at a shore station listening for enemy radio transmissions heard the Japanese signals and pressed the key of his own spark transmitter to jam those signals.

As a result of that jamming effort, the Japanese bombardment caused little damage and few casualties.

The wireless jamming at Port Author was the first recorded use of electronic warfare in combat. On another occasion in that conflict, a Russian squadron sent out on a raid was able to deduce from intercepted Japanese radio traffic that it had been detected and was able to avoid steaming into a trap.[6] Those were the first examples of the impact that electronic warfare could have on naval operations. The Russian commanders usually preferred to conceal their presence by maintaining radio silence, and when possible they would attempt to listen to and exploit Japanese transmissions and on rare occasions to jam them. Despite those efforts, the Russians were decisively defeated in the overwhelming Japanese naval victory in Tsushima Strait—between Honshu, Japan, and the Korean Peninsula—in May 1905.

Also, beginning in the early 1900s, in peacetime, available warships and even the naval auxiliaries of several nations that were sent on normal cruises into foreign waters were fitted with radio intercept equipment and carried specialist technicians. Thus, when visiting foreign ports or observing naval exercises at times, those ships were able to gain useful intelligence by intercepting radio transmissions.

The Russians continued to use land-based radio intercept stations to support their naval operations and established radio intelligence posts within the Baltic and Black Sea areas by August 1914, when World War I erupted. Several naval officers fluent in German and with experience in cipher work were assigned to those intercept stations. The intelligence thus gained from their intercepts of German and Turkish radio communications helped guide several successful operations by Russian warships until the revolution was ignited in 1917.[7]

The First World War

World War I (1914–18) was the first conflict in which all the belligerents made widespread use of radio communications both ashore and at sea. From the outset there were attempts at radio jamming. On 4 August 1914, the day before Britain entered the war on the side of Belgium and France against Germany and Austria, the British battle cruisers *Indomitable* and *Indefatigable* passed close to the German cruisers *Goeben* and *Breslau* in the Mediterranean. Both forces were moving at high speed, neither knowing whether the other was likely to open fire. No shots were fired. The German force commander, Admiral Wilhelm Souchen, later wrote, "The British cruisers merely attempted to jam systematically our wireless communications."[8]

Radio messages to and from ships at sea obviously could be received, or read, by those for whom they were intended and by the enemy as well—whomever was within range. Historian Robert M. Grant, in addressing the communications in that period, wrote:

> Secret messages are usually made secret in two ways. First, they are "coded." This means that a message is translated into a highly artificial language by means of a codebook used by the sender and the receiver. Second, they are "enciphered." The language of the codebook is modified by substitutions and alterations of various kinds, In order to break into an enciphered message one must first decipher and then decode it. The whole process is sometimes called "decryption."[9]

Shortly after World War I began, German U-boats attacked British and French merchant shipping. In response, beginning in September 1914, the British established radio intercept stations ashore in an attempt to listen to the German shore-to-submarine and submarine-to-submarine communications. Soon fourteen ground intercept stations were operating in the British Isles, all with direct land telegraph lines to the Admiralty in London, plus an intercept facility on the island of Malta in the Mediterranean and two sites in Italy: Anconia and Otranto.[10]

The British were able to greatly exploit the German Navy's radio communications through an outstanding code-breaking effort. The Royal Navy's code-breaking efforts—centralized in Room 40 of the Admiralty headquarters in London—benefited from the capture of German codes, including the fortuitous recovery of a codebook from a German warship by the Russians. That success occurred when the German light cruiser *Magdeburg* ran aground in the Gulf of Finland on 26 August 1914; the Russians seized her and recovered three German codebooks, one of which they passed to the

British in October 1914.[11] (Apparently the British made little if any use of shipboard radio intercept capabilities during the conflict.)

During World War I, the submarine became a principal weapon of war at sea. The advent of submarines provided still another intelligence platform, although they made less of a contribution as spy ships than could surface ships because of their limited electronic equipment and their need to remain submerged when in hostile waters. Among the notable submarine intelligence efforts were British and Australian submarines conducting surveillance in the Turkish Straits–Dardanelles area in World War I, Russian submarines landing scouting parties in the Black Sea area in 1916, and U.S. submarines running numerous reconnaissance missions against the Japanese in the Western Pacific in World War II.

World War II

In the Battle of the Atlantic during World War II (1939–45), the German shore-based intercept stations were able to use High-Frequency/Direction-Finding (HF/DF) to locate Allied convoys through their radio transmissions and then direct U-boat attacks on those British and U.S. merchant ships. At the same time, Allied escort ships employed HF/DF to detect German submarines.[12] Captain Donald Macintyre, Britain's leading "U-boat killer," wrote that during the war,

> ship-borne direction-finding, H/F D/F or "Huff-Duff" as it was called, had by now [mid-1943] attained efficiency, in trained hands, which could give reliable warning of a threat to a convoy.
>
> Provided therefore that the H/F D/F set was listening on the frequency selected by the U-boat, or provided there was a sufficient number of sets in the escort group to cover all of the frequencies used by the U-boats, these reports would be intercepted and . . . were an immediate indication that the convoy was being shadowed or attacked by a U-boat. As the bearing could also be obtained it was then possible to send out an escort or an aircraft out to hunt for the U-boat in its estimated position and keep it down while the convoy steered a drastically new course.[13]

During World War II, the Germans used radio communications extensively to and from U-boats and shore stations, and between submarines at sea. The large number of circuits for serving all areas in which U-boats were operating—from the Caribbean to the Indian Ocean and throughout the North Atlantic—facilitated Allied HF/DF and interceptions.

In August 1944, the Germans began using the Kurier, a system of high-speed "flash" transmissions using special sending and receiving equipment to communicate with U-boats. Kurier was almost impossible to intercept by Allied facilities. The German system could send about ten letters of encoded text in a couple of seconds. (The Kurier system reappeared during the Cold War when, in the early 1960s, the Soviet Navy developed burst encoding systems for its own submarine communications.)

The Cold War

As the Cold War evolved after World War II, the Soviet Union and then the United States developed specialized intelligence collection ships. Those ships spied on potential enemy and neutral communications and other electronic emissions, observed naval exercises, and, subsequently, intercepted telemetry links during missile tests and space events, such as orbiting reconnaissance satellites. Their spy ships and submarines also undertook major at-sea efforts to collect equipment and debris from the missiles and torpedo tests.

In many respects, the Cold War—the Soviet Union and its Eastern European allies against the Western states—was unique. Historian Michael A. Palmer wrote: "During the Cold War no major fleets contested by force the control of the sea. For more than forty years, the Soviet and American navies stalked each other on, above, and under the surface of the world's seas in preparation for a conflict that never came."[14]

On occasion, warships also were used to glean intelligence when visiting foreign ports. For example, when the Soviet cruiser *Ordzhenikidze* carried Premier Nikita Khrushchev to England in April 1956, the ship carried a team of electronic intercept specialists. (During the cruiser's visit to Portsmouth, British Commander Lionel [Buster] Crabb was decapitated, apparently while examining the ship's underwater hull. It is widely believed that he was detected while near the ship and killed by the Soviets.[15])

Intelligence collection—spying—was a major factor in the 45

years of Cold War confrontation between the United States and its allies and the Soviet Union and its followers. Naval ships and submarines served as vital intelligence collectors in that period, although both the United States and the Soviet Union (and afterward Russia) had also extensively developed land-based communications intercept stations, specialized aircraft, and, subsequently, satellites as major gatherers of intelligence. (The first U.S. Electronic Intelligence [ELINT] satellite was the Navy's GRAB project, initially orbited in June 1960; the Soviet Union orbited its first ELINT and ocean surveillance satellites in 1970.[16]) Surface ships and submarines continued to serve as important intelligence collectors when this volume went to press.

This study of spy ships concentrates on the efforts and programs of the Soviet Union/Russia and the United States; the characteristics of their intelligence collection ships are provided in appendixes A and B, respectively. Several other navies and government agencies have operated intelligence ships, generally in "ones" and "twos" except for China and Norway. Both of those nations have sailed significant numbers of those ships, some of large size with extensive capabilities. China has become a major maritime power in the twenty-first century, with special interests in the South China Sea and with increasing hostility toward the United States. Norway, a member of the North Atlantic Treaty Organization, has occupied a critical location on the western maritime border of the Soviet Union/Russia. Those Chinese and Norwegian intelligence collection ships, as well as those of several other countries, are addressed in appendix C of this work.

ACKNOWLEDGMENTS

The authors are in debt to many individuals for their assistance in this project, especially:

Captain 3rd Rank Nikolai Artamonov (aka Nicholas Shadrin), Soviet Navy

A. D. Baker III, author and former intelligence analyst

Rear Admiral Thomas A. Brooks, USN—director of Naval Intelligence, historian, and author

Dr. A. Jay Cristol, captain, USNR—historian and author

Vice Admiral Robert Dunn, USN—deputy chief of naval operations (air) and aircraft carrier commander

Vice Admiral Donald Engen, USN—director of the National Air and Space Museum, carrier commander, and author

Robert Richard Fredlund Jr., executive officer of the USS *Banner*

Vice Admiral F. J. Harlfinger, USN—director of Naval Intelligence and submarine commander

Keith Jacobs, Soviet and Chinese military analyst

Tohru Kizu, managing director of Kaijinsha Co.

Marvin E. Nowicki, U.S. Naval Security Group intercept operator

Dr. Dominic A. Paolucci, captain, USN—submarine commander, naval analyst, and author

Bernard Prézelin, longtime editor of *Flottes de Combat*

Commander Jonathan (Jonty) Powis, Royal Navy, submarine commander

Rear Admiral Micha Ram, Israeli Navy—commander in chief and missile boat commander

Dr. David A. Rosenberg, captain, USNR—naval analyst, historian, and author

Bruce Rule, senior Sound Surveillance System (SOSUS) analyst

Alexandre Sheldon-Duplaix, historian and author

Yasumitsu Takada, editor, *Ships of the World*

Dr. Don Walsh, captain, USN—submarine commander, author, and Navy hydronaut No. 1

Matt Zullo, Naval Security Group operator and author

Also most helpful have been University of Nebraska Press staffers Taylor Rothgeb, Tom Swanson, Andrea Shahan, Ann Baker, and Leif Milliken.

ABBREVIATIONS

CCB	Communications Ship (*see* SSV)
CIA	Central Intelligence Agency (U.S.)
CNO	Chief of Naval Operations
COMINT	Communications Intelligence
DF	Direction-Finding
DIA	Defense Intelligence Agency (U.S.)
DSSP	Deep Submergence Systems Project (U.S.)
ELINT	Electronic Intelligence
FS	Freight and Supply (U.S. Army)
GRU	Glavnoye Razvedyvatelnoye Upravlenie (Main Intelligence Directorate) (Soviet/Russian)
GS	*Gidrograficheskoye Sudno* (hydrographic ship)
GUGI	Glavnoye Upravleniye Glubokovodnykh Issledovaniyx (Main Directorate of Deep-Sea Research)
GUPPY	Greater Underwater Propulsion Project (U.S.)
HF/DF	High-Frequency/Direction-Finding
HMS	Her/His Majesty's Ship (British)
HSV	High-Speed Vessel
IDF	Israel Defense Forces
KGB	Komitet Gosudarstvennoy Bezopasnosti (Committee for State Security) (Soviet)
MRIS	Missile Range Instrumentation Ship
MSTS	Military Sea Transportation Service (U.S.)
NATO	North Atlantic Treaty Organization
NGA	National Geospatial Agency (U.S.)
n.mile	nautical mile (1.15 statute miles)
NSA	National Security Agency (U.S.)
NSG	Naval Security Group (U.S.)

NURO	National Underwater Reconnaissance Office (U.S.)
OP-( )	Office of the Chief of Naval Operations (U.S.)
RIMPAC	Rim of the Pacific (exercise)
RIU	Radio Intelligence Units
SESS	Space Events Support Ship
SIGINT	Signals Intelligence
SNCP	Special Naval Collection Program
SOD	SIGINT Operations Department
SOSS	Soviet Ocean Surveillance System
SOSUS	Sound Surveillance System
SSV	*Svyazi Sudno* (communications ship)
SURTASS	Surveillance Towed Array Sensor System
SWATH	Small Waterplane-Area Twin Hull
TRS	Technical Research Ship
TELINT	Telemetry Intelligence
USNS	United States Naval Ship (MSTS/MSC)
USS	United States Ship

U.S. NAVY SHIP AND SUBMARINE DESIGNATIONS

U.S. Navy ships and Coast Guard cutters have alfa-numeric designations originally based on Navy General Order 541 of 17 July 1920 that prescribed ship designations. Many designations since have been added and deleted. The following designations apply to the U.S. Navy and Coast Guard ships and submarines cited in this volume.

The prefix "T-" indicates a civilian-manned ship operated by the Navy's Military Sealift Command, previously the Military Sea Transportation Service. The prefix "W" indicates a Coast Guard ship (designated "cutter" by the Coast Guard).

AE	ammunition ship
AG	miscellaneous auxiliary
AGB	icebreaker
AGER	environmental research ship
AGI	miscellaneous auxiliary intelligence
AGM	missile range instrumentation ship
AGOS	ocean surveillance ship
AGS	surveying ship
AGTR	technical research ship
AK	cargo ship
AKA	attack cargo ship
AKL	light cargo ship
AKV	cargo ship and aircraft ferry
AM	minesweeper
ARD	auxiliary repair dock
ARL	repair ship—landing craft
AS	submarine tender
ASR	submarine rescue ship

ATF	fleet tug
BB	battleship
CA	(1) armored cruiser; (2) heavy cruiser
CL	light cruiser
CLG	guided missile light cruiser
CV	aircraft carrier
CVA	attack aircraft carrier
CVAN	attack aircraft carrier (nuclear propulsion)
DD	destroyer
DDG	guided missile destroyer
DE	destroyer escort
DER	radar picket destroyer escort
DSRV	deep-submergence rescue vehicle
DSSV	deep-submergence search vehicle
DSV	deep-submergence vehicle
FF	frigate
IX	unclassified—miscellaneous
LPH	amphibious assault ship
LST	tank landing ship
PG	gunboat
PR	river gunboat
PY	gunboat (converted yacht)
SS	submarine
SSBN	ballistic missile submarine (nuclear propulsion)
SSGN	guided missile submarine (nuclear propulsion)
SSN	attack submarine (nuclear propulsion)

SPY SHIPS

1

The Dawn of Spy Ships

The first spy ships of the modern or electronics era were U.S. Navy and Imperial Japanese Navy ships carrying especially trained operators during the 1920s and 1930s who sought to monitor foreign radio communications. The earlier use of ships for intelligence collection lacked the primary means of modern, technological espionage—the interception of electromagnetic transmissions (radio, radar, laser, etc.)—to obtain information that the target nation wanted to keep secret.

Communications Intercept

During World War I, the U.S. Army and Navy had very different exposures to the arts and science of electronic warfare. Arriving in France in 1917, the American Expeditionary Force was welcomed with enthusiasm by the French Army, which not only trained radio intercept teams of the U.S. Army's Signal Intelligence Service but also provided equipment and access to the years of French code-breaking experience.

The U.S. Navy had established the Code and Signal Section within the Office of the Chief of Naval Operations in 1916.[1] Following the United States' entry into the war in April 1917, the U.S. Navy's signals intelligence effort received very little support from the British, sharply contrasting with the close relationship that the U.S. Army had with the French.

However, Rear Admiral William S. Sims, the commander of U.S. naval forces in Europe, did receive the daily intelligence summary from the Royal Navy's intelligence staff under Captain William R.

(Blinker) Hall. Still, Hall refused to share Britain's code-breaking expertise with the Americans.[2]

Subsequently, in July 1922, the U.S. Navy's director of communications formally established OP-20-G—then called the Research Desk—with the primary goal of breaking into foreign codes and developing an understanding of their weaknesses and vulnerabilities to help in developing U.S. Navy codes that would be more secure against decryption efforts. The OP-20-G office was not originally envisioned as a source of foreign military intelligence; thus, it was placed under the Navy's communication branch rather than the intelligence office.[3]

Asiatic Fleet Efforts

The first application of electronic spying from U.S. Navy ships was initiated by OP-20-G in efforts to establish radio intercept sites in the Asiatic Fleet area. In 1923 the chief of naval operations (CNO) requested that ships of the Asiatic and Pacific Fleets and Navy shore radio facilities "listen in" to foreign encrypted radio traffic.

That effort targeted Japanese military communications, which were mostly katakana transmissions—katakana being Japanese syllabary, similar to an alphabet, but with each symbol representing a consonant-vowel pair. U.S. Navy radiomen began self-training to recognize and intercept katakana on the U.S. Asiatic Fleet's flagship, the armored cruiser *Pittsburgh* (CA 4); on the alternative fleet flagship, the armed yacht *Isabel* (PY 10); and at the Fourth Marine Regiment's headquarters in Shanghai.[4]

In 1924 Lieutenant Laurance F. Safford of OP-20-G purchased four Underwood katakana typewriters and sent three of them immediately to the Far East: one each to the Navy's radio station in Shanghai; the armored cruiser *Huron* (CA 9), then serving as the Asiatic Fleet's flagship; and the destroyer *Pruitt* (DD 347).[5] Those devices were invaluable in recoding radio intercepts.

In 1925 a U.S. Navy land-based Pacific intercept station was established at Wailupe, Oahu, in the Hawaiian Islands (called Station Hypo). A year later additional Navy radio intercept stations were set up in Peking (Beijing), China; on the island of Guam; in San Francisco; and on the minesweeper *Bittern* (AM 36), which then was operating in Chinese and Philippine waters. In 1927 the shore

Photo 1. Serving as the U.S. Asiatic Fleet's flagship in the 1920s, the armored cruiser *Pittsburgh* (CA 4) carried specialists attempting to intercept Japanese naval communications. The development of radio and subsequently radar led to the development of electronic intercept efforts by almost all the world's navies. / U.S. Navy.

station at Shanghai (Station Able) was transferred to the Navy station ship based there—first to the cargo ship *General Alava* (AG 5) and then to the gunboat *Monocacy* (PG 20).[6]

Lieutenant Commander Ellis M. Zacharias—a former assistant U.S. naval attaché in Tokyo, an intelligence officer, and a Japanese linguist—was assigned to the American Consulate in Shanghai in 1926 and given temporary command of the destroyer *McCormick* (DD 223) serving in Chinese waters. During a transit from Chefoo, China, to Hong Kong, the *McCormick* conducted radio intercepts against Japanese naval communications as a test of the Asiatic Fleet's intercept capabilities.

Zacharias was excited by the intercept potential demonstrated by the test and requested that specially trained radio operators be dispatched to the Far East to monitor the Japanese Navy's forthcoming, 1927 triannual fleet maneuvers. Based on the *McCormick* intercepts, Zacharias wrote the first comprehensive intelligence report on the Japanese Fleet while never having come within visual distance of any of the exercising Japanese ships.[7] Also included in the report was his opinion that Japanese Navy radio operators were undisciplined and did not use high frequencies, and he commented on the U.S. Navy's need to develop high-frequency/direction-finding capabilities in the Far East.[8]

Navy intercept teams from Peiping (Beijing) sailed aboard the light cruisers *Memphis* (CL 13) and *Trenton* (CL 11) off the coast of China in September 1928, seeking to evaluate the ability of warships to operate as intercept sites while in transit.[9] The former Shanghai station ship—the gunboat *Monocacy*—moved to Guam in March 1929, and the Navy/Marine intercept station at Shanghai shifted ashore to the American Embassy in Peking. It operated there until July 1934, when it moved back to Shanghai, where it continued to operate ashore until December 1940.[10]

Radio intercept personnel from Guam (Station Baker) departed on the armed yacht *Isabel* in October 1929 to survey several locations in the Philippines for an additional intercept station. They selected the Olongapo Navy Yard at Subic Bay. The intercept group subsequently moved to Mariveles (1935), then to Cavite (1936), and, finally, to the island of Corregidor in Manila Bay (1939). Designated Station Cast, it evolved into the Navy's most capable signals intelligence intercept station west of Hawaii.

As the time neared for the triannual Japanese Fleet maneuvers of 1930, the U.S. Navy had established radio intercept stations at Peking, Hawaii, Guam, and Olongapo, as well as afloat intercept teams on the cargo ship *Gold Star* (AG 12) operating out of Guam and on the Asiatic Fleet flagship, the heavy cruiser *Augusta* (CA 31), usually sailing off the coast of China.[11]

Those Asiatic Fleet intercept stations in the 1920s and 1930s were not operationally interconnected. They acted independently under the overall coordination of the Asiatic Fleet staff (on the fleet flagship) and independently recorded intercepts of Japanese Navy radio transmissions. They sent their intercepts by courier or registered mail to the Navy Department in Washington DC for decryption, review, and analysis.

The Japanese naval maneuvers of 1930 revealed a simulated defense of the Western Pacific against the U.S. Fleet and involved a complete mobilization of the Japanese Navy, local defense forces, and the naval shore establishment. Decrypts revealed a simulated capture of Guam and the Philippines, and a defense against a U.S. air strike on Tokyo. The decryptions also suggested that the Japanese had accomplished accurate high-frequency/direction-finding from a moving ship—ten years ahead of the U.S. Navy.[12] (As early as 1921, during the Washington Naval Conference, the American "Black Chamber" cryptographic team had been reading the Japanese government/diplomatic ciphers; that effort continued into World War II.)

Asiatic Spy Ships

In 1932 the commander of the U.S. Asiatic Fleet noted that his only active intercept sites were in Peking, on Guam, and on the heavy cruiser *Houston* (CA 30), his flagship. The Hawaii intercept station remained active in the Pacific Fleet area.

Just prior to the 1933 Japanese fleet maneuvers, the U.S. Navy reached an arrangement with the Dollar Steamship Line to host Navy personnel on its ships to obtain increased coverage of Japanese radio traffic. A 1932 trial run on board a Dollar Steamship Line passenger ship by Radioman 2nd Class James Pearson was shown to have great potential and resulted in the 1933–34 arrangements with the Dollar Line. The firm agreed to embark a Navy communications intercept operator plus a four-man team from the U.S. Weather Bureau to cover the Japanese fleet maneuvers of 1933 and on cross-Pacific round trips in 1933–34.[13]

With great-circle transits from Seattle, along the eastern coast of Japan, and ending in Manila, each Dollar Line transit had ports calls that included Yokohama, Kobe, Nagasaki, Nagoya, and/or Shimizu in Japan, and Shanghai and/or Hong Kong in China.

The round trip averaged 44 days. That program provided the U.S. Navy with unique exposure to low-power Japanese naval communications. U.S. Navy intercept operators participated in more than a score of round trips during a 13-month period on five different ocean liners. Upon completion of each voyage, the communications intercepts along with an analytic summary were sent directly to the Navy's headquarters in Washington via registered mail. In that incarnation of a spy ship, the Dollar Ship program lacked direction-finding capabilities.[14]

And Japanese Efforts

The Tokumu Han (Special Section) in the Communications Department of the Navy's General Staff in the 1920s concentrated on deciphering Chinese communications.[15] The Navy analysts found that the Chinese ciphers were based on a simple, commercial codebook. China had become the prime target for Japanese espionage in the 1920s, not only because of interests in that country, but also for intelligence related to the great powers that were grabbing territory and seeking to influence the Chinese government. Those exploiters included the United States, Britain, France, Germany, and Italy.

Significantly, the Tokumu Han cryptanalysts failed to break into the relatively simple codes used by the U.S. State Department and Navy, although they briefly could read the communications of the U.S. naval attaché in Peking. A young naval officer, Hideya Morikawa, led a nighttime break into the American Consulate in Kobe and obtained photographs of certain U.S. codes and the M-138 cipher machine.[16]

In 1924 the Japanese Navy equipped a cruiser and the specially outfitted intelligence collection ship *Sata* to monitor segments of the successive U.S. fleet exercises off Hawaii. That effort had only limited success. The U.S. Navy used two-digit substitution codes for the exercises that were not difficult to solve provided that sufficient coded messages were intercepted.

However, while the Japanese ships could intercept the U.S. Navy's medium- and long-wave radio transmissions, in the early 1930s they had no receivers for shortwave (high-frequency) transmissions. Because the U.S. Navy reflected shortwave transmissions from the West Coast off of the airship *Shenandoah* to the fleet, the Japanese could not tap into that source of intelligence.

By the 1930s the Japanese had established radio intercept and direction-finding stations at the following:

Bako (island off the western coast of Formosa/Taiwan, now Magong)

Ashizuri (end of the Japanese home island of Shikoku)

Hamamatsu (southeast of Yokohama on Honshu)

Owada (near Tokyo)

In time those intercept efforts were able to provide the Japanese with an almost complete understanding of the U.S. Navy's War Plan Orange—the secret plan for fighting a Pacific war!

To monitor the U.S. fleet exercises of 1932, the Japanese outfitted the innocuous oil tanker *Erimo* with "banks of sophisticated electronic equipment humming below decks."[17] Throughout the month of March, the Japanese intercept operators monitored Fleet Problem XIII in Hawaiian waters. From the analysis of signal intelligence collected by the *Erimo*, the Japanese Tenth Subsection (code research) was able to break the two-digit encipher system then used by the U.S. Navy.[18] The Japanese Navy continued to have eavesdropping teams aboard ships to monitor subsequent U.S. fleet exercises. And the small, intelligence collection ship *Iroo* sailed along the coast of California, seeking military radio transmissions.

More Japanese intercept capability was achieved with the opening of the so-called L-Unit intercept site in Mexico. That five-man unit was tuned to the frequencies of the U.S. Atlantic Fleet and to the Navy's primary transmitter in Washington DC.

The Japanese intercept station at the town of Owada, some 20 miles northwest of downtown Tokyo, was employed in large part to monitor military attaché traffic of the foreign embassies in Tokyo. However, according to the Royal Navy's Vice-Admiral Sir Arthur Hezlet, "They had little success . . . against the U.S. naval ciphers. It was, of course, very difficult, for lack of signal data with reduced traffic, to break into naval ciphers in peacetime."[19] (On the eve of World War II, the Japanese were able to read American diplomatic traffic, while simultaneously the United States was reading Japanese diplomatic—*not military*—communications.)

Commenting on the Japanese successes, military historians Williamson Murray and Allan Millett observed,

> The greatest danger was that a service would tilt too much toward one technical option; the Japanese Navy, for example, stressed radio direction-finding intelligence, which gave it excellent data on the U.S. Navy. It became, however, complacent about the security of its own radio communications despite the knowledge that the U.S. Navy had broken Japanese codes in 1921–1922 and knew the Japanese negotiating positions at the Washington Conference.[20]

U.S. Navy Traffic Analysis

Lieutenant Joseph N. Wenger, an early U.S. Navy cryptologist, in 1933 sought to demonstrate that valuable intelligence could be obtained solely by traffic analysis.[21] Traffic analysis provides information that can be obtained without decrypting a coded message. It had the potential to provide a commander with comprehensive and timely information without awaiting decryptions from naval intelligence headquarters in Washington. Wenger was aboard the cruiser *Houston*, then the Asiatic Fleet flagship anchored at Tsingtao, China.[22] That fleet's intercept stations were ashore and afloat, with the latter on both the *Gold Star* and *Isabel.* The three shore stations had about ten intercept operators each, with the *Gold Star* and *Isabel* each having three on board. Immediately prior to the start of the 1933 maneuvers, Wenger sent a chief petty officer to Olongapo on the gunboat *Sacramento* (PG 19), and during the transit he monitored Japanese pre-exercise radio traffic.[23]

Without access to decrypted messages, Wenger used traffic analysis to develop an understanding of the Japanese Navy's communications system and to determine the intentions of Japanese exercises. The ultimate test would be to compare his conclusions with decrypted texts developed in Washington after the fact. Subsequently, Wenger was rotated back to Washington. In his report on the 1933 maneuvers, Wenger was successful in demonstrating the effectiveness of traffic analysis, accelerating the Navy's recognition of its value to communications intelligence.

Admiral Frank B. Upham, the commander in chief, U.S. Asiatic Fleet, provided an endorsement to Wenger's report to the CNO, stating that it contained several significant "discoveries" based on traffic analysis, including "Indications of Approaching Hostilities." It predicted, more than six years before the Pearl Harbor attack, that "any attack by [Japan] would be made without previous declaration of war or other intentional warning."[24] Wenger's report has been called possibly "the single most important historical document in the development of U.S. signals intelligence and radio traffic analysis."[25]

Also, beginning in the late 1930s, with the advent of high-frequency radio used in long-range communications with ships at sea, it became possible to monitor transmissions sent from shore stations and ships thousands of miles distant. As ground intercept sites proliferated in the 1940s, shipboard intelligence interception faded in strategic value. Shipboard radio signal intercepts became almost exclusively tactical in nature during World War II.

By 1940 the U.S. Navy had 16 high-frequency/direction-finding stations in the Atlantic and Pacific areas and in United States, manned by a total of 65 operators. Thus, HF/DF became one of the Navy's primary tools for locating Japanese ships just prior to and during World War II.[26] High-frequency/direction-finding equipment did not become available on U.S. warships until late 1942.

Not a Spy Ship

In the 1930s, China was wracked by civil war with much of the country divided by local warlords and with troops of Western nations occupying portions of the country. Foreign citizens working in China were protected by naval ships and gunboats from the navies of Britain, France, Italy, Japan, and the United States that mainly operated on the Yangtze and Yellow Rivers. The situation became critical in July 1937, when the Japanese Army in Manchuria provoked the so-called Marco Polo Bridge incident that led to a full-scale Japanese invasion of China.

Photo 2. The U.S. river gunboat *Panay* (PR 5) at speed. One of her two 3-inch/50-caliber guns was mounted forward of the bridge; the Shanghai-built ship also was armed with machine guns. One of a score of Western gunboats on Chinese Rivers before World War II, the *Panay* and her sister ships collected intelligence on Chinese and foreign activities. / U.S. Navy.

On 20 August 1937, the U.S. Asiatic Fleet flagship *Houston*, while anchored off Shanghai, was caught in the crossfire between Chinese and Japanese troops. One American was killed and 18 wounded on the ship; which side had fired those specific shots could not be determined. On 30 August, the Dollar Steamship Line's passenger ship *President Hoover*, at anchor off Shanghai, was bombed by Chinese aircraft, killing one and wounding six people. (Chinese officials apologized and paid reparations for that attack.)

On Sunday morning, 12 December 1937, the U.S. river gunboat *Panay* (PR 5) and three commercial oil tankers on the Yangtze River, all flying the American flag, were strafed and bombed by Japanese naval aircraft without warning.[27] All four ships were evacuating civilians from the Chinese capital of Nanking (now Nanjing), which the Japanese occupied the following day.

Early that same morning, a group of Japanese soldiers had come on board the *Panay*; they were cordially greeted and, after discussing the local situation with the ship's commanding officer, they had departed. Apparently, the subsequent air attack—by Japanese naval aircraft—had no relationship to the army's visit that morning.

In the bombing attack, the *Panay* and one of the oil tankers were sunk, and the other two tankers were set afire. On the *Panay*, two crewmen and one evacuee were killed, and 22 of the crew and five civilians were wounded; the seriously wounded included the commanding officer, Lieutenant Commander James Hughes, and the executive officer, Lieutenant Arthur F. Anders. The Japanese aircraft strafed swimmers in the water and fired on the boats shuttling survivors ashore as the ships were sinking. The air attack was made despite the Japanese commanders having issued orders not to attack neutral shipping, and the *Panay* was marked as a neutral with large American flags spread on her awnings.

(Earlier that day, Japanese shore guns also had fired on the British river gunboats *Ladybird* and *Bee*, killing one sailor and wounding others.)

The *Panay* has been characterized as having been a "spy ship," reporting on Japanese military activities in the area and monitoring Japanese radio traffic. The *Panay* did report on significant political and military events that her officers observed, but speculation that the ship was monitoring Japanese radio transmissions for intelligence purposes has not been supported by official records or personal accounts.

The *Panay* was the first U.S. Navy ship to be sunk by aerial attack and may have been the first naval ship of any nation to be sunk solely by aircraft. Twenty-three crew members were awarded the Navy Cross, and the executive officer was awarded the Distinguished Service Medal. (The Japanese government subsequently apologized for the attack and paid reparations.)

The Approach of War

In 1937 beginning with the destroyer *Hatfield* (DD 231) at anchor at La Rochelle, France, U.S. Navy ships in European waters began intercepting Spanish, Italian, and German radio communications. Due to a lack of intercept training, the efforts of the *Hatfield*'s radio team were not productive.[28]

A year later, OP-20-G ordered a communications intercept typewriter with German characters from the Underwood Typewriter Company. It was sent with an intercept receiver and operators to the light cruiser *Omaha* (CL 4) in the Atlantic Fleet. From April to June 1939, the *Omaha* deployed to the Black Sea to monitor German activities in Romania, Hungary, and Bulgaria.[29] In June 1939, the light cruiser *Trenton* took aboard a radio intercept team that monitored radio transmissions for almost a year as part of Squadron 40-T, the small U.S. task force protecting American interests during the Spanish Civil War of 1936–40.[30]

Closer to home, in the late 1930s the U.S. intelligence agencies became concerned over the possible political inroads of the Nazis and Japanese in South and Central America. The Office of Naval Intelligence directed naval attachés and intelligence officers in every major Latin American capital to be aware of possible "enemy" activities. A Navy-manned civilian yacht cruised the Caribbean and the northern and eastern coasts of South America in search of suspicious craft. That action was undertaken at the specific direction of President Franklin D. Roosevelt.[31]

In August 1939, the U.S. Naval Research Laboratory in Washington DC, forwarded an experimental "radio fingerprinting" system to OP-20-G. It was intended to identify minute differences between radio operators and their transmitters, and to help link an individual transmitter or operator to a specific ship no matter how often the ship changed her radio call sign. Transmitter fingerprinting would continue to develop in World War II and afterward, becoming a major component of radio traffic analysis.

Vice-Admiral Hezlet later wrote: "The influence of the electron on sea power during the period between the wars was substantial. The range of radio communications and the increase in the number of channels made world-wide communications possible without having to rely on cables."[32]

War in Europe

In September 1939, Germany invaded Poland, leading to the declaration of war by France and Great Britain against Nazi Germany. After several attempts by the German Navy to send major surface warships into the North Atlantic as commerce raiders, the naval war between Germany and the Allies soon settled into German U-boats attacking British convoys. German commerce raiders, both surface and submarine, had high-frequency radio transmitters and receivers but only for communications, not for the interception of British shipboard communications or for high-frequency/direction finding in direct support of tactical situations—that is, to locate convoys.

Only during the period from early 1943 to early 1944 did Germany send B-Dienst intelligence intercept operators with English-language skills to sea on specific U-boats to provide intercepts and translations of Allied convoy transmissions, with *medium*-frequency/direction-finding equipment.[33] B-Dienst was the department of German naval intelligence that dealt with the interception, recording, decoding, and analysis of enemy radio communications.

The B-Dienst equipment in U-boats was reportedly able to intercept ground waves below 30 kilocycles (medium frequency) accurately over a distance of some 40 to 55 n.miles. The first known instance of U-boats using medium-frequency/direction-finding to intercept a convoy occurred in November 1943. Still, by February 1944, that effort was allowed to fade away due to technological deficiencies and to the development of other, more productive methods that the German Navy had for generating convoy contacts—especially directions derived from HF/DF by land intercept sites combined with intelligence derived from decrypted British radio messages.

The British, having to track the convoys and the German commerce raiders—both surface and submarine—established an extensive HF/DF network of Atlantic area shore sites from the Caribbean northward to the coasts of Canada and Iceland. The British also expedited the development of HF/DF equipment for warships as small as corvettes. By the close of 1942, most British convoy escort commanders had HF/DF available, and by late 1943 almost all convoy escorts were so equipped. Those systems enabled each convoy commander to determine the location of U-boats in his area by their high-frequency transmissions. Shore-based intercepts and direction finding of U-boat transmissions could ascertain the location of the transmitter to an accuracy of 85 to 100 n.miles, sufficient to allow the rerouting of convoys away from known U-boat concentrations.

The U.S. Navy became engaged in the so-called Battle of the Atlantic—as an observer—on 4 September 1939, when the CNO ordered the Atlantic Squadron to establish a combined air and ship patrol to observe and report the movements of ships of warring nations within an area extending east from Boston to 65 degrees west and thence south to the 19th parallel and seaward around the Leeward and Windward Islands. Obviously, the U.S. Navy provided some of the intelligence that it garnered to the British.

When the United States actively joined the effort to protect Atlantic convoys in 1941, the Navy's HF/DF network joined the British effort to detect and locate U-boats. By the time of the country's formal entry into the European war in December 1941, the U.S. Navy had an appreciation of U-boat tactical communications and procedures, and was preparing to provide destroyers and larger warships with shipboard HF/DF equipment for tactical employment in convoy operations.

Three Small Spy Ships

In late November 1941, with war raging in Europe since September 1939 and Japanese forces threatening war in the Pacific, the U.S. Asiatic Fleet commander in chief, Admiral Thomas C. Hart, began overflights by Manila-based PBY Catalina patrol aircraft across Japanese-held Cam Ranh Bay in French Indochina (now Vietnam). On 27 November, the headquarters of both the U.S. Army and Navy in Washington DC, sent "war warnings" to their field and fleet commanders. The Army's message contained the sentence: IF HOSTILITIES CANNOT, REPEAT CANNOT, BE AVOIDED, THE UNITED STATES DESIRES THAT JAPAN COMMIT THE FIRST

OVERT ACT. Those words were inserted on the direct order of President Roosevelt to Secretary of War Henry Stimson.[34]

On the 28th, U.S. Army intelligence reported a large force of Japanese ships sailing south from the home islands. And on 1 December, the United States intercepted Japanese messages instructing their diplomats in London, Hong Kong, Singapore, and Manila to destroy their code machines.

The U.S. chief of naval operations on 4 December 1941 ordered U.S. naval activities on Guam and other "endangered outposts" in the Western Pacific area to destroy all classified publications except those essential for ongoing day-to-day operations.[35] The Guam station ship, the cargo ship *Gold Star* with her productive team of katakana intercept operators, withdrew southward.[36] (The six radio technicians remaining on Guam were captured when Guam fell to the Japanese on 10 December; five were executed, and one survived the war.)

Also on 28 November, President Roosevelt instructed Admiral Hart to outfit three small ships, each commanded by a U.S. naval officer, with sufficient armament—one small cannon and one machine gun—to be classified as "U.S. men-of-war." Their crews could be largely Filipino.

Those small ships were to take up positions in the path of the Japanese convoy then heading south and to "report the movements of the Japanese." The president's order was recognized as a "suicide mission" that would provide the United States with the political advantage of the Japanese firing the first shots of a war.[37]

The U.S. Navy's armed yacht *Isabel*, still in her bright white Asiatic Fleet paint scheme, received instructions on 3 December 1941 to be stripped for war and fueled. The ship stood out of the Cavite navy yard in the Philippines that same day to make a reconnaissance of the coast of Japanese-occupied French Indochina. Two days later, while off Cam Ranh Bay, she was notified that a Japanese fleet was 50 miles away and closing.[38]

On 4 December, Lieutenant Kemp Tolley received "oral, informal" orders to take command of the civilian-owned, U.S. Navy–chartered, schooner-rigged, diesel-powered yacht *Lanikai*; to arm her with a cannon and a machine gun; and to commission her as a

Photo 3. The sailing ship *Lanikai* was intended to observe Japanese naval activity off the coast of Indochina. She was hastily armed with a 3-pounder cannon and a machine gun. With a crew of Filipinos and Americans, the craft was placed in commission in the U.S. Navy on 5 December 1941. / Authors' collection.

U.S. man-of-war with a partial Filipino crew.[39] Admiral Hart advised Tolley that the Cavite yard had been directed to give work on the *Lanikai* the highest priority: "Anything you ask for within reason. Of this you can rest absolutely assured; the President himself has directed it." The president's message, carrying the highest security classification, had said the order was to be executed "as soon as possible and in two days if possible." The *Lanikai* would relieve the *Isabel* on station as the U.S. spy ship off the Indochina coast.

(The *Lanikai* was a U.S.-built, German-owned yacht that was in Honolulu at the outbreak of World War I. After the U.S. government seized her, the yacht saw service during the war from April 1918 to January 1919 as the USS *Hermes*, working as an inter-island patrol craft. Decommissioned in 1919, she went through a series of private owners from 1926 to 1941.)

At 0700 on 5 December, the *Isabel* was 40 n.miles from Cam Ranh Bay when a Japanese plane closed on her. Aircraft shadowed the *Isabel* for the remainder of the day. At 1910 on the seventh (the sixth, Hawaii time), Admiral Hart ordered her back to the Philippines. The *Isabel* was about 70 n.miles from Manila when the Japanese began their surprise attack on Pearl Harbor.

The third small ship was never dispatched. During the afternoon of 7 December (6 December Hawaii time), Admiral Hart radioed to Washington: HAVE OBTAINED TWO VESSELS. ONE NOW EN ROUTE INDOCHINA COAST. SECOND ONE SAILING SOON AS READY. ISABEL RETURNING. WAS SPOTTED AND IDENTIFIED WELL OFF COAST HENCE POTENTIAL UTILITY OF HER MISSION PROBLEMATICAL. HAVE NOT YET FOUND THIRD VESSEL FOR CHARTER.[40]

Signals Intelligence in the Pacific

The United States and Japan fought a conflict over an ocean that stretched more than 5,000 miles between their respective homelands. Thus, both nations turned primarily to high-frequency radio signals for both long-range communications and for the interception of enemy radio transmissions. A result of that geography was that the U.S. and Japanese signals intelligence (SIGINT) organizations were almost mirror images of one another.

Both nations established ocean-wide networks of interception and high-frequency/direction-finding shore stations, which were augmented by new network nodes and shore sites as the tactical situation developed. The Japanese Navy's communications units exploited enemy communications with a network of shore stations and embarked mobile teams in aircraft carriers and battleships with operators capable of translating English voice transmissions.

Like the U.S. SIGINT organization, the Japanese mobile SIGINT teams were equipped for HF/DF, having developed that shipboard capability almost a decade before the U.S. Navy. The Japanese also had established a transmitter identification (radio fingerprinting) system at shore intercept sites that were similar to the U.S. and British systems. While U.S. radio equipment was superior to Japanese electronics early in the war, by 1943 the Japanese were operating radio and radio intercept equipment as capable as that of the Allies.

Beginning in March 1944, Japanese communications intercept units, each consisting of a petty officer and three seamen, were assigned to convoy escorts in an effort to avoid American submarines and to detect patrol aircraft. Generally, those surface escort SIGINT teams were judged as effective, but escort commanders could not use them to the fullest extent because the escorts usually were not equipped with HF/DF equipment.[41]

The U.S. Navy gunboat *Isabel* arrived at Cavite on 10 December, the same day that 68 Japanese aircraft bombed the navy yard. Several bombs that splashed close aboard the *Isabel* failed to detonate, while her gunners were credited with shooting down one of the Japanese bombers. That night she slipped out of Manila Bay in company with the submarine tender *Holland* (AS 3), steaming south to the Dutch East Indies. En route her crew painted the *Isabel* haze gray.

In the East Indies, the *Isabel* had an encounter with the surfaced Japanese submarine *I-55*. The *Isabel* took the submarine under fire and, assisted by a PBY Catalina flying boat, was credited with sinking her prey, which actually escaped and survived the war.[42] For the remainder of the war, the *Isabel* served as a training ship at Fremantle, Australia.[43]

Before she could deploy to relieve the *Isabel* off the Indochina coast, the sailing ship *Lanikai* was caught in Manila Bay when the Japanese struck on 8 December. Her commanding officer, Lieutenant Tolley, for weeks thereafter patrolled—under sail—outside the entrance to Manila Bay.[44] On 24 December, the *Lanikai* was called alongside the pier to help evacuate the Asiatic Fleet staff. She departed Cavite the morning of the 26 December with a crew of 18 and six staff officers for a three-month, 4,000-mile journey. Sailing by night and hiding from Japanese aircraft along shorelines by day, the *Lanikai* reached Australia on 18 March 1942.

(The *Lanikai* was decommissioned at Fremantle on 22 August 1942 and transferred to the Australian Navy. She served on harbor defense duties during the remainder of the war.[45])

Spy Ship and Shore Capabilities

Spy ships generally require a permissive environment, and World War II erased the protection of peacetime rules of the sea for non-warships engaged in that role. The U.S. Navy's OP-20-G staff ashore grew exponentially from about 1,000 men and women at the end of 1941 to more than 10,000 in 1945, including the organization of intercept operators that in the future would be known as the Naval Security Group (NSG).[46] The wartime growth largely was in land-based radio intercept stations and headquarters personnel in Washington DC, and in nearby Arlington, Virginia.

Shipboard intercept teams—called Radio Intelligence Units (RIU)—were routinely assigned to U.S. fleet and major task force flagships. In the Pacific, those ships usually were large-deck aircraft carriers, some battleships, and, on occasion, a heavy cruiser or—on rare occasion—even a destroyer. Those units provided direct support to commanders by detecting and translating enemy voice tactical communications, interceptions of Japanese reconnaissance aircraft transmissions, and other Japanese voice and other unencrypted transmissions. Additionally, the RIUs provided strategic support by receiving Washington-level communications intelligence for fleet and task force commanders. The size of the RIU in a ship was determined by the tactical situation and the space available in the ship.

Shore-based high-frequency/direction-finding networks were established in both the Atlantic and Pacific theaters to give location information on the enemy's forces. Tactical HF/DF receivers were available as early as May 1943 and were on most U.S. warships to provide direct support for tactical operations.

During the Korean conflict (1950–53), only eight U.S. Navy mobile RIUs were in the Pacific area; they were almost always assigned to large-deck aircraft carriers operating in the Western Pacific. In the early 1950s, the United States initiated Binnacle operations—after 1968 called Holystone—with small naval signal intelligence teams embarked in submarines involved in the close surveillance of Soviet and Chinese naval exercises, ports, and harbors.

The National Security Agency (NSA) was founded in 1952 to coordinate all U.S. signal and electronics intelligence, including the operations of the security services of all military branches: the Army Security Agency, the Air Force Security Service, and the Naval Security Group (formerly OP-20-G). In the 1960s, both the U.S. Navy and the National Security Agency adopted the concept of having dedicated intelligence ships.

2

Western Spy Submarines

Submarines have been effective platforms for intelligence missions, primarily against enemy harbors and coastal installations, albeit with major operational limitations.[1] Initially submarines made periscope observations, with cameras later being fitted to the periscopes. While a periscope protruding some two feet above the water had a very limited field of vision, the clandestine nature of submarine operations generally made even those observations valuable.

The most numerous and effective submarine reconnaissance missions of World War II were carried out by U.S. submarines in the Pacific.[2] On several occasions, those submarines were used to spy out Japanese-held islands to determine the location of enemy forces. The first recorded use of a periscope-mounted camera occurred when the U.S. submarine *Pompano* (SS 181) conducted surveillance against Wake Island and the eastern Marshall Islands in December 1941–January 1942. More "recon" missions by U.S. submarines followed during World War II. In a few of them, the submarines put swimmers into the water to reconnoiter enemy beaches prior to amphibious landings.

On rare occasions U.S. and British submarines did land personnel behind enemy lines; the Americans usually did so to support guerrillas in the Japanese-conquered Philippine Islands. One British submarine intelligence deception operation was especially notable—the landing of a dead body in Spain in Operation Mincemeat.

Mincemeat was an ingenious British deception ploy during World War II to make the German high command believe that the Allies would invade the Balkans in mid-1943 instead of Sicily, the real objective. The operation called for making the Germans think that they had, by accident, intercepted highly confidential documents that foretold Allied war plans.

British naval intelligence took the corpse of a man who had recently died in England and preserved his body in dry ice. The intelligence officers quickly developed a persona for "Major Martin" of the Royal Marines. They outfitted the corpse in a Royal Marine uniform, complete with service ribbons; identity disks and papers; theater ticket stubs; pound notes; loose change; a statement from his club for lodging in London; and so on. Most important, chained to him was a locked briefcase with official documents and a personal letter from one senior Allied officer to another mentioning the Balkans operation. The documents indicated that Major Martin was en route by aircraft from England to Allied headquarters in North Africa.

The intelligence officers then placed Major Martin in a sealed steel canister and put it on board the British submarine *Seraph*, which sailed to a position off Huelva on the coast of Spain. There, early on 30 April, the uniformed body was fitted with a life jacket, the 39th Psalm was read, and the body gently was pushed into the sea, where the tide would bring it ashore. It previously had been announced by radio that several British officers had died when their aircraft was lost at sea en route to Gibraltar.

German operatives in Spain quickly learned of the body washing ashore. While British officials demanded its return, the briefcase was provided to German officials who carefully opened it and photographed the contents, rushing the pictures to Berlin for analysis. The British Chiefs of Staff wired Prime Minister Winston Churchill, then in the United States: "Mincemeat Swallowed Whole." Churchill's chief of staff, General Hastings L. Ismay, later wrote: "The operation succeeded beyond our wildest dreams. To have spread-eagled the German defensive effort right across Europe, even to the extent of sending German vessels away from Sicily itself, was a remarkable achievement."[3]

("Major Martin" was laid to rest in the graveyard at Huelva. His real name was not revealed until 2003, when he was identified as Glyndwr Michael, who had committed suicide in London. He was 34 years old.)

Cold War Missions

During the Cold War that erupted soon after the end of World War II, submarines—and especially U.S. undersea craft—provided a major source of intelligence on foreign surface warship and submarine characteristics and their operations, and at times on targets of opportunity ashore. In addition to general surveillance, submarines were specifically equipped to collect Communications Intelligence (COMINT), Electronic Intelligence (ELINT), and Telemetry Intelligence (TELINT); they also undertook trailing enemy ships and submarines, and "gate keeping." The last mission entailed keeping watch off an enemy port to observe and possibly trail ships and submarines entering and departing it. In addition, several U.S. submarines were fitted to plant and service recording devices that were clandestinely attached to enemy seafloor communication cables, and the submarines also recovered debris on the ocean floor from missile tests.

Probably the earliest U.S. submarine intelligence foray into Soviet sea areas—and the first into the Barents Sea—was undertaken by the USS *Cochino* (SS 345). The *Cochino*, placed in commission in August 1945, was one of the last U.S. submarines to be completed during World War II. Subsequently, she was modernized under the Greater Underwater Propulsion Project (GUPPY) to enhance her underwater performance.[4]

Equipment to monitor Soviet missile tests—TELINT—was installed in the *Cochino* at Portsmouth, England, in early August 1949; her destination was the Soviet Navy's operating area off the port of Polyarnny on the Kola Peninsula. The *Cochino* departed Portsmouth on 12 August for the Barents Sea. Also in the area was the GUPPY submarine *Torsk* (SS 423). By 20 August, the two submarines were in the Barents Sea. The *Cochino* recorded some Soviet voice transmissions, but no missile test telemetry was intercepted.

Withdrawing from the area, on 25 August, the *Cochino* encountered a violent polar storm off the northern coast of Norway. Giant waves slammed the submarine. The pounding ignited an electrical

Photo 4. The U.S. submarine *Cochino* (SS 345), shown leaving Portsmouth, England, for the Barents Sea in 1949. U.S. and other NATO submarines regularly operated in Soviet areas for a variety of intelligence collection missions. The *Cochino*, a modified World War II–built submarine, was lost to a battery explosion in 1949. / U.S. Navy.

fire and battery explosion that caused the release of deadly hydrogen gas. The nearby *Torsk* attempted to help save the stricken submarine for 14 hours as her crew performed acts of skillful seamanship in the storm-lashed, freezing seas. A second battery explosion on the 26th forced the crew to abandon the *Cochino*. The crewmen made a highly dangerous crossing across a wooden plank over to the *Torsk*, which was lashed alongside. (The *Cochino*'s only fatality was Bureau of Ships technician Robert W. Philo. The *Torsk* lost six of her own crewmen who drowned while trying to help the *Cochino*.)

The *Cochino* sank in the Norwegian Sea some 15 hours after the initial fire erupted.[5] Six hours after she sank in waters some 950 feet deep, the *Torsk* pulled into a Norwegian port with the survivors.

U.S. submarines continued to carry out intelligence missions off the Soviet Arctic and Far Eastern coasts. Improved electronic intercept equipment was developed and installed first in diesel-electric and then in nuclear-propelled submarines that carried out spy missions. According to Captain Alfred McLaren, who rode those submarines:

> Although always in international waters, we were operating in an area where we knew we would not be welcome if detected. . . . Both torpedo rooms also maintained a full state of readiness, with a self-defense snapshot tube ready for immediate action if need be.[6]
>
> • • •
>
> We prepared and armed for and conducted each mission as if we were on an actual war patrol, because relations were such between the United States and its allies and the Soviet bloc that the steady tension and friction could erupt into an unexpected attack and exchange of weapons at any time.[7]

(A "snapshot" refers to the launch of an acoustic homing torpedo from a ready-to-fire torpedo tube as soon as the tube's outer door could be opened. Ideally, the torpedo could be launched within 30 to 45 seconds of the initial detection of an enemy submarine.)

In 1961 Secretary of the Navy John Connally reported that in the previous ten years diesel-electric and nuclear submarines had conducted 175 intelligence collection patrols in international waters. Those patrols, he stated, provided valuable information on Soviet submarines and anti-submarine efforts that was "not available from other sources."[8]

Almost two decades after the *Cochino*'s loss, the diesel-electric submarine *Ronquil* (SS 396) suffered a fire while operating submerged off the Soviet Far Eastern coast. Ironically, a few months earlier, the submarine had been used in filming the Cold War thriller *Ice Station Zebra*.[9]

In that fire incident, the *Ronquil* was "surrounded by Soviet destroyers which attempted to force it to the surface," according to press reports. The submarine "eluded the Russian destroyer gauntlet and escaped to safety." Neither that incident nor any operation against Soviet interests is mentioned in the U.S. Navy's official, online history of the *Ronquil*.[10]

U.S. Navy clandestine undersea operations by "special projects" submarines from 1969 through 1976 were the operating component of the National Underwater Reconnaissance Program. The National Underwater Reconnaissance Office (NURO), a national intelligence agency, was established in 1960 for the employment of advanced deep-submergence technology. Founded by Captain James F. Bradley Jr., formerly the head of the Navy's Undersea Warfare Division in the Pentagon, and Ernest J. (Zeke) Zellmer of the Central Intelligence Agency (CIA), the joint efforts of the CIA and the Navy were immediately applied to Projects Azorian and Declension (see below). As a national agency, the NURO joined the NSA, the National Reconnaissance Office (NRO), and (in 1996) the National Geospatial Intelligence Agency (NGA) within the Department of Defense to provide resources to meet national intelligence objectives.

At the Mare Island Naval Shipyard in California, the special projects submarines were modified by inserting an almost 100-foot-long compartment into the center of the submarine. The new section contained the apparatus to deploy a deep-tow sensor sled and a remotely operated claw for recoveries to depths as great as 20,000 feet, to attach and retrieve multiton seafloor cable recorders ("bugs"), and to deploy and support divers to work at depths as great as 600 feet.

With the conclusion of Project Azorian in 1973, the CIA withdrew most of its personnel from the NURO, and the Navy-operated effort was renamed the Special Naval Collection Program in 1976 and put under the direction of the director of naval intelligence.[11] That national intelligence program has survived to the present.

The U.S. submarine missions into Soviet or Chinese sea areas initially were given the codename Binnacle, then Holystone, Barnacle, and Bollard. The U.S. submarines periodically encountered Soviet undersea craft, and several experienced collisions as well as near misses when they penetrated Soviet operating areas. For example, on 15 November 1969, the nuclear-propelled *Gato* (SSN 615) collided with the Soviet submarine *K-19* at the entrance to the White Sea, near Norway, while at a depth of some 200 feet. The *K-19* was a nuclear-propelled, ballistic missile submarine (Project 658, with the NATO reporting name Hotel). The impact destroyed the *K-19*'s bow sonar and mangled the covers of her forward torpedo tubes. The Soviet submarine returned to port for repairs; the *Gato* was relatively undamaged and continued her patrol.[12]

In 1976 the U.S. House of Representatives released a report stating U.S. nuclear-propelled submarines in Soviet waters had collided nine times with "hostile vessels" in the previous ten years. Five incidents were known to involve Soviet nuclear-propelled submarines, and, according to the report, all the submarines involved were carrying either nuclear torpedoes or missiles.[13] The report noted that no U.S. submarines were sunk, and "presumably" no Soviet craft were lost. At one point an American submarine was only one mile from Soviet territory because of a navigation error, the report acknowledged. The report also listed some incidents in the Pacific.

The increase in collisions was caused, at least in part, because U.S. submarines were conducting surveillance and "gate keeper" patrols outside major Soviet bases to record naval ship and submarine movements. Apparently, those assignments began off the Pacific submarine bases of Petropavlovsk and Vladivostok as early as 1956. Admiral Arleigh A. Burke, the chief of naval operations, wrote:

> The normal submarine patrols in the Pacific are off of Petropavlovsk, in the Sea of Japan off Vladivostok, in the Yellow Sea off Darien, Kwantung and Tsingtao and off the China coast south of Formosa [Taiwan]. Periodically we have a patrol in the Sea of Okhotsk.[14]

Although the U.S. submarine operations tapping into Soviet seafloor cables were classified top secret with "special access" clearances required, references to U.S. submarine operations in Soviet home water and the term "Holystone" began appearing in the American press in 1974.[15] Laurence Stern, one of the first journalists to address the subject, wrote: "Sources familiar with the submarine eavesdropping operations say that the monitoring has been conducted within the Soviet Union's three-mile territorial limit since the late 1960s." And, he continued, "the underwater eavesdropping program . . . is probably the most hush-hush of all U.S. electronic intelligence operations which are also conducted by spy satellite and aircraft. The subs are equipped to gather a wide variety of electronic, communications and radar intelligence."[16]

Royal Navy Submarines

British and a few French and Dutch submarines also made forays into northern waters to conduct intelligence missions against the Soviet Union. The first British attempt to penetrate Soviet northern waters was a failure: The diesel-electric submarine *Alcide* departed Rothesay, Scotland, on 30 August 1952 for the Barents Sea. En route the submarine suffered damage to her fuel tanks and had to abort the operation.

The first British submarine to reach the Barents Sea on an intelligence mission, also in 1952, was the diesel-electric *Artful.* Another foray was planned for February 1953, specifically to observe a Soviet naval exercise. That mission was canceled when Prime Minister Churchill was advised that the submarine had little or no possibility of observing the exercise.

Thus, the *Totem* is believed to have made the next British submarine spy operation in 1954, reaching a position off the Kola Peninsula. She recently had been modernized, and her commanding officer, Commander John Coote, "was a highly competent submariner and during the 1953 Summer War Exercise he had earned a reputation for unconventional thinking."[17]

The *Totem*—with Churchill's approval—made another foray into the Barents Sea in 1955. On that mission, a Soviet warship closed on the submerged *Totem*, which immediately descended to 120 feet. The surface ship released a pattern of depth charges. Coote took the *Totem* deeper, to 280 feet. The attack continued.

The submarine was able to escape her antagonist and reached open water. Upon surfacing, the crew's inspection revealed that the *Totem*'s periscopes and snorkel mast were bent and unusable; the guardrails, the sonar dome, and some fittings were blown away; and the forward hatch was warped and jammed. The submarine was able to safely return to a British port.

In November 1956, the British again tried an intelligence collection mission into the Barents Sea, that time with two diesel-electric submarines: the *Artful* and *Tabard.*[18] They were seeking to detect any unusual naval activity that could indicate that the Soviets were preparing for war. In response to the attack on the *Totem* the year before, those submarines were not to "approach the Russian coast nearer than between 50 and 100 miles."[19] Their patrol, while uneventful, did provide excellent training for the submarine crews. They observed scores of merchant and fishing vessels but few naval ships.

British submarine intelligence missions into Soviet home waters continued. Following the completion of the first British nuclear-propelled submarine, HMS *Dreadnought*, in 1963, nuclear undersea craft joined and eventually replaced British diesel-electric submarines on those clandestine missions.[20] Historians Peter Hennessy and James Jinks related:

> Some [commanding officers] were cautious and remained well clear of Soviet territorial waters, while others were daring and tended to patrol as close as they could get. One naval officer, John Coward, then an intelligence watch keeper on board HMS *Oracle* under the command of Robin Morris, recalled one particular patrol off Murmansk: "Morris didn't have any respect at all for the Russians. He'd spent his life in intelligence and he just wanted to patrol as close to the coast as possible preferably with the radio aerial up so he could listen to the [soccer] match. That was quite hair raising. . . . If the Russians detected you and they thought you were not one of theirs they fired."[21]

Reportedly, those submarine commanding officers who suspected that they were being trailed "would try all sorts of tricks to shake off the opposition, stopping dead in the water, diving or climbing abruptly, or rapidly reversing course. . . . Submarine COs [commanding officers] might also order the outer doors of the torpedo tubes to be opened, one of the most obvious preparatory stages in the firing process, and quite easily heard by another submarine at close range."[22]

Beginning in 1972–73 with HMS *Swiftsure*, several British nuclear submarines received a "special fit" for intelligence collection. The equipment included special hull-mounted sonars, towed acoustic arrays, and "an unusual range of other sensors that enabled them to pick up a variety of information about Soviet submarine operations."[23]

An interesting British mission occurred in early 1981, when the nuclear submarine *Spartan* was assigned to intercept a Soviet

Victor (Project 671) returning to the Northern Fleet area from the Mediterranean. As the submarine sailed through the Norwegian Sea, the *Spartan*'s commanding officer, Commander James Taylor, recalled:

> Off Bear Island, some 200 miles north of Norway . . . we saw the Victor set about a different pattern of operations, with more frequent zigs and then a rectilinear pattern. All this indicated that the Victor was either operating with another unit, anticipating the arrival of another unit, sanitizing an area, or trying to ensure—ineffectually as it transpired—that a Soviet SSBN [ballistic missile submarine] was not being trailed by a SSN [attack submarine].
>
> As *Spartan* moved in closer, we detected the signature of a Delta SSBN and observed the sanitization take place. Reckoning that the attention of the Victor would be concentrated on his Delta, I saw this as the time to move closer still.[24]

The *Spartan* then shifted targets and trailed the Delta ballistic missile submarine as she sailed into the North Atlantic. Taylor soon discovered that he had "bagged" *two* Delta SSBNs sailing together. After trailing them for a period, the *Spartan* was ordered to seek out a Charlie (Project 670) cruise missile submarine, homeward bound from the Mediterranean. The *Spartan* also detected that submarine. According to journalist-author Jim Ring, "Taylor brought back an intelligence treasure-trove that merited the plaudits he received."[25]

British nuclear submarines also were employed in efforts to "snatch" Soviet towed sonar arrays. In the mid-1970s, HMS *Churchill* made two attempts to cut and capture an array towed by Eastern Bloc ships. On one effort, British journalist Stuart Prebble wrote,

> there was a brief and dramatic tug of war at sea, which led to explosives being dropped over the side of the trawler. The *Churchill* had become ensnared in the array and enough damage was done to the submarine's planes to oblige her to return urgently to Faslane [Scotland] for repairs.[26]

Another nuclear submarine—HMS *Conqueror*—undertook a similar intelligence collection mission in August 1982. The *Con-*

Photo 5. The British submarine *Conqueror* participated in several intelligence-related activities and was the world's only nuclear-propelled submarine to sink an enemy ship in combat, the Argentine cruiser *General Belgrano* in the Falklands conflict in 1982. Here the *Conqueror* is accompanied by the frigate *Penelope*. / Royal Navy.

queror had conducted training with her special equipment for Operation Barmaid in September and October 1980. The equipment, designed in the United States, consisted of "pods" fitted to both sides of the submarine's hull, with each pod containing a "grabber" and a "cutter" device for "stealing" a Soviet towed acoustic array from a surface ship; the objective was the three-inch-thick steel cable used to tow the arrays.

As the Barmaid submarine encountered the towed array, it would be pulled along the side of the British craft until it could be grabbed and severed. The submarine then would move away from the target while pulling the towed array with her. Then, in darkness, the submarine would surface, and the crewmen would recover the array section and stow as much as possible in the "trench" of the submarine's torpedo loading hatch.

During the *Conqueror*'s workup, "there were complex hydraulics to get right, ultra-sensitive manoeuvring to seek to perfect, a whole new system of communications within the submarine to work out and then practice."[27] In November the *Conqueror* sailed into northern waters to intercept a Polish trawler and steal her Soviet-made towed acoustic array. Despite stalking the target for two weeks, the submarine was unable to close with the trawler and carry out the snatch.

Although the *Conqueror*'s crew continued to practice with her special equipment, there was no opportunity to undertake a Barmaid mission before April 1982, when the Falklands conflict erupted in the South Atlantic. The *Conqueror* raced southward under Commander Christopher Wreford-Brown. On 2 May, the submarine torpedoed and sank the Argentine cruiser *General Belgrano*, becoming the first nuclear submarine of any nation to sink a ship in combat.[28]

Coming north after the Falklands conflict, at Faslane the *Conqueror* again was fitted with pods containing the grabbing and cutting devices. There were reports that two Polish trawlers were operating in the North Atlantic with towed acoustic arrays. The submarine went to sea on 12 August, seeking to intercept one of the trawlers towing the approximately two-mile-long acoustic array.[29]

The *Conqueror* located a target, carefully came up behind her, and, with the pod-fitted devices, she was able to grab and cut the three-inch-thick steel tow cable. She then held onto the severed section to prevent the array from sinking to the ocean floor. Later, in more secure waters, the *Conqueror* surfaced, and four divers were able to retrieve the array and partially stow it within the submarine's torpedo loading hatch complex. Upon returning to Faslane, the prize was unloaded from the *Conqueror*, taken by truck to Prestwick airport, loaded aboard an aircraft, and flown to the United States for analysis.

"The Barmaid mission was complete, the triumph was absolute," wrote Prebble. Prime Minister Margaret Thatcher "was jubilant, and was heard to say 'thank goodness it was one of our submarines which had done it.'"[30] The special Barmaid equipment and several *Conqueror* crew members were transferred to the nuclear submarine *Valiant*, then under the command of Wreford-Brown, in the event that another opportunity should occur to "snatch" a Soviet towed acoustic array. No further efforts to steal an acoustic array have been publicly reported.

After taking the *Valiant* south for a 90-day patrol near the Falklands, Wreford-Brown returned to Faslane. While at the base, he was ordered to sea to counter a Soviet Victor II (Project 671RT) nuclear attack submarine detected in the area. The *Valiant* then trailed the Red submarine for three weeks in the area west and northwest of Ireland, a lengthy and challenging operation.

British nuclear submarines operating in Arctic waters also suffered some "incidents" involving Soviet undersea craft. In October 1968, HMS *Warspite*, on her first mission into the Arctic, reportedly collided with an Echo II (Project 675) cruise missile submarine that she was trailing in the Barents Sea. The *Warspite* was battered and "rolled" in the collision but was able to return safely to port.

That same year, on 27 December, HMS *Splendid* on a separate operation in Arctic waters encountered a Soviet Akula (Project 941/NATO Typhoon) ballistic missile submarine. At some 35,000 tons submerged displacement, the Typhoons were the world's largest undersea craft. The two submarines "grazed" each other. Neither was seriously damaged, although the *Splendid* lost her towed sonar array in the incident. British and American nuclear submarines continued to undertake spy missions into Soviet waters at least through the end of the Cold War.

Dutch diesel-electric and French nuclear-propelled submarines also made a few intelligence collection forays into Soviet northern waters. Along with U.S. submarines, they also carried out intelligence collection missions in the Mediterranean Sea. While usually less contentious than submarine sorties into Arctic waters, "Med ops" did have some dangers. For example, in 1983 the Dutch submarine *Zwaardvis* was monitoring Soviet warship activity in the Mediterranean and trailing a submerged Foxtrot-class (Project 641) submarine when within the Dutch craft sonar operators shouted out:

> "Torpedo, Torpedo, Torpedo!" The message hit everyone like a bombshell! A Soviet torpedo had been launched and was racing through the water at breakneck speed. Was this an exercise or was this torpedo meant for the *Zwaardvis*? The control room remained absolutely silent. Everyone knew the Soviets might be on exercise, but nobody had expected a torpedo.[31]

And then, "at last sonar reports indicated that the torpedo was not heading for the *Zwaardvis*. 'Torpedo run ended,' said a sonar operator from the sound room and everyone breathed a sigh of relief."

From June 1968, until the demise of the Soviet Union in December 1991, six Netherlands Navy submarines carried out some 60 covert intelligence collection activities in both the Soviet Arctic and Mediterranean areas. One of the longest Dutch patrols occurred in 1984, when the *Tijgerhaai* was submerged in the Mediterranean while observing Soviet naval activities for 37 consecutive days except for a few, very brief, nighttime surfacings so that her crew could conduct periscope-head "window washes" using gin because of its alcohol content.[32]

British diesel-electric submarines joined Baltic-area NATO submarines in occasional intelligence collection forays in the Baltic. They observed Soviet activities and attempted to listen in to their communications.

In the Pacific, Japanese diesel-propelled submarines were sent into the Sea of Okhotsk, the Sea of Japan, and the East China Sea on intelligence missions during the Cold War and later.

After the Cold War

The Soviet regime collapsed in 1991. The U.S. submarine operations into Arctic waters continued as did the underwater collisions: The USS *Baton Rouge* (SSN 689) collided with the nuclear submarine *Kostroma* (K-239, Project 945/NATO Sierra) in the Barents Sea on 11 February 1992.[33] U.S. officials claimed that the incident occurred in international waters, beyond the 12-n.mile territorial zone recognized by the United States, while Russian officials declared that the collision, off the port of Murmansk, was within their territorial waters.[34]

Apparently, the *Kostroma* was surfacing when she collided with bottom of the U.S. craft. Both submarines were damaged. Two weeks after the incident, when the American craft returned to Norfolk, Virginia, divers found scrapes, dents, and gashes to her hull. The *Baton Rouge* was taken out of service in January 1993, the first *Los Angeles* (SSN 688)–class submarine to be decommissioned. She had served 15½ years, or about half of her predicted service life. The *Kostroma* suffered slight damage to her sail. She was laid up in 1997 because of funding limitations.

Speculation in the Western press was that the two nuclear submarines had been playing cat-and-mouse games in a study of tactics. That was not the real situation. Rather, the *Baton Rouge* appears to have been attempting to intercept radio communications.

In a rare acknowledgment of that incident, U.S. secretary of defense Richard Cheney said that he was not surprised by the incident and saw no reason to change the nature of U.S. submarine operations in the area. "We have several submarines operating there," he noted. "This is an important element of our security and I have no reason to think that any kind of fundamental problem exists here which requires us to change our policies."[35]

One year later, on 20 March 1993, the U.S. submarine *Grayling* (SSN 646) collided with the Russian ballistic missile submarine *Novomoskovsk* (K-407, a Project 667BDR/Delta III), which normally carried 16 nuclear missiles with multiple warheads. That incident occurred under Arctic ice, about 90 n.miles north of the Murmansk coast. Indications are that the *Grayling* was trailing the Russian submarine. Neither submarine suffered significant damage, and after repairs, both continued in service.

That incident occurred a week before a planned summit meeting of American president Bill Clinton and Russian president Boris Yeltsin. Both governments had enraged reactions to the second clash between U.S. and Russian submarines within the year. In an unprecedented action, on 5 April 1993, Clinton apologized for the collision to Yeltsin. He told a press conference, "I told President Yeltsin I very much regretted the submarine incident and that I had ordered a thorough review of the incident as well as the policy of which the incident happened to be an unintended part."[36]

Several members of the Congress as well as naval officers voiced concern over President Clinton's apology to the Russian leader. Retired Admiral Thomas H. Moorer, a former chairman of the Joint Chiefs of Staff, said that it was a mistake for the president to imply that the U.S. Navy was at fault for the collision. He explained, "We have had this surveillance for some time, and it has been very successful and useful. I think it's important that we continue to maintain up-to-date information on former Soviet military forces."[37]

A leading Soviet/Russian submarine designer, academician Sergei Kovalev, told why he believed so many collisions occurred between U.S. and Soviet submarines during intelligence collection operations: A submarine making a possible detection of another submarine would slowly, carefully head toward the source of the sound. As she drew nearer, the other submarine would make a possible detection, and she would carefully head for the source of that sound. This detection and closing process by both submarines would be continued until—he slapped his hands together—"Bang!"[38]

Trailing the Enemy

Beyond penetrating into Arctic waters to collect intelligence, U.S. nuclear-propelled submarines also endeavored to trail Soviet submarines leaving their regional waters, both to see what they were up to and to garner intelligence about their operating procedures. That was especially true when the Yankee (Project 667A) ballistic missile submarines began deploying into the Western Atlantic in the late 1960s. The Yankee SSBNs were equivalent—albeit not similar—to the U.S. Polaris submarines with each type carrying 16 nuclear-tipped ballistic missiles.

One of the longest submarine trail operations occurred in the spring of 1978, when the USS *Batfish* (SSN 681) took up shadowing a Yankee missile submarine on 17 March 1978 in the Norwegian Sea and continued until 5 May 1978, when the Soviet submarine reentered the Norwegian Sea.[39] That comprised the Yankee's entire patrol, including a 19-day "alert patrol" steaming west of the Azores in April, presumably ready to move into a ballistic missile firing location.

Early in that trailing operation, the *Batfish* encountered heavy weather in the Iceland–Faeroe Gap that led to brief loss of contact with the Soviet craft. It was reestablished with the help of a

U.S. Navy patrol aircraft that was able to detect the Soviet submarine. The *Batfish* was in contact the Soviet submarine for 50 days, believed to be the longest trail ever recorded of a Soviet SSBN by a U.S. submarine.

Of particular significance, as the Yankee transited to her patrol area at speeds of nine to 11 knots, every one or two hours the SSBN maneuvered to "clear its baffles." The term "baffles" refers to the insulation between the submarine's bow sonar and hull to mask the noises of submarine machinery from the sonar. The SSBN maneuver enables the submarine to search behind with passive sonar to determine if there was a "trailer." That usually involved a ten-minute, 90-degree turn. (While in the alert status, clearing the baffles involved a 135-degree course change at a speed of seven knots or fewer.)

The target submarine being trailed may have detected the *Batfish* and then resumed course, as she later used the active sonar known by the NATO designation "Blocks of Wood." As that trail occurred after the North Koreans' capture of the U.S. spy ship *Pueblo* (AGER 2) in 1968 that gave the Soviets access to U.S. intelligence documents, Moscow also could have advised the Soviet submarine that a U.S. submarine was trailing her. The Soviets had several years of success in reading the U.S. submarine broadcast communications due to the *Pueblo*'s capture and the treason of U.S. Navy communications technician John Walker.[40] While the submarine's active sonar emissions may have been employed to search for a trailing submarine, they also could have been a means of signaling to an escorting Soviet nuclear attack submarine as there were occasions when deploying Soviet SSBNs were escorted to their patrol areas by torpedo-attack submarines.

And in the Pacific

The earliest U.S. post–World War II submarine surveillance and espionage operations in the Pacific were undertaken against China following the Communist takeover of the country in 1949. As the defeated Nationalist forces were established on Taiwan (formerly Formosa), some 100 miles off the coast of mainland China, the U.S. government became immediately concerned about either a possible Chinese invasion of Taiwan or the Nationalist forces seeking to reenter China. The diesel-electric submarine *Pickerel* (SS 524) was deployed to patrol the Chinese coast from 23 July to 30 July 1950 and to report on possible preparations for an amphibious assault against Taiwan.[41]

The *Pickerel* then operated off Soviet Far Eastern ports in September 1950. While off Vladivostok, her commanding officer, Paul Schratz, later wrote, "I was faced with the awkward choice of failing to carry out the mission if we remained within the assigned area or of penetrating the Soviet restricted area and succeeding in the mission. . . . We would penetrate the [restricted] area as far as necessary to do the job."[42]

On 19 August 1957, the diesel-electric submarine *Gudgeon* (SS 567) was conducting surveillance near the port of Vladivostok when she was detected by Soviet anti-submarine forces. A casualty to her garbage-ejection tube prevented her from going deep (i.e., to her 700-foot maximum operating depth). After some 30 hours of cat-and-mouse moves and countermoves with her antagonists, the American submarine was forced to the surface. Her pursuers allowed her to sail away. (The *Gudgeon* had sailed from Pearl Harbor on 8 July 1957; after her encounter off Vladivostok, she entered the port of Yokosuka. Shortly thereafter she began a history-making cruise around the world, becoming the first American submarine to circumnavigate the globe. The *Gudgeon* returned to Pearl Harbor on 21 February 1958, eight months and 25,000 miles after her departure.)

U.S. submarine operations off Soviet ports continued. In 1964 the nuclear attack submarine *Sargo* (SSN 583) was operating off Soviet ports in the Far East, observing missiles tests and trailing Red submarines to record their propulsion sounds and photograph them. During that deployment, a Soviet destroyer chased the *Sargo*, and a hydraulic failure almost caused the loss of the submarine.[43]

Six years later, on 26 June 1970, the Soviet cruise missile submarine *K-108* (Project 675/Echo II) collided with the U.S. submarine *Tautog* (SSN 639) off Petropavlovsk. Both submarines were at a depth of some 150 feet. Although both nuclear submarines were damaged, they were able to return to their respective ports. Another collision of an apparent gatekeeper occurred in May 1974 when the USS *Pintado* (SSN 672) collided with a Soviet submarine off Petropavlovsk. The Red submarine was a Yankee (Project 667A) nuclear-propelled ballistic missile craft. The submarines were said to have collided "virtually head-on" at a depth of some 200 feet. Neither suffered major damage.

U.S. submarines also attempted to trail Soviet submarines in the Pacific. In May 1972, in response to the mining of North Vietnam's Haiphong harbor by U.S. carrier-based aircraft, five Soviet cruise missile submarines were ordered into the South China Sea. The submarine *K-184* (Project 675/Echo II), deploying from Vladivostok to the Gulf of Tonkin, was trailed for 25 consecutive days by the U.S. submarine *Guardfish* (SSN 612).[44]

U.S. submarines also continued to patrol off the Chinese coast, albeit conducting fewer operations than those off Soviet ports. Still, on 29 July 1964, the Chinese government broadcast its 300th "serious warning" against U.S. submarine violations, calling them "provocations."[45] The Chinese occasionally detected a Binnacle or Holystone U.S. submarine within their territorial waters and responded with depth charge attacks. In the 1960s and 1970s, U.S. submarines occasionally had to sneak into Pearl Harbor after dark because of visible damage to their sails and/or periscopes from Chinese attacks.

"Special" Submarines

The most audacious U.S. submarine spy missions of the Cold War undoubtedly were those that involved the nuclear-propelled submarine *Halibut* (SSN 587) and her especially modified successors. The *Halibut* was constructed as a Regulus guided missile submarine, being completed in 1960. With the subsequent termination of the Regulus missile program, she was modified in 1965 to a special operations, intelligence collection platform. Her massive missile hangar provided substantial space for technicians and special equipment, and she was provided with facilities for lowering towed sensor sleds, or "fish."[46] The towing cable for the *Halibut*'s fish was more than 20,000 feet long![47]

Reportedly, the *Halibut*'s first mission after modification was with the Winterwind Project, searching the seafloor for dummy warheads and missile debris from Soviet missile tests in the Pacific. About 1960 the Soviet Union had begun test launches of long-range

Photo 6. The *Halibut* (SSGN/SSN 587) was built as a Regulus cruise missile submarine. Subsequently converted for special operations, she is shown here in 1970 carrying a "DSRV simulator"—in reality, a lockout chamber for divers engaged in the clandestine tapping of Soviet seafloor cables. / U.S. Navy.

ballistic missiles into the North Pacific, most launched from Tyuratam, near the city of Baikonur (formerly Leninsk). The CIA and the Naval Security Group intercept stations in Iran, Pakistan, and Turkey, as well as satellites, were able to detect precursor events to provide a warning of missile launches.[48]

Identifying the impact locations was based upon observations made by U.S. surface ships that watched the actions of Soviet missile range instrumentation ships. Augmenting U.S. land-based radars in the Aleutian Islands, two U.S. missile range instrumentation ships (designated AGM) and four destroyer escorts with small NSG detachments embarked were deployed to the Western Pacific to track the reentry phase of the missiles. Under an operation that began in 1964, the four destroyer escorts had special intercept equipment installed to record the terminal reentry of Soviet ballistic missile tests and nose cone splashdowns. The ships also would shadow Soviet missile range ships in the Pacific area and seek indications of imminent missile tests.[49] The U.S. ships' deployments to the missile impact areas were codenamed Painted Fox, while overall Pacific-area collection efforts were named Ivy Green until 1971 and after that Pony Express.

The submarine *Halibut* made two trips to those predicted missile impact areas. On those forays, in 1967 and 1968, she used her towed sensor sled but was unable to locate any missile debris. Subsequently, in 1968, the *Halibut* was dispatched to find the sunken Soviet ballistic missile submarine *K-129* (Project 629/Golf II) that had gone down in the North Pacific.

The *Halibut* had a key role in the efforts to locate and salvage the *K-129*. At about midnight of 11/12 March 1968, while the *K-129* was sailing at periscope depth some 1,600 n.miles northwest of Oahu, the submarine suffered three small, internal explosions, each being the equivalent of between five and ten pounds of TNT.[50] They may have been caused by the activation of an emergency method of blasting away the missile tube covers. That action probably was caused by the submarine's fire control system suffering a massive malfunction during a training event.[51]

Seconds after the third explosion, one of the submarine's three R-21 (NATO SS-N-5 Serb) ballistic missile engines ignited inside of its launch tube. Six minutes later, a second missile engine ignited. Both missile engines burned to fuel exhaustion within the submarine. The damage was horrific as the missile exhaust plumes reached some 5,000 degrees Fahrenheit and pulsed through the submarine. All 98 crewmen died instantly.

Completely flooded, the *K-129* sank rapidly to a depth of some 16,000 feet. Because of the missile propulsion damage, the engineering compartments broke away from the forward hull as the submarine plunged to the ocean floor.

A U.S. Air Force seafloor acoustic system detected the sounds of the submarine sinking. Thus, the United States knew the approximate location of the sinking; the Soviets did not. Soviet air and naval forces searched in vain for the submarine.

The *Halibut* was dispatched to the area of the *K-129*'s remains indicated by the seafloor acoustic system. The American subma-

Photo 7. The massive *Hughes Glomar Explorer* was built specifically to secretly lift a sunken Soviet missile submarine from a depth of some 16,000 feet. The "cover story" was that millionaire Howard Hughes was harvesting manganese nodules from the ocean floor. The *Glomar Explorer* operated with Soviet ships observing the operation. / Authors' collection.

rine searched the area with her towed sensor sled and precisely located the wreckage of the *K-129* on 20 August 1968. Reportedly, during the next three weeks, the *Halibut* took more than 20,000 close-up photos of the wreckage with her towed sensor sled. The *Halibut*'s detailed photography of the wreckage enabled the recovery of a portion of the *K-129* in 1972 by the clandestine salvage ship *Hughes Glomar Explorer*.[52] While the U.S. ship only raised the forward 38 feet of the submarine, she did provide U.S. intelligence with the remains of two nuclear torpedoes and some documents. The primary objective of the salvage effort—recovering the nuclear warhead of the *K-129*'s surviving third R-21 ballistic missile—was not accomplished.

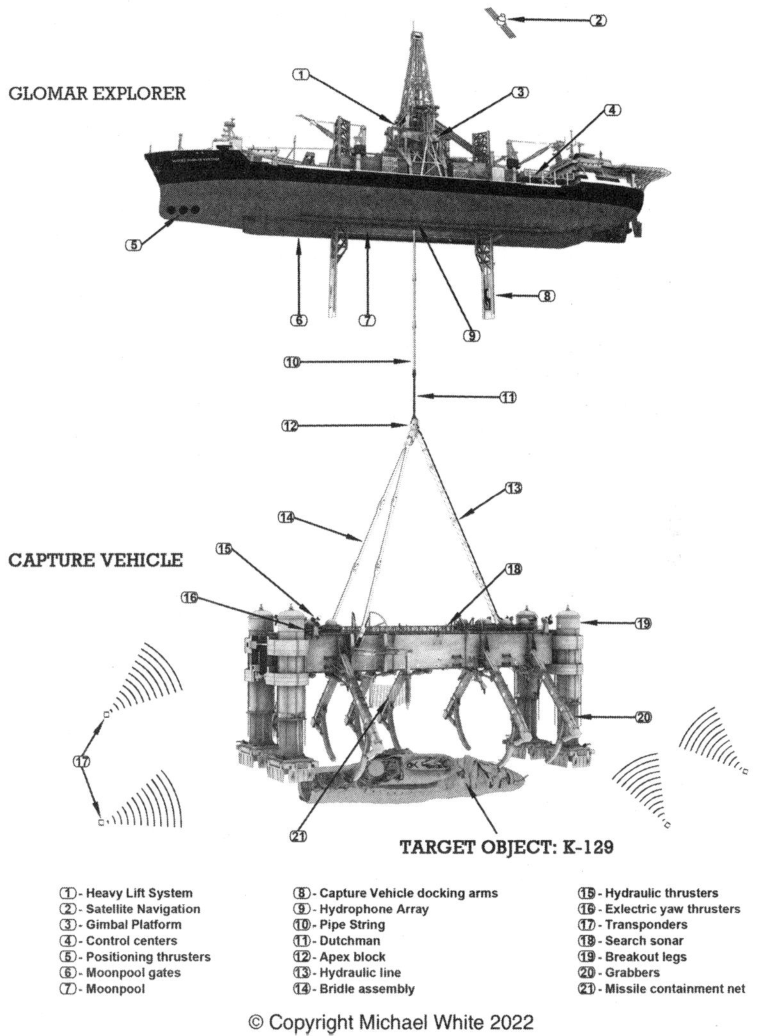

Fig. 1. The Project Azorian concept of the *Hughes Glomar Explorer* and the 2,000-ton "capture vehicle" built specifically to lift the remains of the sunken Soviet ballistic missile submarine *K-129* from the ocean floor. A material failure of the lift device enabled only the forward 38 feet of the submarine to be recovered. / © Michael White.

(The U.S. Navy had planned to return to the scene with the *Glomar Explorer* to recover the breakaway section that held the third, intact R-21 missile. The Soviets learned of the original effort and warned that a return attempt could lead to war.)

From 1968 to 1970, the *Halibut* underwent further modifications at the Mare Island Naval Shipyard. Ducted thrusters were installed for underwater station-keeping, and she was fitted to carry and support saturation divers. Additional sonars were provided, "legs" or "skegs" were installed so that she could "sit" on the ocean floor, and other special gear was added. The most obvious feature was a diver lockout chamber mounted atop the submarine's after hull. From that structure, saturation divers could leave and enter the *Halibut* (see "The Special Submersibles" section).

The story was put out that the *Halibut* carried a rescue submersible "training platform." Thus converted, in reality, the divers could install and retrieve tapes in a recording device attached to seafloor cables, with the divers remaining at the equivalent ambient (ocean) pressure while living in the *Halibut*.[53] The former hangar for Regulus cruise missiles in the submarine's bow was converted to three-level work and equipment spaces. That so-called Bat Cave was approximately 50 feet long, 28 feet wide, and some 30 feet at its highest point.[54]

Beginning in 1971, in a program popularly but incorrectly known as Ivy Bells and actually called Declension, the *Halibut* was employed to install recording devices for tapping into an underwater communications cable at a depth of some 400 feet in the Sea of Okhotsk off the Kamchatka Peninsula. The cable "bugging" concept was developed by Captain Bradley, a surface warfare specialist who spent much of his career in intelligence work. He believed submarines could "tap" into offshore communication cables. Bradley successfully gained support for his theories from the National Security Agency as well as the Office of Naval Intelligence and the Central Intelligence Agency. Secretary of the Navy John Lehman would later call Ivy Bells/Declension "one of the most consequential intelligence developments of the Cold War."[55]

Thus, in 1971 the submerged *Halibut* slowly traced the coastline of the Kamchatka Peninsula, searching for visible warning signs for ships not to anchor near seafloor cables. She found them. The seafloor communications cables, between Petropavlovsk on the remote peninsula and the Far Eastern coast, carried highly classified military as well as civilian communications.[56]

The *Halibut*'s saturation divers were able to exit the submarine to attach a recording device to the cable without being detected. At a later time, the *Halibut* returned to retrieve the recording tapes from the device. Those recordings revealed substantial intelligence about Soviet submarine operations, problems, schedules, and more. Although the communications on the tapes were weeks or months old when they were recovered and replaced, they still were valuable to intelligence analysts.

The dangers in such spy sub operations were not only from their possible detection (and attack) by Soviet forces but also from the environment. In their outstanding book *Blind Man's Bluff*, journalists Sherry Sontag and Christopher Drew wrote that on one occasion when the *Halibut*'s divers were replacing the tapes in the device,

> abruptly, their routine was broken. A storm above began boiling beneath the surface. The divers were trapped outside, unable to climb back into the [lockout] chamber as the *Halibut* strained against her anchors one moment and slammed into the seafloor the next. All the men could do was try to keep a safe distance and watch.
>
> An hour passed, then another. Then there was a loud crunch. Both steel anchors snapped at once, broke so easily that they could have been rubber bands.
>
> Outside, the divers watched as *Halibut* began to drift upward. The men were still linked to the submarine through their air hoses. They knew that they would die if *Halibut* pulled them up before they could decompress. If they cut themselves loose, they would suffocate. Inside, the officer of the deck was well aware of the danger when he shouted a desperate order: "Flood it!"[57]

The *Halibut*'s ballast tanks were quickly flooded, and the submarine crashed down onto the ocean floor. The divers hastily entered the lockout chamber and then into their pressurized haven within the submarine.

Periodically the *Halibut* transported divers to retrieve and replace the tapes until 1976, when the extensively modified, nuclear-propelled submarines *Seawolf* (SSN 575) and then the *Parche* (SSN 683) took on the cable-tapping task. Completed in 1957, the *Seawolf* was the U.S. Navy's second nuclear-propelled submarine, but she was plagued with engineering problems.[58] The modifications to the *Seawolf* (and later the *Parche*) for the Declension/Ivy Bells operations included the submarine being cut in half and an additional midships section (of 99 feet for the *Parche*) inserted for housing and locking out saturation divers, having legs (skegs) installed so that the submarine could sit on the ocean floor, and being provided with an under-midsection device for retrieving debris off the ocean floor from Soviet missile tests (the last activity known as Operation Sand Dollar).

The *Seawolf* thus serviced the Sea of Okhotsk cable. In 1980 she suffered a fire in her engineering spaces, but by the summer she was able to sail into the Sea of Okhotsk and again replace tapes in the bugging device. She made another Declension/Ivy Bells foray in 1981. On that mission, the *Seawolf* encountered a typhoon. Although the water depth was only 400 feet, the *Seawolf* tried to ride out the storm on the ocean floor. Her water intakes for reactor cooling ingested sand, which damaged the reactor plant. The submarine became stuck in the bottom mud, where she was battered by underwater waves. Damaged and with her crew exhausted, the *Seawolf* finally reached deep water and was able to return to her home port of Mare Island.[59]

The *Parche*, placed in commission in 1974 and extensively modified for the Ivy Bells/Declension operation, became the principal submarine for servicing the seafloor bugging devices. On what is believed to have been her first spy mission, the submarine's divers installed a second device atop the first in the Sea of Okhotsk to increase the intercept capacity.

The *Parche*'s second Declension mission, in 1979, took her north from her home port of Mare Island, through the Bering Strait between Alaska and Siberia, under the polar ice, and to the Soviet Arctic coast. Off the Kola Peninsula, she deployed a towed sensor "fish" to locate a communications cable believed to run from submarine bases in the Murmansk area to the massive shipyard complex at Severodvinsk. Having located the cable and made a connection,

> it would take the spooks at least two weeks to sift electronically through the hundreds of lines running through the cable and choose which lines to record—and at what times—over the next year. The process relied on educated guesses and luck. Certain channels would probably be best in the summer months when the ice cleared from the Barents and the Soviets conducted naval exercises. Missile tests tended to be seasonal as well. But lines connected directly to headquarters could be active and profitably tapped year-around.[60]

Having located the "right" lines, the *Parche*'s saturation divers installed an advanced bugging device. The *Parche* is believed to have made a total of six runs up to the Barents Sea for the undersea cable-tapping operations. Her intelligence forays resulted in the *Parche*'s becoming the most decorated ship in U.S. Navy history with nine Presidential Unit Citations and ten Navy Unit Commendations.

The *Parche* subsequently was joined by another nuclear submarine in those bugging operations—the *Richard B. Russell* (SSN 687). Completed in 1975, the *Russell* served in the Atlantic and Mediterranean areas, apparently in typical nuclear attack submarine activities, until she was transferred to the Pacific in 1982. After her conversion at the Mare Island shipyard for deep-submergence search and recovery, the *Russell* spent much of the next few years in Winterwind and Sand Dollar recovery operations, as well as other highly classified intelligence missions. Of the last three commanders of the *Russell*—from 1987 to 1994—two achieved the rank of vice admiral, and one became a four-star admiral.[61] During the command of Commander Charles L. Munns in 1990–92, the *Russell* received the Presidential Unit Citation, two Navy Unit Commendations, and three Battle Efficiency "E" Awards.

A Soviet technology expert, Lieutenant General Nikolai Brusnitsin, has described a U.S. cable-tapping device:

> The device is a steel pipe more than five meters [16½ feet] long and about 120 cm [4 feet] across, marked "property of the United States of America." The hermetically sealed pipe contains several tons of electronic equipment to amplify the reception and demodulate

> signals picked up from the cable. Conversations are recorded by 60 automatic tape-recorders which operate when the line is busy and stop when the line is dead, being switched on automatically when conversations are resumed. Each tape recorder is intended for a 150-hour operation, so the total volume of taped conversations adds up to about 3,000 hours. . . . The device weighs a little more than 100 kg [220 pounds] in water.[62]

General Brusnitsin added, “You can imagine how much all of those contraptions must have cost the American taxpayer.” He also observed, “It is highly improbable that . . . the system for tapping seabed cable lines (which are little used by the USSR) has been created solely to spy on two Soviet lines—Magadan-Kamchatka and Sevastopol-Varna—while there are tens of thousands of kilometers of similar lines operating on sea and ocean beds across the world.”[63]

The Kamchatka seafloor cable tapping continued until 1981, when U.S. satellite photos showed Soviet salvage ships working in the Sea of Okhotsk over the exact location of the recording device. Subsequently, when the *Parche* next attempted to recover and replace tapes, the device was gone. With the 1985 arrest of Ronald Pelton, an NSA analyst who was selling secret information to the Soviets, the U.S. government learned that he had revealed the cable-tapping operation to them in 1980.[64]

Picking up Debris

Some of the submarines participating in the cable-tapping missions also were involved in Sand Dollar and Winterwind missions. The Sand Dollar sorties sought to recover cruise missile components on seafloor in the Sea of Okhotsk, the impact area for the Soviets test firings of their cruise missiles, while the Winterwind missions attempted to locate and recover reentry vehicle debris off the deep ocean floor after Soviet ballistic missile test firings into the Pacific. Reportedly, those recovery missions had several successes. Although details are not publicly known, a U.S. submarine in the Far East recovered a Soviet Shkval hypercavitating torpedo, probably lost during tests. That was the world’s fastest torpedo-type weapon with a speed of almost 200 knots.

In addition, there were reports that the *Parche* may have recovered fragments from Chinese ballistic missile tests in 1995–96. During the Taiwan Strait crisis of that period, the Chinese launched unarmed DF-15 and DF-21 missiles into the sea around Taiwan. The *Parche* was in that area and was equipped, trained, and experienced in locating and recovering missile debris.

The *Parche* served in the spy ship role until late 2004, when she was retired. The *Jimmy Carter* (SSN 23) was placed in commission in early 2005, having been extensively converted during construction for intelligence collection and recovery activities. As with her predecessor, the *Carter* had a 100-foot-long amidships section installed to support saturation divers with lock-out facilities and seafloor recovery devices, thus increasing the submarine's length to 453 feet. Auxiliary maneuvering devices also were fitted to enable precise maneuvering over seafloor objects. Those modifications increased the submarine's submerged displacement to 12,139 tons compared to 9,150 tons for the two other units of the class: the *Seawolf* (SSN 21) and *Connecticut* (SSN 22). The *Carter* remained in service when this book went to press.[65]

U.S. Navy submarines also carried out intelligence collection missions against China, Cuba, Libya, and North Korea during the Cold War era—and afterward.

At least one Canadian submarine is known to have carried out an intelligence mission against North Korea: The diesel-electric submarine *Chicoutimi* in 2017–18 deployed to the Far East, the first patrol by a Canadian submarine into Asian waters in some five decades. The *Chicoutimi* operated off the coast of North Korea, monitoring sea traffic relative to the United Nations sanctions placed against that country. During that deployment, she made port visits to Guam and Japan.[66]

Ghost Submarines

Soviet/Russian officials blamed the loss of three of their submarines to collisions with U.S. submarines that were—or probably were—on intelligence collection missions or were trailing Red submarines. Those officials claimed that the *K-129* was sunk in a collision with the USS *Swordfish* (SSN 579), which was reported

Table 1. U.S. special operations submarines

No.	Name	Commissioned	Special Operations
SSN 587	*Halibut*	1960	1965–68, 1970–75
SSN 575	*Seawolf*	1957	1974–86
SSN 683	*Parche*	1974	1978–87, 1992–2003
SSN 687	*Richard B. Russell*	1975	1986–92
SSN 23	*Jimmy Carter*	2005	2005–?

Note: SSN 587 began as SSGN 587 and was redesignated SSN on 15 April 1965.

to have been trailing the Soviet submarine. At the time that the *K-129* was lost, according to the U.S. submarine's log, declassified contemporaneous records, and interviews with crew members, the *Swordfish* was on patrol off Vladivostok. She later entered a Japanese port with a bent periscope; the Soviets contend that it was damaged in the collision. All evidence indicates that it was damaged when the submarine struck an ice floe off Vladivostok.

Similarly, the Soviets blamed the USS *Augusta* (SSN 710) for colliding with the ballistic missile submarine *K-219* (Project 667A/ Yankee) while submerged at a depth of 130 feet some 680 n.miles northeast of Bermuda on 3 October 1986. The actual cause of the Soviet submarine's loss was water coming in contact with the highly volatile liquid fuel of one of her missiles. (A similar accident had earlier caused the welding shut of one of that submarine's 16 missile tubes.)

The *K-219* was able to surface, but she soon sank with the loss of several crewmen. Later, her commanding officer, Captain 2nd Rank Igor A. Britanov, when asked the number of times that he was called upon to be a guest lecturer, he replied: "None—I do not tell the story the way my government wants me to tell it. I did not collide with an American sub."[67]

In addition, the Russian nuclear-propelled cruise missile submarine *Kursk* (Project 949A/Oscar) sank in the Arctic from an internal torpedo explosion on 8 August 2000. All 118 men on board died. Once again, Russian officials immediately claimed that a U.S. submarine observing the naval exercise in which the *Kursk* was participating had collided with her. Later it was determined that the cause of that disaster was the explosion of a torpedo within the submarine.

Other Western submarine intelligence collection operations in Western Pacific areas as well as in the Atlantic and Arctic areas have continued.

The Special Submersibles

During the Cold War era, the U.S. Navy acquired several submersibles that at times have been engaged in intelligence collection activities. In 1959 the Navy purchased the bathyscaph *Trieste*; it and the French FNRS-3 were the world's deepest diving submersibles. In January 1960, piloted by U.S. Navy lieutenant Don Walsh and Swiss engineer Jacques Piccard, the *Trieste* reached the deepest known point in the world's oceans—35,800 feet in the Mariana Trench.[68]

The *Trieste* and two subsequent variants of that craft—all given the same name—carried out numerous deep-ocean research *and recovery* operations, some of the latter being highly classified. As modified, the craft had a 20,000-foot capability, which encompasses some 98 percent of the world ocean depths. The *Trieste* vehicles suffered from requiring surface ship transport and support, limiting their ability to conduct secret activities, and their seafloor mobility was limited. Still, they were invaluable vehicles for intelligence as well as research and scientific work.

One of four reentry vehicles—the RV-3—from a Hexagon spy satellite with 54,083 feet of film taken over the Soviet Union and other areas of interest was deorbited on 10 July 1967. The capsule suffered a parachute failure and hit the water at high velocity some 300 n.miles northwest of Oahu. It immediately sank to a depth of 16,400 feet. The capsule was located by surface-towed sensors and marked with sonar devices, and the *Trieste* was dispatched to the scene. Modified to recover the reentry vehicle and after being twice towed from Pearl Harbor to the capsule's location, the *Trieste* finally recovered the spy film capsule.

But near the end of a nine-hour dive on 26 April 1958, as the *Trieste* neared the surface, the capsule began to break apart, shedding the film. The 30½ feet of film that was recovered aboard the *Trieste*'s support ship had been exposed to salt water and divers' lights—and had no intelligence value. Other *Trieste* clandestine operations were far more successful.[69]

Prior to the Hexagon recovery attempt, the *Trieste* had been about to be retired. "The Hexagon effort resurrected the *Trieste* program and propelled it into high-visibility status within the Navy Department. The next several years would see plans and programs to build a more effective system around the *Trieste*."[70]

Following the loss of the nuclear submarine *Thresher* (SSN 593) with all 139 men on board in April 1963, the Navy developed a comprehensive deep-submergence program that included deep-ocean rescue and search systems. The Navy had planned to build six deep submergence rescue vehicles (DSRVs) and two deep-submergence search vehicles (DSSVs), with the latter having a 20,000-foot capability. Both types would be transported and supported by submarines. The DSSVs were intended for seafloor exploration and recovery, and to be capable of clandestine operations, unlike the *Trieste* and other search vehicles that required surface ship support.

Budget issues reduced the rescue vehicle program to only two rescue vehicles: the *Mystic* (DSRV-1), delivered in 1970, and the *Avalon* (DSRV-2), delivered in 1971. They were in service until 2008 and 2000, respectively, never having participated in an actual rescue operation. Those craft had a maximum operating depth of 5,000 feet.[71] The DSRVs were 50 feet long and could be carried, launched, and recovered by attack submarines (SS/SSN) while fully submerged or by two specialized surface ships.

A DSRV had a crew of three and could carry up to 24 rescuees in two pressurized compartments. They could be transferred directly into the "mother" submarine without exposure to external water pressures. Obviously, saturation divers also could operate from the pressurized compartments of a DSRV to conduct clandestine underwater tasks. (The two surface mother ships also were fitted to support saturation divers who operated from the submersibles.[72])

The two DSRVs were involved in classified operations while operating from mother submarines. Details of those missions are still classified. Dr. John Craven, the first head of the Navy's Deep Submergence Systems Project (DSSP), which developed the rescue vehicles, wrote:

Photo 8. The deep submergence rescue submersible *Avalon* (DSRV-2) "mated" to the nuclear-propelled submarine *Cavalla* (SSN 684) at Pearl Harbor. The Navy's two DSRVs were effective in clandestine operations, being transported and supported by submerged submarines. / U.S. Navy.

> There were many highly classified missions associated with national security that could not be accomplished without a DSRV system. The specific operational needs for those missions could not be anticipated but they were certain to occur. Thus a DSRV designed, constructed, and deployed for every conceivable rescue mission would also be available for the intelligence "mission impossible" that were sure to occur.[73]

As noted previously, the two planned, 20,000-foot-capability DSSV search vehicles were budget casualties and never built. However, the bathyscaphs known as *Trieste* provided limited, manned,

20,000-foot search and recovery capabilities until the last craft of three vehicles in that series was retired in 1984.

The U.S. Navy also funded the surface-supported research submersibles *Alvin*, *Sea Cliff*, and *Turtle* that participated in several classified seafloor recovery operations. The *Alvin* was operated by the Woods Hole Oceanographic Institution and the two others by the Navy.[74]

In several respects, the most interesting submersible developed by the United States was the nuclear-propelled *NR-1*, a project personally promoted by then-Vice Admiral Hyman G. Rickover, the longtime head of the Navy's nuclear propulsion program.[75] The *NR-1* was built specifically as a test platform for a small submarine nuclear power plant and was successfully employed as a deep-ocean search, recovery, and work vehicle. In explaining the craft's significance, Rickover told a U.S. congressional committee, "You will be looking at a development that I believe will be as significant for the United States as was the *Nautilus* [SSN 571]."[76] Rickover envisioned a series of similar craft, hence the designation *NR-1* for his first nuclear reactor submersible.

The veil of secrecy that Rickover imposed on the *NR-1* was partially lifted on 18 April 1965 when President Lyndon Johnson publicly revealed her development in a White House press release. The president cited the severe endurance and maneuverability limitations of existing research submersibles and stated:

> The development of a nuclear propulsion plant for a deep submergence research vehicle will give greater freedom of movement and much greater endurance of propulsion and auxiliary power. This capability will contribute greatly to accelerate man's exploration and exploitation of the vast resources of the ocean.[77]

The *NR-1*'s nuclear plant gave her a theoretically unlimited underwater endurance with the craft having an operating depth of 3,000 feet. While that depth was not as great as other U.S. Navy manned submersibles (i.e., the *Trieste* bathyscaphs and DSRVs), the underwater endurance of those craft was measured in hours versus days for the *NR-1*, and their electrical power for sonar, lights, and other equipment was limited.

Photo 9. The nuclear-propelled submersible *NR-1* was a unique craft employed for deep-ocean exploration, search, and recovery activities. "NR" indicated nuclear reactors, with the organization headed by Admiral H. G. Rickover, the longtime head of the U.S. Navy's nuclear propulsion program. / Giorgio Arra.

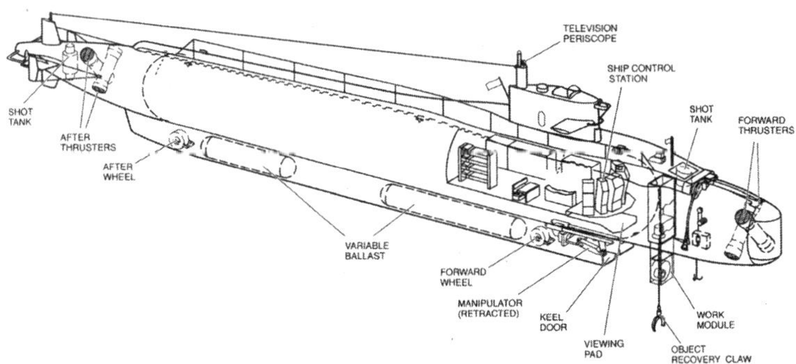

Fig. 2. The after section of the *NR-1* was devoted to the nuclear reactor and propulsion plant; it was sealed off from the forward living and working/control spaces. / Authors' collection.

The *NR-1*, fabricated of HY-80 steel, had her living and working spaces located forward, with the after portion of the craft containing the sealed reactor and engineering spaces. She was fitted with two large, retractable wheels to enable her to roll on and rest on the ocean floor. In addition to her twin screws, which provided a submerged speed of 3.5 knots, the craft had paired ducted thrusters fitted in the hull, forward and aft, that provided a high degree of maneuverability. Extensive external lights, viewing ports, close-range sonars, a remote-controlled mechanical arm, and a recovery cage provided considerable capabilities. The *NR-1* crew normally consisted of five Navy operators plus two scientists. The crew's endurance was limited only by oxygen, which she could replenish with electroanalysis, and the amount of food that she carried, but the "capacity of the [human] waste tank was, in truth, the single most important factor in determining how long the boat could remain submerged."[78]

With an overall length of 145¾ feet, the *NR-1* had a surface displacement of 365.5 tons and submerged was 393 tons. Launched on 25 January 1969, the *NR-1* underwent initial sea trials that summer and was placed in service on 27 October of that year. The principal operational limitation of the *NR-1* was her deployment mobility. Because of her slow speed, she had to be towed to her operating areas either by a surface ship or (underwater) by a nuclear submarine. Her surface towing speed was up to six knots; submerged it was less than four knots.

The *NR-1* conducted numerous research, ocean engineering, and deep recovery missions in addition to supporting the Navy's extensive seafloor Sound Surveillance System (SOSUS). The submersible's publicized operations included searching for the wreckage following the space shuttle *Challenger* disaster in 1986, discovering and excavating Roman-era shipwrecks in the Mediterranean, exploring plant and marine life in the Gulf of Mexico, and recovering a Phoenix missile from an F-14 Tomcat fighter that crashed off the coast of Scotland and the wreckage of an F-15 Eagle fighter off the coast of North Carolina.

The *NR-1* also carried out several highly classified missions, the details of which have not been made public. (The *NR-1* had not been able to locate the wreckage of the Israeli submarine *Dakar* that sank in the Mediterranean in 1968 after a collision with a merchant ship.)

The *NR-1* was taken out of service in November 2008, almost 40 years after being completed. Despite Admiral Rickover's prediction that the *NR-1* would be the first of a fleet of nuclear-propelled submersibles for research, ocean engineering, and other tasks, no additional vehicles were built. An *NR-2* submersible was planned as a test platform for HY-100 steel, but that project never came to fruition.[79] Still, Western submarines and submersibles of several sizes and types were used for clandestine missions during the Cold War era.

Projects Winterwind and Underdog

During the 1960s, the U.S. Navy and Air Force undertook comprehensive operations to recover missile components from the ocean floor following Soviet missile test launches in the Pacific. Navy studies had concluded such deep-ocean search and recovery operations were feasible and gave the project the codename Winterwind. A parallel plan codenamed Underdog was developed for a covert capability to locate and recover practice torpedoes and cruise missile components from shallow water—that is, less than 2,000 feet deep.

The original Winterwind concept of operations had four phases:

- Hydrographic survey and bottom mapping by the USS *Compass Island* (AG 153)
- Submarine search by the USS *Halibut* with towed search sleds and later by the USS *Seawolf* (SSN 575)
- Recovery of objects by the third, specially built version of the bathyscaph *Trieste*
- Surface support by the floating drydock *White Sands* (ARD 20), which was towed to operating areas.

Obviously, the surface-supported *Trieste* could not possibly participate in the clandestine recovery of objects of interest. For several reasons, the only Winterwind element that was active from 1964 to 1967 was the seafloor mapping by the *Compass Island*. That ship was a converted Mariner-type merchant ship configured for the development and evaluation of an advanced navigation system in support of the Polaris ballistic missile submarine program. But work on the other elements of Winterwind was underway at the Mare Island shipyard, the Lockheed and Westinghouse firms, and the Navy's Deep Submergence Systems Project. And, as noted earlier, the *Halibut* was sidetracked from Winterwind in 1968 to locate the sunken Soviet missile submarine *K-129* and determine if the craft's remains could be recovered.

In early 1969, the Winterwind and Underdog projects were combined, with surface-based location and recovery systems discarded in favor of more clandestine, submarine-based search and recovery capabilities. In the mid-1970s, the debris of several nose cones from Soviet intercontinental ballistic missile tests was recovered from Pacific impact areas, providing significant technical intelligence that was not available to the United States from any other source.

The *Halibut* and successor special projects submarines undertook other clandestine operations. At times, they employed the Navy's three covert submersibles that could be deployed and supported by submarines: the *Mystic* (DSRV-1), *Avalon* (DSRV-2), and *NR-1*. When retired, those submersibles were replaced not by *manned* submersibles but by towed search and recovery devices and by remotely operated unmanned vehicles.[80]

Computer Age Exploitation

Radiant Gemstone was a suite of submarine-mounted equipment for "computer network exploitation." The program focused on both political and military targets, including the interception of cell phones and other low-energy transmissions.[81] The countries of interest were Afghanistan, China, India, Iran, Iraq, and Russia. Vice Admiral Michael Connor, then commander of the Atlantic Fleet submarine force, explained, "We have a remarkable ability to take the sensors that we have . . . and put them in the place they are the most relevant, because we can get *closer*."[82] After being "captured," the intercepts were run through a National Security Agency program called Blinddate to generate information for intelligence analysts.

The Radiant Gemstone equipment first was installed in the attack submarine *Annapolis* (SSN 760) in 2003 for a "field test."

The system also was tested on the high-speed research ship *Joint Venture* (HSV-X1) in 2006 and in a Tiger Shark aircraft drone in 2008. Testing was conducted on a second nuclear submarine, the *Montpelier* (SSN 765), in April 2008. Subsequently, it may have been installed in later *Los Angeles*–class submarines.[83]

The only publicly documented operational installation of Radiant Gemstone was obliquely referenced by the commanding officer of the *Annapolis*, upon the submarine's return to her home port in September 2015, when he revealed that the *Annapolis* had engaged in four missions of critical national importance. The submarine had operated in the Indian Ocean, the Red Sea, and the Mediterranean during that deployment.

In addition to acting as a very sensitive platform to intercept low-powered electronic transmissions, the Navy reportedly was preparing for submarines to have a more active role in cyber warfare. "There is . . . an offensive capability that we . . . prize very highly," said Rear Admiral Michael Jabaley, previously the U.S. Navy's program executive officer for submarines.[84]

Thus, in the twentieth century, submarines opened new sources of communications intelligence to meet national objectives, including the tapping into undersea cables. In the early twenty-first century, the employment of submarines for intelligence missions has grown more complex and versatile.

3

The Cold War

The Red Side

> An important condition for ensuring the high combat readiness of the Soviet Navy from the start of the '60's has been the systematic reconnaissance of the forces of the probable enemy in all possible regions in which they are located while still in peacetime.
>
> —Captain 1st Rank V. P. Kuzin and Captain 1st Rank V. I. Nikol'skiy

As the Cold War evolved after World War II, the Soviet Union initially had little interest in maritime matters, although Soviet dictator Josef Stalin had pronounced that he would build a large navy.[1] As early as 28 July 1943, Stalin had declared that in the postwar period "the Soviet people wish to see their fleet grow still stronger and more powerful." The war had made the Soviet Union a great power, and Stalin had not forgotten the limitations of the Soviet Union in the Spanish Civil War of 1936–39, when Red merchant ships carrying aid to the Republican forces were at the mercy of fascist warships and airplanes. He also had recognized the value of navies in several World War II campaigns. However, his grandiose plans for the country's becoming a major naval power died with him in March 1953.

The Soviet Navy commander in chief, Fleet Admiral N. G. Kuznetsov, on 1 September 1951, issued an order establishing a program to develop and send to sea specialized intelligence collection ships with trained intercept technicians. Until dedicated spy ships could be provided, the Red fleet employed readily available craft—with minimal modifications and very limited capabilities—in the reconnaissance role. These early efforts included the

American-built submarine chaser *Irtek*, formerly the *SC-646* built in 1942; she was provided to the Soviet Union in May 1945 under the Lend-Lease program. The 148-ton, 110⅚-foot ship served in the intelligence role in the early 1950s until sunk in 1956. Also in the 1950s, the Soviet Union acquired 13 East German–built fishing trawlers that were employed as intelligence collection craft. Most of those craft were assigned a few SIGINT technicians in addition to their Navy crews, usually sailing in civilian garb. Those craft operated in several regional areas, with most observing Western naval operations. They initially were called messenger ships by the Soviets (and tattletales by NATO navies).

The Soviet defense establishment became increasingly interested in the U.S. Navy in the early 1950s, in large part because of the increasing threat from nuclear-armed strike aircraft launched from U.S. aircraft carriers. Thus, the Soviets initiated specialized intelligence ships in the 1950s. Those intelligence ships also supplemented the limited number of overseas listening posts then available to the Soviet intelligence community.

During the Cold War, two U.S. Navy intelligence officers, Lieutenant George Stuart and Lieutenant Commander Linda Taylor, wrote: "A significant element of the unparalleled growth of Soviet sea power since 1956 has been the emphasis placed on expanding the country's intelligence collection fleet. . . . This fleet, under the centralized control of the Soviet Navy, remains the principal 'eyes and ears' of Soviet naval intelligence."[2]

Those intelligence collectors reported to the deputy chief for intelligence of the Main Navy Staff. That officer was "double hatted" as a deputy head of the Main Intelligence Directorate of the Soviet armed forces, the GRU (Glavnoye Razvedyvatelnoye Upravlenie).[3] The GRU appears to have no relationship to the state security organs that are responsible for Soviet/Russian internal security and political interests. However, like the other state security agencies, the GRU operates networks of "illegals" in other countries to collect military intelligence, and it maintains personnel under diplomatic cover in Russian embassies, consulates, and other agencies around the world. All naval and military attachés are trained GRU officers.[4]

Along with other state intelligence agencies, the GRU maintains worldwide SIGINT collection operations, including satellites, aircraft, warships, submarines, and dedicated spy ships. The only type of intelligence activity that is not duplicated is internal security, which is the exclusive domain of other agencies.

Each of the four Soviet/Russian fleets—Northern, Baltic, Black Sea, Pacific—have an intelligence directorate. Those directorates manage naval intelligence collection activities within their area, including the control of some assets, such as the dedicated spy ships. Those directorates coordinate the collection operations by warships and submarines, as well as collection efforts by merchant ships, fish factory/support ships, and fishing vessels when opportunities are available. Ashore the directorates maintain an analysis and correlation center in each fleet area to support afloat operations and to provide intelligence to the Main Naval Staff.

Each of the fleet intelligence directorates is reported to have five principal divisions:

- Reconnaissance/collection activities
- Agent operations within the fleet area
- Naval special forces (Spetsnaz) operations[5]
- Correlation and distribution of intelligence collected within the fleet area and with intelligence provided by the Main Naval Staff
- COMINT and ELINT operations

All of those intelligence activities in the past contributed to the Soviet Ocean Surveillance System (SOSS)—a Western term. The SOSS sought to maintain a current picture of the world's oceans, plotting the location of Western naval ships and, to the extent possible, Western submarines. There were several contributors to SOSS:

- Space: photo, ELINT, radar satellites, manned spacecraft
- SIGINT/radio direction: KGB (Komitet Gosudarstvennoy Bezopasnosti [Committee for State Security]), GRU, and Navy systems
- Naval/maritime: AGIS (intelligence ships), naval ships, naval aircraft, merchant ships, fishing ships, oceanographic research ships
- Open source: Western press articles
- Spies: KGB, GRU

At Navy headquarters in St. Petersburg, the Intelligence Department of the Main Naval Staff is headed normally by a vice admiral who also is a deputy chief of the GRU. That office coordinates the input from the fleet intelligence staffs and distributes intelligence information to various departments, commands, and agencies as appropriate. Reportedly, the following fleet command units operate the AGIs:

Baltic Fleet: 72nd Separate Division based at Baltiysk

Black Sea Fleet: 519th Separate Division based at Sevastopol

Northern Fleet: 518th Separate Division based at Severomorsk

Pacific Fleet: 515th Separate Division based at Vladivostok

The Soviet Spy Ships

Although often depicted in the Western press as disguised fishing trawlers, even the early Soviet intelligence collection ships were readily identifiable. Those ships were manned by Navy personnel and fitted with extensive arrays of electronic antennas; many had their designations of GS (hydrographic) or CCB (SSV in English, for communications) painted on their hulls.[6] Most of the early Soviet intelligence ships were built on trawler hulls, and some had large, refrigerated cargo holds that were readily adaptable to electronic spaces. Trawler hulls also provided long endurance, had good seakeeping qualities, and were in series production. Western navies assigned the designation "AGI" to those ships—miscellaneous auxiliary, intelligence.

The published material is unclear in details of the early Soviet AGIs. Reports indicate that the Soviet ships employed in that role first appeared around Johnston Island in the Pacific during the 1958 atmospheric tests of U.S. nuclear weapons.[7] The first specialized ships probably were the *Izmeritel'* and *Protraktor*, which were converted during construction from tuna fishing ships being built in Japan. Completed in 1959, their conversion to intelligence collectors included adding a small deckhouse abaft the funnel and being fitted with electronic intercept equipment. Those ships were 1,050 tons full load with a length of 171 feet. Both ships served in the Pacific (see appendix A).

Photo 10. Looking well-worn and tired, a Mayak-class AGI heads for her home port. Many of the crew are on deck, "watching the watcher." These small and relatively crowded intelligence collectors made lengthy deployments. They often were refueled and provisioned by Soviet/Russian fish factory ships. /U.S. Navy.

Large numbers of intelligence collection ships followed, both conversions of existing designs and, subsequently, new designs. At least 15 intelligence ships were adapted from the small, Okean-class trawlers, of which more than 100 were constructed in East German shipyards between 1959 and about 1967. That was the most numerous series of intelligence collection ships; they had a full-load displacement of 700 tons with a length of 166⅔ feet. (A Moma-class hydrographic survey ship carried the name *Okean*—i.e., "ocean.")

As an example of their endurance, the *Lotlin* of the Okean series once remained on station for 201 days. In 1967, while operating off the U.S. East Coast, the *Lotlin* suffered a propulsion casualty; after her crew rigged a sail, the spy ship was able to sail more than 300 miles to reach the *Dauriya*, a Soviet fish factory ship operating off Newfoundland. The *Lotlin* was able to take advantage of the north-flowing Gulf Stream in her odyssey, averaging some two to three knots for the voyage. After repairs and taking on provisions from the *Dauriya*, the *Lotlin* returned to her nefarious activities.

Also in the 1960s, eight Mayak-class AGIs were converted from side trawlers. Those ships displaced 912 tons with a length of 177¾ feet. At least one Mayak was armed with machine guns. But there were CIA reports that two of those AGIs were fitted with four 16-inch (406-mm) tubes for anti-submarine torpedoes, four RBU-1800 anti-submarine rocket launchers, and a twin 25-mm/80-caliber anti-aircraft gun mount.[8] Anti-submarine weapons were not reported to have been fitted to any other AGIs. (Those two ships may have been trial ships for anti-submarine weapons.)

In time most Soviet AGIs were provided with intercept systems for Communications Intelligence and Electronic Intelligence. The larger ships also had optical tracking devices to monitor Western missile launches.

While the early AGIs were based on trawler- and other fisheries-type hulls, the three large ships of the Polish-built *Nikolay Zubov* class were converted in the 1960s from oceanographic research ships; they were 3,100-ton ships with a length of 297 feet. Among the largest AGI were the six ships of the Primor'ye class of the 1970s that had on-board intelligence processing as well as collection capabilities. Those ships were based on the hull design of fish factory trawlers and are believed to have been the first Soviet ships to be constructed and fitted specifically as intelligence collectors. They displaced 4,340 tons with a length of 277½ feet.

In particular, the Primor'ye class and the subsequent four ships of the Bal'zam class had massive superstructures amidships to house equipment and space for analysts, providing the ships with intelligence processing capabilities, and mounted extensive satellite communications antennas. The electronic systems in those ships have continually been upgraded, with some ships having optical trackers or cameras to monitor missile tests—both Russian and

Photo 11. The *Aziya* was one of the four Bal'zam-class large, highly capable AGIs. Those ships were distinguished by their two large radomes atop the forward superstructure and by their size. This class was the first Soviet ship design that was intended from the keel up specifically for the intelligence collection role. / Japan Maritime Self-Defense Force.

foreign. Probably beginning with the subsequent Bal'zam class, the larger Soviet AGIs also were armed with 30-mm AK-630 rapid-fire (Gatling) guns and the Strela (arrow) surface-to-air missile launchers (NATO SA-N-5 Grail). Those weapons were superior to the armament being fitted to U.S. spy ships—that is, 20-mm cannon and .50-caliber machine guns. The Bal'zam ships displaced 4, 500 tons full load with a length of 346⅙ feet.

The next AGI class was the seven-ship Meridian series. The lead ship—named *Fedor Golovin*—was completed in 1985. Built in Poland, those purpose-built ships displaced 3,470 tons at full load with a length of 309½ feet. Each also was armed with AK-630 rapid-fire guns and Strela missiles.

Russia has continued to construct specialized intelligence ships in the post-Soviet era with two ships of the *Yuriy Ivanov* class, completed in 2015 and 2018, with additional ships planned. Thus, there apparently was an interval of almost three decades between the completion of the last of the Meridian class and the first of these ships. The later ships are large, displacing some 4,000 tons with a length of 315 feet. Reportedly, these ships have more advanced intelligence collection capabilities with a high degree of automation and systems integration. These ships also are armed.

In addition to the specialized AGIs, the Soviets constructed and converted several large, space event support ships and missile range instrumentation ships to monitor manned and unmanned space operations, and missile tests. Obviously, those ships could be employed in the intelligence collection role, as when the *Chazhma* observed the clandestine salvage of the submarine *K-129* by the *Hughes Glomar Explorer* in the North Pacific. However, those Soviet ships normally lacked the specialized electronics and the intercept and translation personnel to perform effectively as spy ships.

Beginning in the 1950s, Soviet AGIs dogged U.S. Navy ships at sea, especially aircraft carrier operations. Senator Robert Griffin of Michigan told a congressional committee, "At least since August 1956, the Soviets have utilized AGIs in intelligence collection operations against U.S. Naval bases, individual ships, and carrier task groups."[9]

During missile test launches by the first U.S. Polaris submarine, the *George Washington* (SSBN 598), some 120 miles off the coast of New Jersey in April 1960, the Moma-class AGI *Vega* attempted to recover debris from those tests. A U.S. intelligence bulletin noted: "The activities of the *Vega* are the most aggressive noted to date, and the first to be related to the Polaris program."[10]

With the deployment of the U.S. Polaris strategic missile submarines in the early 1960s, the AGIs additionally began patrolling off the submarine bases of Guam; Holy Loch, Scotland; Kings Bay, Georgia; and Bremerton, Washington. Those spy ships sought to intercept radio transmissions related to the missile submarines and possibly tried to pick up their trail as they departed bases for their forward patrol areas. Soviet spy ships also were seen off Cape Canaveral, Florida, when military-related space launches were occurring. The AGIs that operated off the East Coast of the United States used Havana for support and replenishment, a practice that continued into the post–Cold War period. (The Soviet Union also established a major SIGINT facility at Lourdes, Cuba, in 1962. At its peak operation, that facility was manned by some 1,500 Soviet military personnel. The facility was closed in 2001.[11])

Soviet spy ships also operated against military facilities in Great Britain in addition to the Holy Loch submarine base. In February 1960, British defence minister Harold Watkinson accused Soviet "trawlers" of being "constantly at sea in close proximity" to British coastal waters while Soviet submarines spied on the weapons testing range at Aberporth, Wales. Prime Minister Harold Macmillan complained about those incidents in a letter to Premier Nikita Khrushchev, stating that such activities brought the Soviet Union "perilously close to a showdown with the West."[12]

The first authorized U.S. action against a Soviet AGI reportedly occurred in 1964, when a Naval Security Group detachment boarded the destroyer *Robert A. Owens* (DD 827). Under Captain John Murphy, the detachment was directed to keep Soviet intelligence ships away from Harpoon missile tests that were being conducted off the coast of Norfolk, Virginia.[13] Murphy reported:

> I became increasingly impressed with the shiphandling skills of the AGI's captain. We would try and come close alongside for photographic coverage and he would "spin on a dime" and head into the sun putting us at a disadvantage. Our destroyer could not "spin" as nicely as an AGI.[14]

In his overall appraisal of the AGIs, Murphy observed, "They may have looked like god-forsaken pieces of junk, but they were manned by talented and capable crews."[15]

Beyond keeping watch on U.S. submarine bases and observing surface ship operations, periodically the AGIs operated in important international waterways, such as the Strait of Gibraltar, the Sicilian Straits, and the Strait of Hormuz. During the Vietnam conflict, when U.S. B-52 Stratofortress bombers began striking targets in North Vietnam in April 1966, the AGI that was deployed almost continuously off the American island of Guam purportedly could warn the Hanoi government of B-52 bomber flights departing the island en route to strike North Vietnamese targets.

An AGI apparently had been assigned to the "Guam station" beginning in 1964 when the submarine tender *Proteus* (AS 19) was based at Guam's Apra Harbor to support Polaris missile submarines deploying in the Western Pacific. Other possible targets for the Soviet intelligence ships off Guam included a master communications station, a SOSUS terminal, and a National Aeronautics and Space Administration satellite-tracking facility.

Watching the Carriers

During the Vietnam War (1964–75), a Soviet AGI almost continuously operated in the Gulf of Tonkin to monitor U.S. carrier operations in that area. Some sources contend that those intelligence ships could have provided warnings to the Hanoi government of U.S. carrier strikes to North Vietnam. The Soviets tracked Western aircraft carriers to provide the regime with intelligence on their operations for "defensive" reasons. They also were interested in observing carrier techniques and practices as the Soviet Navy had begun constructing aircraft carriers in the 1960s. Navy Department historian Dr. David Winkler related the tactics that two future U.S. chiefs of naval operations used when AGIs steamed close to U.S. ships during Tonkin Gulf operations when flying strikes in the Vietnam War.[16]

Admiral Thomas B. Hayward, commanding the carrier *America* (CVA 66), first ordered all aircraft tied down securely. Then he executed a hard starboard turn into the path of the AGI, "sending an immediate signal to its captain that we didn't appreciate his action and that he should clear the area immediately. It worked."[17]

Admiral James L. Holloway III, when commanding the nuclear-propelled carrier *Enterprise* (CVAN 65), once ordered his 95,000-ton warship to full speed and turned to head straight toward the trailing AGI. "And it got the hell out of our way," recalled Holloway.[18] There were no recorded collisions of AGIs with U.S. aircraft carriers.

According to a Russian source, from 1964 to 1974, the Soviet Pacific Fleet operated 17 "reconnaissance ships" in the Vietnam area. Reportedly, they made 94 cruises lasting three to four months.[19]

Photo 12. The Soviet spy ship *Gidrofon* observes the U.S. aircraft carrier *Coral Sea* (CVA 43) during operations in the Gulf of Tonkin in 1989. Soviet AGIs continuously monitored U.S. carrier activities in the area during the Vietnam conflict. / U.S. Navy.

Periodically, Soviet warships, especially destroyers, would serve as tattletales tracking Western warships in the Mediterranean and in open-ocean areas. Some of those destroyers had aft-firing anti-ship missiles, which led to speculation that if war erupted those ships would report on the location of the Western carriers and then clear the area at high speed while adding their missiles to the potential carnage.[20]

During the 1973 war between Israel and several Arab states, both the United States and the Soviet Union reinforced their Mediterranean squadrons. In close quarters, the U.S. Sixth Fleet reached a peak of 60 ships and submarines, including three attack carriers, while the Soviet Fifth Eskadra (squadron) reached 96 units, including 23 submarines.[21]

During that confrontation, Soviet cruisers and destroyers trailed the U.S. attack carriers, while Soviet AGIs monitored the U.S. amphibious squadrons in the Mediterranean, with the latter including two helicopter carriers. At most times there was an AGI tattletale with the attack carriers, possibly "capable of providing midcourse guidance to [surface-to-surface missiles] fired from elsewhere."[22]

Apparently, "in effect, Moscow was sending Washington a signal that interference with its resupply operations [of Arab forces] would be met with force."[23] The October 1973 conflict between Israel and the Arab states was overwhelmingly a victory for the Jewish state, and the armed forces of neither the United States nor the Soviet Union became directly involved.

The Soviet warships shadowing Western aircraft carriers often would maneuver close aboard the larger warships. On 9 November 1970, during a NATO exercise in the Mediterranean, the Soviet destroyer *Bravyy* steamed close in to the British task group, crossed ahead of the aircraft carrier *Ark Royal*, possibly to observe and make an apparent effort to disrupt flight activities. The carrier put her engines full astern to avoid a collision; still the two ships made contact, with the destroyer being struck on the port side and rolled to starboard. Seven Soviet sailors were thrown overboard; only five men were recovered. Both ships sustained minor damage. The day after that collision, the Soviet government accepted a long-standing invitation from the United States to hold bilateral talks "on incidents at sea."[24]

Numerous other "near misses" of Soviet AGIs and trailing destroyers with U.S. and British warships occurred as the Red ships maneuvered close-in to collect intelligence. They also sought to determine how Western naval ships would react in certain situations.

(One Russian AGI was sunk in a collision with a merchant ship. On 27 April 2007, the *Liman* collided with a merchant ship on the Black Sea coast, just north of Istanbul. The spy ship, a former naval survey ship, sank following the collision with the Togo-flagged merchant ship *Youzarsif H* in heavy fog conditions. Of the 78 personnel on board the *Liman*, 63 were rescued by the Turkish coast guard and 15 by the merchant ship, which suffered minor damage.)

Photo 13. The *Ark Royal*, backing astern, collides with the *Bravyy* after the Soviet destroyer attempted to cross ahead of the aircraft carrier, forcing her to back down during operations in the Mediterranean on 9 November 1970. Two Soviet sailors were lost in the collision. The destroyer was "shadowing" the British flattop. / Royal Navy.

Separate from the Soviet-Western confrontations of the Cold War that involved intelligence collection, during the Falklands conflict of 1982 the Soviet Union employed more than a dozen SIGINT-fitted ships to monitor the British ships and operations. The *Primor'ye* followed the British task force as it sailed south to the Falklands in April 1982, after the Argentine seizure of the islands. Possibly she was seeking to intercept the communications between London and the British ships.[25]

Subsequently, the fishery research ship *Akademik Knipovich* anchored at the Argentine naval base at Ushuaia, although the exact purpose of her visit is not known. Several other Soviet ships, apparently in the SIGINT role, sailed into the conflict area, violating the 350-n.mile exclusion zone that the British had proclaimed around the Falklands during the conflict.

The Soviet Union also developed "underwater situation illumination" ships. Those ships had the large Dnestr sonar fitted for long-range submarine detection, in part as compensation for the

Photo 14. Like many AGI classes, the configurations of the six Primor'ye-class ships differed greatly. The *Zaporozh'ye*, shown here in 1989 off the U.S. Atlantic coast, was fitted with a two-face, fixed-array radar amidships for missile tracking. Like most AGIs, those ships were based on a commercial, fisheries industry design. / U.S. Navy.

country not being able to effectively deploy fixed, seafloor acoustic systems, such as the American SOSUS.[26] Those ships were based on a large, refrigerator trawler design. The lead ship, named *Kamchatka*, completed in 1986, displaced 5,700 tons full load with a length of 347¾ feet. With the end of the Cold War, the second unit was completed for Ukraine in 1992.

A significantly larger ship that began as a "submarine search ship" was laid down in Leningrad in 1987 as the *Povolzh'ye*. Unfinished, she was transferred to an Italian shipyard and completed as a merchant ship.

The Soviet Union operated more than 60 AGIs when the Cold War ended in 1991. They had been highly effective in garnering Western secrets. However, there were "liabilities." In the mid-1980s, Lieutenant Stuart and Lieutenant Commander Taylor listed three principal liabilities:

> Although they have been increasingly used in crises or hostile environments, most are unarmed and therefore defenseless against

attack. . . . The *Balzam* has been armed, and efforts are apparently under way to arm other classes. The second disadvantage is their slow speed, ranging anywhere from twelve to twenty knots, which means that they can easily be outdistanced by many of the ships they are directed to monitor. Finally, the majority of these ships are technically inflexible in that all of their electronics systems are believed to be permanently wired into the ship. Although modularization is possible on some classes, in most cases, these ships could not be modernized without great difficulty.[27]

A Very Brief Career

Ironically, the largest and most impressive Soviet-era spy ship never spied. The *Ural* (Project 1941) was large—35,200 tons at full load and 869 feet in length—with a combination steam-nuclear propulsion plant. Her design was based on the *Marshal Nedelin*–class space event support ships.[28] The *Ural* was reportedly intended to serve in the intelligence collection as well as communications relay and spacecraft-tracking roles. Other than aircraft carriers, the *Ural* was the world's largest nuclear-propelled ship, being larger than the U.S. and Soviet missile cruisers with nuclear propulsion.

Given the NATO codename Kapusta (Russian for cabbage), the *Ural* was laid down in 1981 at Leningrad's Baltic Shipyard, which also constructed the four nuclear-propelled battle cruisers of the *Kirov* class (Project 1144). The *Ural* had the same, twin-reactor propulsion plant as the cruisers.

The *Ural* was launched in 1983 but not placed in service until 1989. The lengthy interval could be attributed to problems with her propulsion plant and to the fitting of advanced electronic equipment. The ship was armed with light defensive guns and surface-to-air missiles.

Upon completion, the *Ural* was transferred to the Pacific Fleet, making the transit on the Northern Sea route in 59 days. When she arrived at Vladivostok, no pier was long enough to accommodate the large ship; thus, she was forced to anchor in the bay with her nuclear plant operating continuously to support the on-board systems and to provide power for crew-related functions. In 1990

Photo 15. The *Ural* (SSV-33) was the largest intelligence collection ship to be constructed. The nuclear-propelled ship had extensive systems to perform multiple roles. Built at the end of the Cold War, she was a victim of the demise of the Soviet Union and never was operational. / German Ministry of Defense.

and again the following year, the ship was reported to have suffered fires. Minimal repairs were undertaken.

Soviet military intelligence "stubbornly required the construction of a second ship of the type, but the Navy objected since the construction of the [*Ural*] interfered with the already sluggish construction of the [*Kirov*] nuclear missile cruisers."[29] The four *Kirov*-class battle cruisers, completed from 1980 to 1996, displaced 28,000 tons with a length of 813½ feet.[30] The *Kirov*s were the largest warships built by any nation after World War II except for aircraft carriers and flight-deck amphibious ships.

In the event, the Baltic yard built only one *Ural*-type ship. With the end of the Soviet regime in late 1991, funding was not available to repair, maintain, and operate the *Ural*, and providing for her 925-man crew became problematic. The *Ural* was decommissioned at the end of 2002, apparently never having carried out an operational mission. She was towed first to Abrek Bay and then to Bolshoy Kamen; scrapping began in 2010. Thus ended the career of the world's largest intelligence collection ship.

The End of an Era

In 1991, on the eve of the collapse of the Soviet Union, the Navy had about 60 AGIs in service. With the demise of the Soviet regime came an immediate reduction in naval forces, including spy ships. By 2020 slightly more than a dozen dedicated intelligence collection ships flew Russian colors and were divided among the four fleets.

Russian surveillance ships have continued worldwide operations. One of the most active had been the *Viktor Leonov*, a large, 3,470-ton unit of the Meridian class. Beginning in 2014, the ship steamed off the U.S. Atlantic Coast for several days on a number of occasions. The *Viktor Leonov* also made visits to Cuba during those cross-Atlantic voyages.

Across the Atlantic, in late 2020 two Vishnaya-class AGIs operated some 20 n.miles off the northern coast of Scotland, or about 35 miles from the large British air force base at Lossiemouth. The base was home to British maritime patrol aircraft as well as to fighters.

In the Pacific, Russian AGIs have monitored the periodic, multination RIMPAC (Rim of the Pacific) naval exercises off Hawaii, with the large AGI *Kareliya* operating in Hawaiian western waters in 2021. (When the *Kareliya* loitered off the coast of Kauai, Hawaii, for several days in December 1988, she caused a delay in a U.S. Missile Defense Agency missile test.) The Russian-era naval activities continue to include spy ship operations in distant waters and off foreign shores, as well as seeking to observe Western naval operations.

The Fishing Fleets

In addition to the dedicated intelligence collection ships, Soviet fishing craft as well as merchant ships have collected intelligence as opportunities permitted, sometimes with naval intelligence officers embarked.[31] By the 1970s, the Soviet oceangoing fishing fleet was the world's largest and the most modern, and in second place in total catch (after Japan).[32] It provided a major source of food for the Soviet population, with the country's per capita consumption of fish more than twice that of the United States. Also, the fishing industry was a significant earner of hard currency through the sales of catches to foreign customers. The large catches also provided important benefits to agriculture in the form of nonfood byproducts, such as feed and fertilizer.

In particular, as flotillas of fishing craft increasingly went to distant seas, there were indications that their accompanying fish factory ships provided suitable platforms for intelligence collection. Award-winning author Martin Cruz Smith pictured that situation in a novel when his hero, detective Arkady Renko of *Gorky Park* fame, discovers that his factory ship *Polar Star* has an intelligence compartment and is fitted with a towed sonar array.[33] (In 1982, for example, 117 of the world's 131 fish factory ships of more than 10,000 gross tons sailed under the Soviet flag.[34])

A U.S. Navy electronics expert, Master Chief Sonar Technician Jim Bussert, has observed, "Due to standardization within the Soviet economic system, fishing and merchant ship equipments are more closely associated with warship equipment than in many Western countries." He added, "In the USSR, non-navy ships are sometimes manned by naval officers and always serve the state's interests."[35]

In 1977 the head of the Canadian Navy, Vice-Admiral Douglas Boyle, stated that at times up to 500 Soviet fishing trawlers were working off the eastern coast of Canada. "We have established that between 10 and 15 percent of these trawlers are intelligence gathers," he said in an interview. "They fish but they are out there doing another job."[36]

Further warnings of the threat posed by the Red fishing fleet came from the U.S. Central Intelligence Agency in 1982:

> Because of its size and equipment, the Soviet Pacific fishing fleet brings with it military and intelligence capabilities. The fleet's travels, for example, put it into position to implant navigation and surveillance devices, collect communications and radar signals,

monitor foreign ships and aircraft, and reprovision naval vessels should the need arise. The repeated return of Soviet fishing and fisheries research vessels to isolated Pacific regions in the face of declining catches there suggests the possible use of the fishing fleets for scientific research, communications and navigation work, military support, or intelligence gathering.[37]

Two years later, in 1984, a Soviet fishing boat captain who had defected a decade earlier, told a U.S. congressional investigating committee, "My ship had special equipment for submarine tracking."[38] The captain, Vladil Lysenko, who was reported to have served more than 30 years in Soviet merchant and fishing ships, claimed to have received the Order of Lenin decoration for his intelligence reporting.

Still another potential threat from Soviet fishing activities was publicized as early as 1959 when five transatlantic cables off Newfoundland were damaged. A multitude of such seafloor cables carry government, commercial, and private communications around the world. The trawler *Novorossisk* was in the area when the cables were damaged.

The U.S. destroyer escort *Roy O. Hale* (DER 336) put a five-man boarding party on the *Novorossisk* when some 120 miles northeast of the port of St. Johns. The captain of the warship said that his men found no evidence that the trawler was engaged in "anything but fishing." The trawler's master was "friendly and co-operative," according to the U.S. Navy.[39] Still, the threat remained that the vast and far-ranging Soviet/Russian fishing fleet could monitor Western naval and commercial activities at sea.

Merchant Ships

From the 1970s through the 1990s, the Soviet Union undertook an impressive buildup of its merchant fleet. That fleet reached the position of number 2 in the world in number of merchant ships—many constructed in foreign shipyards—and was fifth in gross tonnage and sixth in deadweight tonnage.[40] The 2,400 merchant ships in Soviet service in 1990 served primarily economic purposes with lesser but still important roles in serving Moscow's political interests (i.e., trade with the Third World) and military activities (providing logistics support of the fleet and overseas military activities).[41]

Some Western observers believed that the merchant fleet also had a significant intelligence collection role. Obviously, merchant ship captains would forward any information on what was observed and considered noteworthy to the appropriate intelligence organs. In 1982 a research specialist at the U.S. Defense Intelligence Agency, Army Captain Robert E. McKeown, wrote: "Many merchant ships and civilian-manned survey, research, and space-associated ships can carry sensors capable of assisting in the area of communications and electronic and signal intelligence collection. Naval personnel are assigned to operate the most sophisticated equipment."[42]

Research and Space Events/Missile Range Ships

The Soviet Union also operated the world's largest fleets of oceanographic/hydrographic research ships and Space Events Support Ships (SESS). At its peak, the former category numbered some 200 ships, more than twice as many as were flying the American flag.[43] In addition, several research submersibles were operated with those ships.

Both the Soviet Navy and the academic and research institutions conducted oceanographic/hydrographic research.[44] Major economic advantages were accrued from their oceanographic research efforts. For example, the efficiency and yield of the large Soviet global fisheries fleet was based in part through the understanding of the dynamics of marine life, due in large part to the work of oceanographic research ships.

From a military perspective, the Soviet oceanographic efforts have centered on submarine operations and anti-submarine warfare. For example, because the performance of acoustic systems depends, in large part, on local oceanographic conditions (salinity, temperature, seafloor sediments, wave action, background noise), the Soviets collected extensive data on worldwide ocean environments. In exercises and operations, Soviet naval forces have used the knowledge of local oceanographic conditions to greatly extend the range of their acoustic sensors; similarly, they have attempted to "hide" submarines behind ocean fronts.[45]

These ships have ranged far and wide. For example, a CIA memo observed that the Soviet Navy first became active in the Indian Ocean in 1957–58 with the dispatch of an oceanographic research ship for intelligence gathering. From then until the mid-1960s, the Soviet presence in that area was the deployment of two or three ships per year on extended oceanographic cruises.[46] (The first Soviet warship to sail the Indian Ocean was a destroyer in 1965.)

The Soviet Union also has operated the largest fleet of Space Events Support Ships for both military and scientific space activities. The first of those ships went to sea in 1959, providing spacecraft monitoring and, in time, control functions for the country's increasing military and civilian space programs. In addition to ships supporting military space activities, Missile Range Instrumentation Ships (MRIS), military space monitoring and control ships, and other scientific support ships are operated under the aegis of the Academy of Sciences and other academic agencies. Although civilian manned, these ships "supported all of the basic tracking tasks of Soviet space craft *and* spacecraft of the probable enemy, and also experimental launches of various ballistic missiles belonging to him."[47]

From the beginning of the space era, Soviet military intelligence considered the MRIS and SESS ships as dual-purpose: to monitor and support Soviet missile and space operations, and to intercept U.S. and other Western nations' telemetry and signals controlling missile and space operations. The military MRIS and SESS ships deployed with teams of intelligence intercept operators. At times Soviet civilian SESS also sailed with teams to intercept non-Soviet space-related telemetry and signals.

The Soviet space events ships were the world's largest. The *Kosmonaut Yuriy Gagarin*, operated by the Academy of Sciences, was completed in 1971.[48] The ship had a standard displacement of 53,500 tons with a length of 760 feet and embarked a crew and scientific/technical staff of 340.[49]

In 1983 the *Marshal Nedelin*, the first of the latest generation of military MRIS/SESS ships, entered the fleet. Displacing 25,300 tons full load with a length of 692¾ feet, the *Nedelin* and similar *Marshal Krylov* could accommodate a crew and scientific/technical staff of almost 400.

Subsequently, the GRU proposed a ship that combined the MRIS/

SESS and communications intelligence roles and with the virtually unlimited operational endurance provided by nuclear propulsion. The result was the huge *Ural.*

And the Beat Goes On

Russia has continued to construct and operate advanced intelligence collection ships in the post–Cold War era. The *Yuriy Ivanov*, the lead ship of a series of large, 4,000-ton AGIS, was commissioned in 2015. A second ship, the *Ivan Khurs*, followed a year later with additional ships planned. Those ships are reported to have advanced collection systems and to be highly automated. In addition, the ships are armed, being fitted with two machine guns and a short-range, surface-to-air missile system. The new AGIS and several older ships provide the Russian forces with a score of AGIS into the third decade of the twenty-first century.

Early in the post–Cold War period, the Russian economy declined precipitously with a major impact on the armed forces. Naval construction programs were severely reduced, with surface ships and submarines already on the building ways having their construction delayed by many years. Some were never completed. With a much smaller fleet in all categories of surface ships, submarines, and aircraft, the Russian Navy has continued intelligence collection efforts, albeit on a scale much reduced from the Cold War years.

4

The Cold War

Red Submarines

The classified Soviet journal *Military Thought* in 1964 published an article by two naval intelligence officers that extensively discussed intelligence collection against Western naval forces and shore facilities.[1] Rear Admiral Boris N. Bobkov and Captain 1st Rank Ivan K. Khurs wrote:

> Submarines, by virtue of their tactical-technical characteristics, can perform a wide variety of reconnaissance tasks against ship groupings at sea, and against ports, bases, and the coastline of the enemy. They can conduct reconnaissance over the entire depth of ocean theaters, covertly negotiating deeply echeloned zones and lines of enemy anti-submarine defense, penetrate defended areas, and carry out covert observation reconnaissance objectives over a considerable period of time.[2]

During World War II, Soviet submarines conducted several reconnaissance missions but were mostly limited in that role to the Baltic Sea area. And as had the submarines of other nations, on occasion they also inserted "agents" into hostile territory. For example, on 7 August 1941, the submarine *Shch-211*, one of the few Soviet submarines in the Black Sea, landed 13 Bulgarians in the service of Soviet military intelligence on the Bulgarian coast. They were led by a Soviet Army colonel.[3]

At the start of World War II, the Soviet Union had the world's largest undersea fleet.[4] During the war, those submarines had very limited success in attacking German warships or merchant shipping because of the poor Soviet naval leadership, the doc-trine with regard to submarine operations, and their restricted operating areas.

After the war, Soviet dictator Josef Stalin undertook a massive naval rebuilding program. Submarines were a small part of that plan, although still significant in numbers, and they soon incorporated advanced German U-boat technology.[5] For example, from 1950 to 1957, the Soviet Navy completed 236 submarines of Project 613, known in the West as the "Whiskey" class; submarines of other classes also were being constructed during that period. (Additional submarines as well as major surface warships were canceled as Stalin's ambitious shipbuilding program was decimated following his death in March 1953.)

The Whiskey-class submarines were considered medium-range craft and operated mainly in Soviet coastal and regional waters. Even the early nuclear-propelled submarines did not undertake long-range operations until well into the 1960s. For example, during the Cuban missile crisis of the fall of 1962, the Soviets deployed only diesel-electric submarines to the Caribbean area.

During the Cold War, the Soviets appear to have relied on submarine-collected intelligence far less than did Western navies for three apparent reasons: First, the West was an open society with military, technology, and even intelligence information being readily available from public sources; second, Soviet intelligence organs were successful in penetrating many Western military and intelligence organizations; and, third, the Soviet Navy's large fleet of intelligence collection ships—both naval and, to a significant extent, civilian—could glean secrets from the West.

There have been reports of Soviet submarines operating off the coast of the United States since the late 1940s. The *New York Times* reported, "By 1947, the United States knew that Russian submarines were patrolling near U.S. bases in the Pacific Ocean," and that year "at least five submarines positively identified as belonging to the USSR were spotted cruising off the Aleutian Islands."[6] But neither official U.S. sources nor Soviet sources could confirm such activities by Soviet undersea craft in that period. The known deployment pattern of Soviet submarines in that period also argues against there having been such operations.

In time, Soviet nuclear as well as conventional (diesel-electric) submarines did undertake distant intelligence collection and monitoring missions. Several incidents revealed that role. For example, in January 1968, when the U.S. nuclear-propelled aircraft carrier *Enterprise* departed San Francisco en route to Pearl Harbor, Hawaii, there was little concern when intelligence sources—primarily the U.S. Navy's seafloor Sound Surveillance System—reported a Project 627/November-class nuclear submarine 400 n.miles off the coast of Oregon. That submarine suddenly reacted to reports of the *Enterprise*'s movement, taking an intercepting southwest course.[7] As the submarine approached the carrier task force, the U.S. warships accelerated.

U.S. naval intelligence previously had estimated that the November had a maximum submerged speed of 23 to 25 knots. Publicly available accounts differ as to the speed reached by that Soviet submarine, but SOSUS is known to have tracked her at a steady 27 knots for almost 36 hours as the U.S. task force incrementally increased speed to 31 knots.[8] That incident uncovered an underestimate of Soviet SSN speeds by the U.S. intelligence community and had a profound influence on the U.S. nuclear submarine program. American submarines were becoming progressively slower as each new class grew larger but retained the same S5W nuclear power plant. The Navy undertook efforts to increase the speed of nuclear submarines in subsequent classes.

Apparently Soviet submarines joined the AGIs in keeping watch on bases for U.S. strategic missile submarine activities. In January 1973, a Victor (Project 671) nuclear attack submarine was detected—and tracked—in the sensitive Clyde approach areas, apparently waiting for U.S. or British Polaris submarines to sail from Faslane or Holy Loch, Scotland.[9] In November 1974, the USS *James Madison* (SSBN 627) departed Holy Loch armed with 16 Poseidon C-3 nuclear missiles. She was en route to a patrol in the North Sea area. Shortly after departing the base, the *Madison* collided while submerged with a Victor-class nuclear attack submarine. Damage to both submarines was light, with the U.S. craft returning to Holy Loch having suffered a nine-foot scrape along the hull.

"Whiskey on the Rocks"

A Whiskey diesel-electric submarine made international headlines when she ran aground: "Whiskey on the Rocks." On 28 October

1981, the *S-363* was discovered hard aground in Swedish territorial waters near the major naval base of Karlskrona.[10] She had run aground the previous night.

Reports of Soviet submarines penetrating Swedish territorial waters had surfaced at least as early as 1962. In that incident, a supposed submarine was detected off Fårö in the Baltic Sea, just north of the island of Gotland. That "target" was depth charged by Swedish forces. Several more submarine penetrations were detected over the next two decades—some real—as the Soviet craft evidently were spying on Swedish naval facilities.

The commanding officer of the *S-363*, Captain 3rd Rank Anatoliy M. Gushchin, told Swedish authorities that bad weather and faulty navigation equipment had caused his predicament. The submarine most likely had been collecting intelligence about the nearby Karlskrona base and other military activities in the area.

The *S-363* had run aground in darkness, and after some ten hours, she was discovered by fishermen—not by the Swedish armed forces. The incident caused an 11-day diplomatic standoff until the submarine was released. Prior to the submarine being refloated and allowed to depart, the Swedish Navy determined that nuclear material—presumably torpedo warheads—was on board.[11] Sweden had obtained Soviet consent to interrogate Captain Gushchin in exchange for granting him personal immunity and promising not to detain the submarine's officers.[12]

(In January 1993, Captain Gushchin stated in a Swedish television interview that he had orders to blow up the submarine if an attempt was made by the Swedes to seize the craft. Other Soviet officers confirmed the directive to destroy the submarine and, if necessary, *the crew*.[13])

Indications of Soviet submarine incursions into Swedish waters continued. One year after the *S-363* incident, in October 1982, a submarine—believed to be Soviet or Polish—was detected near the Muskö naval base, some 20 miles from Stockholm. Swedish warships dropped 25 depth charges in an effort to force the submarine to surface, while nets and wires were spread across Horsfjarden Bay in an effort to trap the culprit.[14] She escaped.

More submarine penetrations into Swedish waters have been reported. A Swedish government commission in 1983 accused the Soviet Union of operating six submarines in that country's territorial waters between October 1982 and early 1983. The commission's report said the six submarines included three midgets with a "bottom-crawling capacity of a hitherto unknown character."[15] Jan Breemer, a former American defense consultant who had written about Soviet submarines, believed that bottom crawlers were used to gather intelligence near Sweden and in the La Pérouse Strait between the northern Japanese island of Hokkaido and Soviet Sakhalin. He said those craft were capable of crawling up onto beaches to unload troops and arms, and "there's no question about it—the photographs taken by the Swedes were made by caterpillar-type minisubmarines."[16]

Later it was determined that the tracks observed on the ocean floor were made by bottom-trawling fishing craft—not submersibles. The Soviet fleet had no such submersibles, according to knowledgeable U.S. and Soviet authorities. While some submersibles had wheels, such as the U.S. *NR-1*, tractor propulsion was impractical for submersibles.

One Western analysis stated that from 1980 to 1990 an estimated 17 to 36 foreign submarines—most or all presumably Soviet—had penetrated Swedish waters.[17] That Rand Corporation study concluded that nearly 200 confirmed incidents and more than 200 suspected incidents of submarine espionage occurred in Sweden's territorial seas between 1962 and 1988. Those operations were reported to have involved submarines, miniature submarines, and combat swimmers.

Of course, the Soviets have denied any submarine violations of Swedish waters occurred except for the October 1981 event. Countercharges are that the Soviet submarine intrusions were "manipulated" or simply invented by Western nations seeking to bring Sweden into the anti-Soviet alliance.[18]

Norway—a NATO member—and Finland also have reported numerous incursions from what were believed to be Soviet submarines. Norwegian warships fired a few weapons at suspected submarines but without success in making such "contacts" come to the surface.

Photo 16. This Victor III submarine became entangled in a U.S. ship's towed acoustic array off the Atlantic coast in 1985. Here the Soviet Moma-class AGI *Nakhodka* and the U.S. destroyer *Peterson* (DD 969) stand by the disabled submarine; subsequently, she was towed (on the surface) to a Cuban port. / U.S. Navy.

Former director of U.S. Naval Intelligence Rear Admiral John L. Butts, in discussing the Victor III (Project 671RTM) nuclear submarine, noted that by the early 1980s, "these submarines often are assigned [anti-submarine] missions off our coasts."[19] A Victor III, the *K-324*, operating off the U.S. East Coast, fouled the towed hydrophone array of the U.S. frigate *McCloy* (FF 1038) in November 1983. The event occurred some 500 miles off the coast of South Carolina while the submarine apparently was observing the frigate. A Moma-class AGI soon arrived on the scene as did a U.S. destroyer.

Subsequently, the Soviet salvage tug *Aldan* towed the submarine on the surface to Cuba for repairs and for recovering a portion of the U.S. towed array fouled in her propeller. It was an intelligence "find" for the Soviets.[20]

By that time, according to the U.S. intelligence community, Soviet submarines were "increasingly being used for reconnaissance near U.S. [ballistic missile submarine] bases on both coasts."[21] The *K-324* may have been conducting that type of reconnaissance off the U.S. submarine base at Kings Bay, Georgia, the Atlantic coast base for Trident strategic missile submarines.

(The last Soviet submarine operation off the U.S. East Coast during the Cold War was reported in 1987. Eight years later, in June 1995, an Akula (Project 971) was detected near the Trident submarine base in Kings Bay—the first such sighting since the end of the Cold War.[22])

In the Pacific, a Victor I nuclear submarine—the *Petropavlovsk* (K-314)—collided with a U.S. aircraft carrier when the submarine was observing a naval exercise in the Sea of Japan, some 150 miles east of the Korean coast. As a squall passed through the area on 21 March 1984, the submarine came up to periscope depth, and her commanding officer saw the carrier *Kitty Hawk* (CVA 63) steaming directly at him. He ordered a crash dive and hard turn.

One of the *Kitty Hawk*'s propellers slashed into the stern of the submarine, shearing off a stabilizer and damaging the craft's propeller. The *Petropavlovsk* was able to surface. The carrier launched a helicopter to offer assistance, and a U.S. frigate stood by the submarine until a Soviet tug arrived on the scene to provide help. The damage to the *Kitty Hawk* was superficial.[23]

Deep-Diving Submarines

The Soviet Union developed and built several deep-diving, nuclear-propelled submarines. Those craft were capable of a range of missions, some of which were highly secretive. The missions are believed to have included:

- supporting submarine weapons and systems development;
- supporting deep-ocean anti-submarine projects, including research into the deep sound layers;
- countering U.S. Navy seafloor cable-tapping activities;

- interdicting seafloor cable networks; and
- conducting seafloor surveys related to military and economic interests in the Arctic.

Soviet/Russian efforts in this field are managed by the Main Directorate of Deep-Sea Research (Glavnoye Upravleniye Glubokovodnykh Issledovaniyx [GUGI]). That organization—established in 1976—is directly under the General Staff of the Armed Forces. The submersibles as well as the specialized surface ships and submarines that support them are based at Olenya Bay on the Barents Sea, some 60 miles east of the border with Norway. The command also includes divers known as hydronauts.

The submarines that have been reported under GUGI are listed in table 2. Reportedly the 29th Submarine Division is the GUGI activity that controls and supports these submarines.

Table 2. GUGI-controlled submarines

Number	Project	Russian name	NATO
1	1851	*Nema*	X-ray
2	1851.1	*Paltus*	X-ray
3	1910	*Kashalot*	Uniform
1	09857	"Losharik"	—
1		BS-64 *Padmokov'ye*	converted Delta IV
1		BS-136 *Orenburg*	converted Delta II
1		K-329 *Belgorod*	converted Oscar II
1	20120	B-90 *Sarov*	modified Kilo

Although in some respects analogous to the U.S. Navy's nuclear-propelled *NR-1*, the small Soviet undersea craft are believed to have titanium pressure hulls, enabling them to operate at greater depths (the *NR-1* was built of HY-80 steel). Also, while the *NR-1* was towed submerged to operating areas, the Russian craft are transported beneath "mother submarines."

The nuclear-propelled Project 1851 *Nema* was a relatively small submarine. That craft also was constructed at the Admiralty Shipyard in Leningrad, being completed in 1986. She displaced approximately 300 tons surfaced and had a length of 98½ feet; her operating depth was listed as in excess of 3,300 feet. The original X-ray was

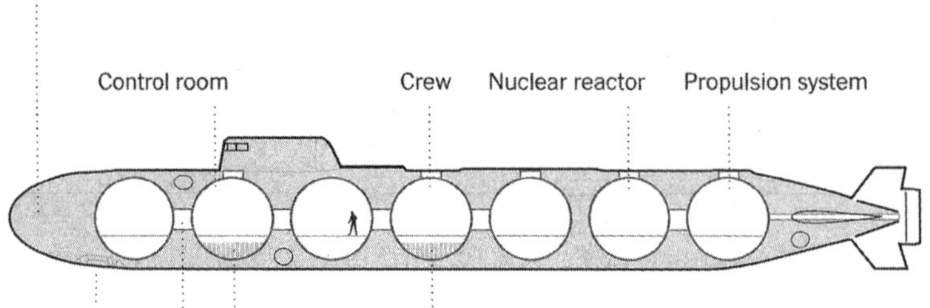

Fig. 3. The nuclear-propelled, deep-diving Losharik has a pressure hull consisting of seven spheres. / Authors' collection.

followed by two similar submarines of the Project 1851.1 *Paltus* (halibut) design, with those craft having been completed in 1991 and 1995; apparently work on a third unit was halted. Those craft—like the *Kashalot* and Losharik—were intended to be carried and supported at sea by modified mother submarines.

The Project 1910 *Kashalot* (sperm whale) was a nuclear-propelled, deep-diving, research and ocean-engineering submarine. The submarine was 226⅓ feet long with a surface displacement of just under 1,400 tons and had an operating depth in excess of 3,300 feet. That craft had extendable legs to sit on the ocean floor, with maneuvering thrusters, and other features for working on the ocean floor. From 1983 to 1995, the Admiralty yard in Leningrad (St. Petersburg) completed three submarines of the Uniform design; a fourth hull was believed to have been left unfinished when the Cold War ended. Reportedly, all three completed units have been laid up in reserve.

The Project 10831—called Losharik by the Russians—undoubtedly is the most unusual of the special-purpose submarines with nuclear propulsion.[24] Her pressure hull is believed to consist of seven spherical, titanium compartments within an outer hull approximately 200 feet in length. Spheres number 1 through 5 are manned, number 6 contains the nuclear reactor, and number 7 houses the propulsion machinery. The latter two spheres are "sealed" when the craft is at sea. That configuration gave the submarine—designated *AS-31* for "nuclear deepwater station"—an operating depth estimated by public accounts at between some 6,600 feet and possi-

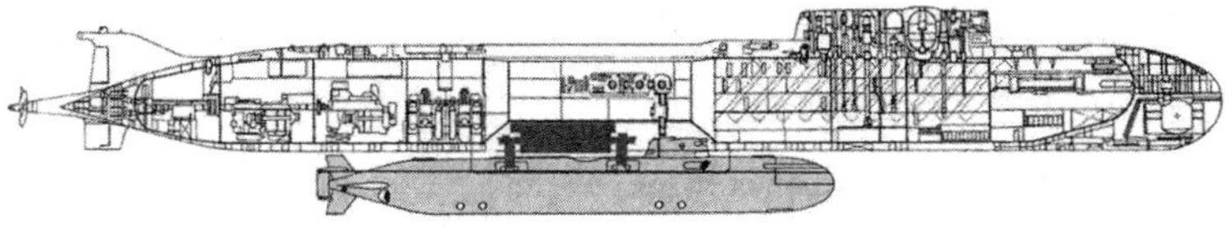

Fig. 4. The Losharik is transported submerged to operating areas docked beneath the "mother" submarine *Belgorod*, converted from an unfinished Oscar-class cruise missile submarine. / Authors' collection.

bly as deep as 20,000 feet. The craft has a hybrid nuclear-electric propulsion plant, extending legs for resting on the ocean floor, exterior lighting, and a claw-like recovery device.

The Losharik was constructed at the Severodvinsk shipyard in the Arctic. Suffering delays after the fall of the Soviet regime, the Losharik was launched in August 2003, some 15 years after having been laid down. The then-commander in chief of the Russian Navy, Fleet Admiral Vladimir Kuroyedov, participated in the launching ceremonies. There were further delays in her construction, with the submarine being photographed at sea in 2007.

In the fall of 2012, in collaboration with the mother submarine *Orenburg* (BS-136), a converted Delta III ballistic missile submarine, the Losharik participated in the research expedition that drilled to a depth of almost two miles into the Arctic seafloor to retrieve soil samples. That operation—known as Arctic 2012—sought to determine the geological nature of the Mendeleev Ridge with the objective of identifying the outer limits of Russia's continental shelf in the Arctic Ocean. The submarine also participated in other, highly secretive operations.

The Losharik suffered a catastrophic fire that was believed in the West to have been caused by battery explosion on 1 July 2019 while at a depth of almost 1,000 feet in the Barents Sea. The event was reported to have occurred while docking with the mother submarine *Padmokov'ye* (BS-64), a converted Project 667BDRM/Delta IV SSBN. Fourteen of the men in the Losharik died from toxic fumes or smoke inhalation; five men were rescued after the craft was able to come to the surface. Her commanding officer, Captain 1st Rank Denis Dolonsky, was one of those killed. The submarine was towed to a Russian base. The large number of senior officers on board at the time of the accident—including seven captains 1st rank—and a single civilian indicated that the submarine most likely was conducting special tests.[25]

The *Sarov* is a modified Project 636/Kilo-class diesel-electric submarine fitted with a small nuclear reactor to provide continuous battery charging. Construction began at the Krasnoye Sormovo yard in Gorky in 1988; completion was planned for 1993. Progress slowed and then halted completely in 1996 when she was 40 percent complete. The unfinished hull was transferred by barge through the inland waterways to Severodvinsk. Work resumed to an extensively revised design in May 2006. She was launched on 14 December 2007 and placed in service on 7 August 2008 with the designation B-90.

The addition of a nuclear reactor compartment and an escape capsule in the sail gave the *Sarov* an overall length of some 323 feet, about 60 feet longer than the later Kilo-class submarines. Her operating depth of some 900 feet is considerably less than the smaller, nuclear-propelled undersea craft described above.

Reportedly, on 27 November 2016, the *Sarov* was involved in a test of the nuclear-powered, nuclear-armed Poseidon unmanned underwater vehicle. In early 2019 the Russian government released a video showing a Poseidon being launched by the *Sarov*.

Thus, the Soviet/Russian state has continued the development and deployment of small, deep-diving submarines as well as mother submarines. They are valuable for a number of clandestine missions. The United States, meanwhile, has largely discarded such manned undersea craft in favor of unmanned, remote-control or autonomous systems.

5

American Spy Ships

Part 1

In contrast to the early Soviet requirement for spy ships, the United States and its Western allies in Europe, the Middle East, and Asia had numerous land installations that effectively could intercept Soviet (and later Chinese) radio emissions and, to some degree, monitor Soviet naval activities. Those intercept capabilities were further enhanced by overflights and peripheral flights by U.S. and British reconnaissance aircraft and, subsequently, by spy satellites.

The concept of employing specialized intelligence collection ships first appears in the U.S. Navy with the use of destroyers on the Taiwan patrol station from 1952 to 1954, when newly established Communist China was threatening to attack the islands of Quemoy and Matsu, occupied by Nationalist Chinese forces, and ultimately to undertake the invasion of Nationalist Taiwan, some 100 miles off the coast of China.[1] Those U.S. destroyers occasionally sailed close inshore to the disputed islands to detect (and prevent) covert Chinese military actions against them.

Addressing destroyer-cum-spy-ship operations in the 1960s, historian David Winkler observed:

> Dissatisfied with the time-share arrangements with NSA, the Navy strapped antenna-laden vans on destroyers and destroyer escorts. . . . However, deploying a warship to perform ELINT duties wasted most of the ship's combat capabilities: it was not a cost-effective use of Navy manpower. Also, a foreign country could interpret the appearance of an American warship steaming slowly off its coastline as a hostile move.[2]

Still, in the early 1960s, the commander, U.S. Seventh Fleet in the Western Pacific, assigned destroyers and other ships that were fitted with radio intercept equipment and embarked small Naval Security Group detachments to cruise just outside the territorial waters of the Soviet Union and China for intelligence gathering. In September 1963, the Navy icebreaker *Staten Island* (AGB 5), with an embarked helicopter, was assigned to observe the annual Soviet convoy across the Soviet Arctic coast, a mission that occasionally was replicated in succeeding years.[3] In April 1964 the submarine rescue ship *Chanticleer* (ASR 7) conducted surveillance off the Soviet port of Vladivostok and along the Soviet maritime provinces bordering on the Sea of Japan. Those operations usually had NSG teams as well as Russian translators embarked in the ships.

Desoto Operations

The first of the so-called Desoto intelligence collection patrols was by the destroyer *DeHaven* (DD 727) in August 1962 along the northern coast of China.[4] Thereafter, Desoto surveillance operations by destroyers were conducted in international waters from the Sea of Japan south to the Java Sea. The Naval Security Group developed "quick vans" that could be transported by helicopter, and within a few hours they could be set up and operating on the helicopter deck of a destroyer. By that method, NSG detachments could develop a familiarity with certain geographic areas and could easily transfer from one ship to another to maintain continuity in that area. To derive maximum collection opportunities, Navy reconnaissance aircraft also were deployed simultaneously into the area to trigger air defense and communication networks for Desoto destroyers to intercept.

The destroyer *Agerholm* (DD 826) extended the Desoto patrols into the Gulf of Tonkin in December 1962. A primary objective of those operations was to obtain information on Chinese and North Vietnamese radars. Chinese patrol craft often trailed those early destroyer forays into the Gulf of Tonkin.

The destroyer *Maddox* (DD 731) was on a Desoto patrol the night of 2 August 1964, when she was attacked by three North Vietnamese torpedo boats in an event since called the Gulf of Tonkin Incident. The *Maddox* fired her 5-inch (127-mm) and 3-inch (76-mm) guns at the torpedo boats, which *may* have launched torpedoes at the destroyer. No significant damage was inflicted on either side.

When the *Maddox* returned two nights later in company with the destroyer *Turner Joy* (DD 951), they reported being attacked by torpedo boats. Subsequent investigations have revealed no attack occurred that night. As a result of those attacks—real and supposed—U.S. aircraft carriers flew strikes against several North Vietnamese military bases, initiating American attacks on North Vietnam in the Vietnam War.

In September 1964, the destroyers *Morton* (DD 948) and *Richard S. Edwards* (DD 950) entered the Gulf of Tonkin with orders to remain beyond 20 n.miles of the North Vietnamese coast while seeking information on the situation in the gulf. On the night of 18 September, the destroyers took under fire two high-speed boats that closed with them; both boats were reported as sunk.

As the Vietnam War raged into the early 1970s, U.S. aircraft carriers, a large number of cruiser and destroyers, and the battleship *New Jersey* (BB 62) operated in the Gulf of Tonkin. Those ships as well as U.S. carrier-based and land-based aircraft collected intelligence against North Vietnamese and, at times, Chinese targets. Those warships, primarily the carriers, were almost continually observed by Soviet AGIs and on occasion by Soviet submarines.

In that same area, during the Sino-Vietnamese conflict of 1979, the Soviet Union was defending a communist state against the People's Republic of China. Three Soviet AGIs as well as reconnaissance aircraft and surface ships operated off the Chinese and Vietnamese coasts to monitor Chinese naval operations.[5] The Soviets also established a major SIGINT facility at Cam Ranh Bay, where there had been U.S. facilities during the Vietnam War. With the naval and air facilities, as well as the SIGINT complex, the Soviets had a peak strength of possibly as many as 7,000 personnel at Cam Ranh Bay in the 1980s.[6]

The U.S. Navy's radio intercept efforts of World War II and the Korean War placed intercept teams on board major U.S. warships to ensure that radio intelligence was readily available to senior commanders, especially in tactical situations. After the Korean conflict, that concept evolved into placing teams—some as small as only two operators—on submarines and surface ships that undertook surveillance missions to provide instantaneous warnings of foreign military action against their mission. Larger Naval Security Group detachments of 25 to 50 cryptologic technicians continued to be assigned to major warships, such as aircraft carriers, amphibious command ships, and fleet flagships. The number of NSG personnel embarked was in proportion to their location and mission. As a "snapshot" of such support, in one year in the mid-1980s NSG teams were provided to three command ships, 14 aircraft carriers, 18 cruisers, 12 destroyers, and the spy ship *Sphinx* (ARL 24), a former landing craft repair ship.

Dedicated Spy Ships

Both the Soviet Union and the United States began developing dedicated spy ships in the mid-1950s. In the United States, the National Security Agency was established in 1952 to intercept radio communications and telephone calls—and later, computer modem and fax machine transmissions—as well as signals emanating from radar and missile guidance systems, and to coordinate military service efforts in those areas.

From 1959 to 1960, the NSA sought the use of specialized intelligence collection ships. Available at that time were hundreds of mothballed World War II–era cargo ships that could be configured for intelligence collection. Their advantages included having innocuous, merchant ship silhouettes and considerable space for electronic equipment and crew and technician accommodations.

The National Security Agency's original justification for a specialized seaborne intelligence collector was for monitoring the eastern Mediterranean, specifically the Greek-Turkish dispute over the island of Cyprus and the tensions between Israel and its Arab neighbors. Called the Technical Research Ship (TRS) program, the first group of ships in the program were considered nominally Navy auxiliaries but under the direct control of the NSA. The ships were envisioned as quick-reaction resources that could respond to emerging situations and work in areas where political or military situations resulted in the loss of American ground intercept sites.[7]

The Navy acquired five mothballed hulls that eventually would be manned by Navy crews and with 125 to 140 Naval Security

Group personnel on board. The Navy initially designated the ships as miscellaneous auxiliaries (AG) ships, but they entered service as technical research ships (AGTR), a euphemism for electronic spy ships (see table 3).

Table 3. U.S. technical research ships

Hull numbers	Name	Navy commissioned
AG 159/AGTR 1	*Oxford*	1961
AG 165/AGTR 2	*Georgetown*	1963
AG 166/AGTR 3	*Jamestown*	1962
AG 167/AGTR 4	*Belmont*	1964
AG 168/AGTR 5	*Liberty*	1964

The ships were to be armed with four .50-caliber machine guns, primarily for protection against boarders. Small arms—rifles and pistols—also would be provided.

Almost simultaneously with the commissioning of the first technical research ship, a second echelon of spy ships was acquired on short notice to meet unplanned intelligence requirements that were arising in 1961 and because of the slow activation process of the TRS ships. That add-on program initially was planned to consist of charters for 11 Military Sea Transportation Service (MSTS) ships—unarmed, civilian-manned cargo ships that were already in naval service—that would carry NSG detachments and be fitted with ELINT equipment. In their new role, those ships were given Navy designations as miscellaneous auxiliaries (AG, with the T- prefix indicating MSTS civilian-manned ships). The first three ships were modified to augment the TRS fleet (see table 4); the eight other planned MSTS ship acquisitions never materialized.

Table 4. U.S. miscellaneous auxiliary intelligence ships

Hull number	Name	Activated as SIGINT ship
T-AG 169	*Pvt. Jose F. Valdez*	November 1961
T-AG 170*	*Lt. James E. Robinson*	January 1962
T-AG 171	*Sgt. Joseph E. Muller*	April 1963

Note: Formerly AKV 3, AK 274.

Photo 17. The *Oxford* (AGTR 1) was the first in a series of large spy ships, part of the U.S. Navy–National Security Agency's Technical Research Ships (TRS) program. Her antenna array is evident in this 1964 photograph. The five AGTRS were among the largest ships employed for intelligence collection. / U.S. Navy.

The first of those technical research ships was modified to provide the NSA with the capability of monitoring political developments in newly independent African counties. However, on 25 November 1961, the Department of Defense implemented a special request from the White House to increase signals intelligence collection off several South and Central American countries because of indications of the possible increase of Soviet influence in those regions.

That new assignment went to the first technical research ship to reach the fleet—the USS *Oxford* (AG 159). A World War II–built, Liberty-type freighter, the ship was converted into the first technical research ship from November 1960 through June 1961 at the Brooklyn (New York) Naval Shipyard. During the *Oxford*'s subsequent shakedown cruise out of Guantánamo Bay, Cuba, in October 1961, the ship proved her ability to obtain a "substantial number of signals of interest," including Russian and Cuban military voice intercepts originating from Cuba.[8]

In port at Norfolk, Virginia, in December 1961, the *Oxford* received the first U.S. afloat "moon-bounce" communications system, a then-unique capability to transmit and receive messages bounced off the moon without revealing the transmitter's location on the earth's surface. On 4 January 1962, the Naval Security Group detachment was activated, and the ship formally was designated as a technical research ship (AGTR 1). The *Oxford* departed for her first deployment that day. Her NSG detachment consisted of six officers and about 110 enlisted technicians.[9]

The *Oxford* was tasked with sampling the signals intelligence environment of the Caribbean and Atlantic coast nations of South America. On the ship's first deployment, she sailed along the Atlantic coastlines of Central and South America from Panama down to the mouth of the Río de la Plata, Argentina, and made port calls at some of the world's finest liberty ports. She returned to Norfolk in June, following the same track on her return voyage. In the several countries sampled, the ship's NSG team had outstanding success in monitoring civilian and military radio traffic, including Cuban voice transmissions and the communications of Polish ships en route to Cuba.

Cuban Missile Crises

The United States regularly conducted radio intercept "hearability" tests with spy ship circumnavigations of Cuba. The first was in July 1960, by the destroyer *Massey* (DD 778), with an NSG team embarked. Those tests determined that a significant portion of Cuban electronic emissions were not being intercepted by existing NSA ground facilities in the United States and, presumably, at certain Caribbean locations. In December 1961, before her first deployment, the *Oxford* also conducted a radio hearability survey off the Cuban coast.

In July 1962, the *Oxford* and other U.S. Navy ships circumnavigated Cuba for further radio surveys that were "very productive" in capturing signals that were not "hearable" from the fixed intercept sites in the United States. That month the *Oxford* was semi-permanently assigned to operate offshore from the capital of Havana to monitor both Cuban and the increasing volume of Soviet communications. The *Oxford* remained steaming off Havana—in international waters—until March 1963, except for brief visits to Key West, Florida, for fueling, provisioning, and changing NSG personnel.

The *Oxford*'s primary contribution to the intelligence collected prior to and during the Cuban missile crisis in the fall of 1962 involved both Communications Intelligence and Electronic Intelligence. Her COMINT ability to intercept microwave telephone conversations became a major source of information on Cuban-Soviet relationships and coordination as the Soviet Union poured troops, strategic missiles and other weapons, and nuclear warheads into the island.[10] She also obtained COMINT on Cuban internal economic problems, counterrevolutionary activities, Soviet shipping in the Caribbean, and so forth. The *Oxford*'s success in intercepting Soviet radars, aviation beacons, and telemetry provided considerable information on Cuban military forces and about the Soviet P-12 early warning radars (NATO designation Spoon Rest) and the status of the Soviet ballistic missiles being installed on the island.

In late October 1962, the *Oxford* was pulled back to the center of the Florida Straits between Cuba and the Florida Keys because of fears that she might come under attack by Cuban forces. Steaming 80 to 90 n.miles north of Havana, she lost the ability to monitor microwave telephone conversations but still was able to collect radar signals from the surface-to-air missile sites being installed on the Cuban coast. The activation of target acquisition radars deployed with those missiles was an important indicator that the Soviets were prepared to shoot down the U.S. reconnaissance planes that were overflying Cuba.[11] On 27 October, a Soviet surface-to-air missile shot down the U.S. U-2 spy plane piloted by Air Force pilot Rudolf Anderson while overflying Cuba.[12]

Admiral Thomas H. Moorer, later the U.S. chief of naval operations, commented that "electronic intelligence acquired by surface ships led to the photographic intelligence which gave us undisputable evidence of . . . Soviet [strategic] missiles in Cuba."[13] The *Oxford* remained as the Havana "station ship" until early March 1963, when she was relieved by the Navy surveying ship *Tanner* (AGS 15) carrying an NSG team. The *Tanner* covered the Havana station until the arrival of the spy ship *Muller* (T-AG 171) at the end of April 1963.

A Strange Partnership

Another highly unusual spy ship operation occurred off Cuba in the early 1960s that teamed a surface ship with a submarine.[14] The Lockheed A-12 was a reconnaissance aircraft built for the CIA by the famed Lockheed "Skunk Works" based on the designs of Clarence (Kelly) Johnson. The A-12, flown from 1963 until 1968, was a precursor to both the Air Force YF-12 interceptor and the renowned SR-71 Blackbird reconnaissance aircraft. Those manned aircraft were the first to incorporate stealth features, such as radar-absorbing material, in their construction.

It was important for the CIA and the Air Force to know if the A-12 could be detected by the Soviet P-14 (NATO Tall King) early warning and SNR-75 (NATO Fan Song) missile control radars. Thus, the CIA initiated Project Palladium to generate "ghost" aircraft on those radars that had been deployed in Cuba. The agency knew from various means the specific location of all radars on the island.

At night a destroyer carrying the Palladium electronics van moved into position off the northern coast of Cuba, remaining just over the horizon. Palladium then electronically generated a ghost aircraft that appeared on the Spoon Rest radar to be making a high-speed run toward Havana. At a predetermined time, a submarine just outside of Havana Bay surfaced and, at intervals, released several balloons carrying calibrated metal spheres of varying sizes.

The plan was to allow the Spoon Rest radar to track the ghost aircraft as it approached the coast. It was hoped that the Fan Song radar would be switched on to initiate a surface-to-air missile engagement. The smallest calibrated sphere that the Fan Song operators detected would indicate the radar cross section of the smallest target that they could acquire.

Cuban fighter aircraft were scrambled and directed toward the point that the submarine had launched the balloons. To draw them away, technicians on the destroyer flew their ghost aircraft out of the area at high speed—and then turned off the transmitter. The fighters searched the area for several minutes, found nothing, and returned to base. Although the destroyer-submarine operation determined that the Soviet radars could detect and track an A-12 aircraft, the CIA continued that program, producing a series of highly successful spy planes.

After a maintenance period at Norfolk, the *Oxford* again deployed in May 1963, sailing back along the eastern coast of South America from Venezuela to Río de la Plata—and once more stopping at excellent liberty ports. She returned to Norfolk in September. On that deployment, the *Oxford* had one additional NSG officer and 17 enlisted men on board for training, bringing her detachment up to almost 170.

Following an extended overhaul from September to December 1963, the *Oxford* sailed for refresher training at Guantánamo Bay in January 1964. Again she deployed to the eastern coast of South America from 22 February to 10 June. Then, after two months back in Norfolk, she departed for her fourth deployment into the Caribbean from early August to early December 1964. Making four transits of the Panama Canal, the *Oxford* cruised along both the eastern and western coasts of South America. In addition to the normally targeted military and government radio traffic, the *Oxford* was able to intercept communications relating to the guerrilla activity in Venezuela and Bolivia.

Following two months in Norfolk, the *Oxford* again went to sea on 3 February 1965, sailing eastward for her first deployment to Africa. She operated along the continent's western coast, monitoring government communications with a special emphasis on anti-Western organizations. There were port visits in the Azores, Nigeria, and South Africa.

And into the Pacific

The commander in chief, U.S. Pacific Fleet, in February 1965 proposed that two technical research ships be assigned to monitor transmissions along the coast of Vietnam as that conflict was escalating with increased American involvement. The *Oxford* and the *Jamestown* (AGTR 3) were selected for that mission.[15]

En route the *Oxford* monitored a Soviet space event from the Gulf of Guinea in April 1965 and then sailed into Cape Town for generator repairs. She departed that port, crossed the Indian Ocean, and arrived at Subic Bay in the Philippines on 16 June. The *Oxford* began her first cruise off South Vietnam in late July, carrying an NSG detachment of 145 that was augmented by 16 translators: ten for Vietnamese, two for Chinese, and one each for Russian, Cambodian, Portuguese, and French.

Upon completion of her first 45-day deployment off South Vietnam, the *Oxford* was given a special assignment—Project Healthy, a 21-day hearability test in the Bay of Bengal, off the Ganges River. Project Healthy sought to determine if a signals intercept ship could replace the CIA land-based intercept site at Peshawar, Pakistan, if that site were lost to political pressures. Of particular importance was determining if the *Oxford* could intercept communications and telemetry from the Chinese atomic testing program at Lop Nur that had begun in October 1964 (and would continue through July 1996, with a total of 45 nuclear detonations).

The results of the project were inconclusive.[16] The signals from Lop Nur could be monitored but were severely degraded during the several months of the monsoon season. That deployment into the Bay of Bengal during August and September 1965 earned the ship liberty visits to Jesselton (now Kota Kinabalu) in Malaysia and in Singapore.

The *Oxford* returned to the South China Sea operating area in September 1965; then she departed for an overhaul period in Sasebo, Japan, from December 1965 to January 1966. En route back to her operating area off South Vietnam, the *Oxford* targeted Chinese military communications as she sailed south. During that transit, the ship was under close surveillance by Chinese naval ships.[17] From the *Oxford*'s return to the South China Sea in March 1965 until her decommissioning in 1969, the *Oxford*, and the *Jamestown*, were almost exclusively engaged in the support of U.S. combat operations in Vietnam, with one or both ships always on station to monitor enemy communications.[18]

The standard tour of duty for the NSG personnel and ship's crew on the *Oxford* and *Jamestown* was one year. The ships had on-station periods of approximately 45 days, followed by brief maintenance periods at Subic Bay in the Philippines. Longer overhauls were undertaken in Japan at shipyards in Sasebo or Yokosuka. Sailing back and forth to Japan usually involved a special intercept effort conducted against Chinese targets, with the ships having liberty calls in Hong Kong, Taiwan, and Bangkok.

In October 1969, the *Oxford* departed the South China Sea for Yokosuka for disposal. After being stripped of usable equipment, she was decommissioned in December 1969 and sold for scrap.

Smaller Spy Ships

Four months after the start of the conversion of the *Oxford*, the director of Central Intelligence tasked the NSA to develop additional coverage of African nations to provide intercepts of their civilian and military communications. The NSA initially chose to make "quick and dirty" modifications to a small, World War II–built freighter. In only six months, the *Valdez* was reactivated from the mothball fleet and fitted as a signals intelligence ship (T-AG 169) to be crewed by MSTS civilian mariners with an NSG detachment. The *Valdez* was equipped to intercept Morse code, voice, and teleprinter communications, as well as radar and other ELINT. She carried an NSG detachment of about 100 personnel.

Unlike the commanding officers of the Navy-manned ships, the *Valdez*'s civilian master was not cleared for signals intelligence, with the MSTS essentially providing transportation and "hotel" services to the embarked NSG military detachment. The *Valdez* sailed from New York in November 1961, just three months after the *Oxford*. However, unlike the *Oxford*, the civilian mariners required no shakedown cruise.

As the *Valdez* operated almost entirely along the western coast of Africa, she obtained normal maintenance and replenishment at Durban or Cape Town, South Africa. She would spend 25 days cruising along the African coast with five days in an African port for liberty, fueling, and provisioning. The ship spent December 1961–January 1962 monitoring Soviet satellite and other space activities from a location off the western coast of Africa. In March 1962, when in port at Cape Town, additional satellite signals intercept equipment was installed.

In addition to civilian and general government radio traffic, the *Valdez* was tasked with monitoring military communications related to guerrilla and anti-colonial activities on the African continent, especially in 1964–65 when several rebel groups were fighting in the Congo. The United States, South Africa, and European countries supported the central Congolese government, while the Soviet Union, China, and Cuba backed the opposition forces. The 1960s and 1970s saw several colonial governments in Africa shift to self-government, and the NSA monitored those transitions, largely with spy ships. (Cuban icon Che Guevara led a force fighting in the Congo in 1965.)

Naval Security Group personnel were flown to and from Cape Town—unofficially the *Valdez*'s home port—for one-year tours on board the ship. She inconspicuously operated from South African ports along both the eastern and western coasts of Africa for more than six years, until a political crisis triggered by an American aircraft carrier's port visit to Cape Town changed the political situation for the *Valdez* and other Africa-centric spy ships.

The aircraft carrier *Franklin D. Roosevelt* (CVA 42) sailed into Cape Town on 4 February 1967 while en route from a deployment off Vietnam to her home port of Mayport, Florida. The *Roosevelt* was the first U.S. carrier to call on the apartheid regime since the *Midway* (CVA 41) visited the port 12 years earlier. President Johnson had personally approved the port visit only a few days previously, but a campaign by U.S. congressmen and civil rights groups rendered the port visit politically indefensible. The almost 500 non-white sailors and airmen (Blacks, Filipinos, and Asians) on board the carrier would not be afforded the same amenities as the 3,300 white American sailors and airmen; thus, liberty was denied to the entire crew. The port visit was shortened to only three days while still allowing thousands of local residents to visit aboard the ship, and time to fuel and provision. But the crew remained on board throughout the visit, much to the embarrassment of the South African regime.

Almost immediately the presence of the *Valdez* and other U.S. Navy auxiliary ships in South African ports became politically unacceptable. Due to a pattern of increasing restrictions imposed on the *Valdez* intercept operations by the U.S. State Department and with Cape Town's facilities no longer available for maintenance, the ship's intercept coverage was reduced by about one-fourth.

Several other ports that the NSA ships had previously used also were declared unavailable due to political or security concerns, resulting in a slow and steady reduction in U.S. shipboard SIGINT effectiveness on the west coast of Africa. Thus, American shipboard SIGINT collection suffered, not only from competition for funds with other intelligence activities and from increasing ship operating and support costs, but also from political circumstances. The reduction of U.S. overseas land-based intercept sites at the end of the 1960s might well have generated an expansion of seaborne operations except for the declining efficiencies and increasingly complex environment of shipboard intercept efforts.

After more than five years away from the United States, the *Valdez* was ordered to return in 1967 via the Mediterranean for a major renovation. On 3 January 1967, the *Valdez* started north along the eastern coast of Africa. En route the ship stopped at Massawa, Eritrea, where she took on board new SIGINT equipment and additional NSG personnel for special tasking when in the Mediterranean Sea. After moving slowly through the Gulf of Suez and the Suez Canal, the ship lingered for a few days in mid-April in the vicinity of Port Said, monitoring Egyptian military forces. Her technicians also sought to identify "tip-offs" of the increasing likelihood of a third Arab-Israeli war. On 23 May, at about the time that the *Liberty* (AGTR 5) was being diverted to the Mediterranean, the *Valdez* departed the Spanish-American base at Rota, Spain, crossing the Atlantic for a major overhaul at Hoboken, New Jersey.

After a three-month overhaul from June to September 1967, the *Valdez* departed New York in late September for another multi-year deployment to Africa, with occasional excursions into the Indian Ocean or the South Atlantic to monitor Soviet space events. Although the *Valdez* operated in Third World areas that appeared to have safer environments than those experienced by U.S. spy ships operating in waters off the Soviet Union, North Korea, and China, following the attacks on the *Liberty* in 1967, she was fitted with destruction devices as a contingency against being seized.

> The USNS *Valdez* has on board devices to scuttle the ship and to destruct electronic devices and documents. An electric ignition and firing method has been provided. . . . The scuttle devices are 14 square shaped explosive charges which will cause a total of 14 approximately 18" square hull penetrations below the waterline in 3 compartments. . . . The file destruct are standard stock items (sodium nitrate) (M-4). The electronic equipment destruct devises [*sic*] standard stock items (thermite) (M1A2). The document and circuit board destroyers are standard stock items (sodium nitrate or sodium tricalcium nitrate) (M-3).[19]

A highly classified (Top Secret UMBRA) history of the technical research ship program noted: "The destruct devices were repeatedly tested for effectiveness. The system was never proven totally satisfactory regarding the 30 minute goal set for destruction; however, it was determined that if allowed to fire, after 30 minutes the process of conflagration would be too great to reverse."[20]

The *Valdez* was again in New York for an overhaul from December 1968 to January 1969 that included the installation of the moon-bounce antenna system. She departed for West African operations on 23 January 1969; however, due to Navy budgetary decisions, the *Valdez* soon was ordered back to the United States for deactivation. The NSG detachment went ashore, and on 7 November 1969, the *Valdez* was taken out of service and laid up. She was stricken in 1976.

In the summer of 1962, the NSA had ordered the activation and rehabilitation of a second small freighter for intelligence collection—the *Sgt. Joseph E. Muller* (T-AG 171). That ship was intended to relieve the *Oxford* off Havana, but the surprisingly poor condition of the *Muller* delayed her delivery by several months. The ship finally arrived off Havana on 30 April 1963, relieving the Navy-manned surveying ship *Tanner*, which had relieved the *Oxford* in March. The *Muller* had no satellite signal interception capability and only about two-thirds of the capabilities of the Navy's larger technical research ships (AGTRS). Her NSG detachment consisted of four officers and 90 enlisted technicians.

The *Muller* operated off Cuba until late 1969, and she was relieved for two months each year by the *Georgetown* (AGTR 2) while the smaller ship entered a U.S. port for provisioning and maintenance. She normally was on station for 25 days each month, with five days per month in Port Everglades, Florida. The *Muller* "bore holes in the ocean" off Havana, usually steaming five-to-12 n.miles offshore but occasionally as close as three n.miles to visually examine Soviet merchant ship loading and unloading activities.

Even before the North Koreans seized the USS *Pueblo* (AGER 2) in January 1968, the Havana station ship—the *Muller* or *Georgetown*—always was accompanied by a U.S. destroyer, with three destroyers based at Key West sharing that duty. Also, on quick alert at the Key West naval air station was an armed fighter aircraft that could be over the U.S. ships within ten minutes of an incident. The commander in chief, Atlantic Fleet, ordered:

> (1) If for some reason the *Muller* is forced to enter [Cuban] territorial waters, the commanding officer of the escort is authorized to pursue. (2) In the event of an engineering or other casualty to *Muller* which causes the ship to drift into [Cuban] territorial waters, every effort shall be made to tow the *Muller* into international waters. The escort vessel, in any case, will remain with the *Muller* to provide protection in the event the *Muller* drifts into [Cuban] territorial waters. (3) In the event [Cuban] forces are declared hostile . . . U.S. forces in self-defense may deliver such fire and perform such tactics as are necessary to provide for defense of the *Muller* as well as themselves, including firing into [Cuban] territorial waters and airspace.[21]

The escorting destroyer assigned to the *Muller* normally maintained a "loose patrol" some four-to-eight n.miles outboard of the spy ship. The requirement for the escorting destroyer remained in effect until the *Muller* ended operations off Cuba. In September 1969, the Navy declared the *Muller* as surplus and deactivated her NSG detachment the following month. The ship was stricken from the Navy List on 16 September 1969 and later sold for scrap.

Look to the Skies

In late 1961, there arose an urgent requirement to monitor Soviet space and missile test events. The MSTS cargo ship *Lt. James E. Robinson* (T-AK 274) was hastily converted for that role in only three days and sailed from New York on 9 January 1962, manned by civilian mariners.[22] The ship's technical manning was unique with the *Robinson*'s military detachment consisting of a combination of NSG and Army Security Agency technicians.

The *Robinson*'s initial role was exclusively to monitor Soviet space events from the Indian Ocean area. As the *Robinson* conversion had been a rush job, the NSA quickly began work on modifying the attack cargo ship *Wyandot* (AKA 92) as a replacement for the *Robinson*, but that plan was abandoned in September 1962.

During April–May 1962, the *Robinson* operated in the Indian Ocean, awaiting a Soviet space launch. After returning to New York for maintenance, from August 1962 through January 1963, the *Robinson* circumnavigated the world, steaming through the Panama Canal, across the Pacific, into the Indian Ocean, through the Suez Canal into the Mediterranean, through the Strait of Gibraltar, and back to the U.S. East Coast. After an overhaul in Norfolk, the *Robinson* returned to the Indian Ocean via the Mediterranean and Suez Canal to continue monitoring Soviet space activities.

In May 1963, the National Security Agency had another urgent collection requirement because of a Soviet space event with the Indian Ocean designated as an alternative recovery area for manned space flights. As the *Robinson* at that time was en route to the United States for maintenance, the U.S. Joint Chiefs of Staff arranged an alternate resource: The Air Force Security Service provided an appropriately equipped van, and the Army Security Agency furnished ELINT operators for the cruise. The ship in which they were embarked has never been publicly identified.

That (unidentified) ship apparently remained on station until the *Robinson* returned to the Indian Ocean in December 1963 (having earlier been redesignated T-AG 170). Thereafter, the *Robinson* monitored Soviet space events and was involved in "normal" communications intercepts off both coasts of Africa. She operated out of Cape Town and Durban, and ranged from Liberia on the western coast of Africa to Kenya on the eastern coast.

The *Robinson* remained on the Indian Ocean–Africa station until April 1964. After returning to New York, in July 1964, she again was redesignated as a cargo ship (T-AK 274) and resumed MSTS cargo duties in the Atlantic. She was taken out of service in March 1976 and later scrapped.

The Technical Research Ships

The former World War II freighter *Robert W. Hart* received an extensive refitting at a shipyard in South Portland, Maine, emerging as the USS *Georgetown* (AG 165) in November 1963. After a 30-day shakedown cruise out of Guantánamo, the ship conducted a peripheral sweep of the southern coast of Cuba, steaming five-to-12 n.miles offshore, and then made a port call to Key West. Subsequently, she returned to Norfolk for installation of additional intercept equipment to enable her to relieve the *Muller* off Cuba.

On 1 April 1964, the *Georgetown* was redesignated as a technical research ship—AGTR 2. The Naval Security Group detachment of 143 officers and enlisted personnel was activated that month, and the *Georgetown* relieved the *Muller* off Havana from 19 April to 26 May.

After returning to Norfolk for most of June, the *Georgetown* departed on her first overseas mission. That deployment was to the northern and eastern coasts of South America, replicating those tracks sailed by the *Oxford* in 1962–63, with nearly identical targeting against communications in Argentina, Brazil, Colombia, Uruguay, and Venezuela. Liberty port calls were made at Rio, Montevideo, and Buenos Aires in the south, and San Juan, Port of Spain, and St. Thomas in the Caribbean. Among the notable accomplishments of that deployment were the initial intercept of Brazilian naval teleprinter communications between Rio, Brasilia, and Recife, and a deepening understanding of Brazilian Army communications, including determining the location of 34 transmitting stations. The *Georgetown* returned to Norfolk on 26 October 1964.

The *Georgetown* next departed Norfolk on 5 January 1965. There were three phases to that deployment: Phase I targeted radio communications in Venezuela and Colombia; Phase II required the ship to transit the Panama Canal to target Ecuador, Peru, Bolivia, Chile, and Argentina, with port calls in Callao, Peru, and Valparaíso, Chile; and Phase III saw the ship transit the canal eastward and from 16 to 29 March conduct a 14-day circumnavigation hearability survey of Cuba. The last was required because of a reduction in U.S. reconnaissance overflights of the island. The *Georgetown* then relieved the *Muller* off Havana from 3 April to 13 May, allowing for the *Muller*'s annual maintenance in a U.S. shipyard. The *Georgetown* returned to Norfolk on 14 May.

After maintenance into July alongside a repair ship in Norfolk, the *Georgetown* deployed to the east coast of South America and sortied as far south as 36 degrees latitude to monitor a Soviet space event. Again the crew's liberty ports were outstanding. The ship returned to Norfolk on 13 October 1965. During the subsequent period in port, the *Georgetown* received the moon-bounce system.

The *Georgetown* again departed Norfolk on 14 December; operated in the Caribbean with a port call at Willemstad, Curaçao, for Christmas; and then sailed to Trinidad for the New Year holiday. Targeted countries on the Caribbean cruise were Haiti, Venezuela, and Colombia. Afterward the ship made a westward transit of the Panama Canal and cruised along the Pacific coast of Colombia and Ecuador, seeking to intercept guerrilla communications. The ship then returned to the Caribbean via the canal, making a port visit to Cartagena, Colombia. On that deployment, the *Georgetown* intercepted extensive Haitian communications, obtained excellent coverage of Ecuadorian networks, and recorded considerable Colombian voice activity. During that crowded schedule, her NSG personnel made the first successful ship-to-ship moon-bounce communications (with the *Belmont* [AGTR 4]), and the crew responded to a civilian ship's emergency call off Colombia. The *Georgetown* returned to Norfolk on 7 March 1966.

Out of Norfolk on her fourth deployment, the *Georgetown* covered Havana for the *Muller* from 18 May to 20 June. On 21 May, a Marine firing from inside the U.S. naval base at Guantánamo killed a Cuban soldier. The Cuban government mobilized reserves and increased the readiness of local defenses. From 27 May through the first week of June, the NSA set a heightened state of SIGINT alert and prioritized the *Georgetown*'s intercept efforts. The ship rode out Hurricane Alma on 8–9 June with winds to 137 miles per hour, causing her to roll up to 43 degrees, with the eye of the storm passing directly over her.

Upon the return of the *Muller* to the Cuba station, the *Georgetown* transited the Panama Canal and began intercept operations against Mexican and Central American targets on 11 July. Notable intercepts included Mexican military networks, limited Nicaraguan military voice nets, and intercepts of El Salvadorian police frequencies. After a port call at Acapulco on 4 August and an unscheduled stop at Puntarenas, Costa Rica, to evacuate an injured crewman, the *Georgetown* transited the canal eastbound and made port calls at Coco Solo, Panama; Cartagena and Barranquilla, Colombia; and La Guairá, Venezuela. The ship returned to Norfolk on 23 August.

After a maintenance period, the *Georgetown* departed Norfolk on 4 October 1966. The principal objective of that deployment was intercepting military-related signals from Venezuela and Colombia. On 21 December, the *Georgetown* returned to Norfolk for the year-end holidays and an extended maintenance period. Also during 1966, the *Georgetown* twice rescued boatloads of refugees fleeing Cuba. Her activities during 1966 won the ship the Navy's Battle Efficiency "E" Award for that year.

The *Georgetown* again departed Norfolk on 7 March 1967, first to track down the Caribbean coast of Mexico, Guatemala, Nicaragua, and Panama. She then operated off Venezuela and Colombia. After suffering a boiler explosion off Venezuela on 25 March, the *Georgetown* spent the remainder of the month and the first half of April undergoing repairs at Cristóbal in the Canal Zone. The ship then made a westbound transit through the Panama Canal and steamed south to Peru, concentrating on military communications of South American governments facing narco-guerrilla activities in Colombia and leftist guerrilla movements in Ecuador and Peru. Upon returning to the Caribbean, the *Georgetown* again relieved the *Muller* off Havana, operating on that station from 15 May through 30 June.

Returning to Norfolk on 3 July, the *Georgetown* underwent an extensive overhaul. Her crew required a refresher course at Guantánamo, after which she returned to the Caribbean. The *Georgetown* operated off Haiti and Colombia before arriving at Rodman in the Canal Zone on 21 November. The next day the *Georgetown* began Pacific operations, but only four days later the ship unexpectedly was recalled and sent to the Mediterranean.

Mediterranean-African Operations

By late November 1967, the Turkish-Greek situation over the island of Cyprus had greatly deteriorated, and the *Georgetown* was ordered to proceed to Naples, Italy, and operate in the area to provide intelligence on the growing crisis. However, tensions between Turkey and Greece soon eased, and the NSA's ground intercept sites on Crete and Cyprus were no longer threatened. The *Georgetown* then was tasked to conduct intercept operations against Egypt and Syria, and she sailed from Naples for the eastern Mediterranean on 31 December. Following the North Korean assault on the *Pueblo* in January 1968, the *Georgetown* was ordered back to Naples because of the government's concern over the vulnerability of passive intelligence collection ships.

On 4 February 1968, the *Georgetown* departed Naples, now escorted by the guided missile destroyer *Lawrence* (DDG 4). On the 11th, the two U.S. ships were overflown by an Il'yushin Il-28 (NATO Beagle) reconnaissance aircraft with Egyptian markings that made three low passes over the ships. The aircraft most likely was flown by a Soviet crew. The Sixth Fleet commander immediately assigned the destroyer *Stormes* (DD 780) as an additional escort for the *Georgetown* and placed the aircraft carrier *Roosevelt* on one-hour notice to provide air support of the spy ship.

The *Georgetown*, steaming to the eastern end of the Mediterranean, was instructed to maintain a standoff range of 35 n.miles from the coast, making it almost impossible to intercept very- and ultra-high-frequency signals. After tracking along the Egyptian, Israeli, and Syrian coasts with very little accomplished, she ceased operations, departed the Mediterranean on 11 March, and arrived in Norfolk on 26 March.

In her final year of operation, the *Georgetown* departed Norfolk on 6 June 1968, scheduled to conduct another circumnavigation of Cuba, but that tasking suddenly was canceled. The *Georgetown* relieved the *Muller* on the Havana station from 8 June to 9 August, when the *Muller* returned after a maintenance period in the United States. The *Georgetown* returned briefly to Norfolk to take aboard additional technical material and then operated off the coasts of Trinidad, Guyana, Surinam, and French Guiana along the northern coast of South America, establishing baselines for the government communications of those nations.

On 27 October, the *Georgetown* steamed eastward across the South Atlantic and around South Africa, arriving off Mozambique on 7 December. The ship's primary mission in the Indian Ocean was to observe the track of a Soviet Zond spacecraft bound for the moon. Later in that deployment, on three occasions the *Georgetown* was directed to specific intercept positions, but all three taskings were frustrated by shipboard equipment failures, or by requiring speed beyond the ship's capability, or cancellation of Soviet launch attempts. After a port call at Port Louis, Mauritius, and a month sailing along the eastern coast of Africa for SIGINT surveillance, the *Georgetown* departed the Indian Ocean on 5 February. She steamed around South Africa and across the South Atlantic to make a port call at Recife, Brazil; she then tracked northward, arriving at Norfolk on 6 March 1969.

The *Georgetown* was scheduled to circumnavigate Cuba and relieve the *Muller* off Havana in July–August 1969, but problems with the ship's main engines made that commitment impossible. The Navy declared the ship was surplus. On 17 December, the NSG detachment was disestablished; the ship was decommissioned two days later and scrapped.

The *Jamestown*

During the same period as the *Georgetown* was refitted, the former Liberty-type World War II freighter *J. Howland Gardner* was converted into the USS *Jamestown* (AG 166/AGTR 3) and was placed in commission on 13 December 1962. Arriving at Guantánamo for her shakedown cruise just 18 days after the *Georgetown*, the *Jamestown*'s Naval Security Group detachment numbered 143.

The *Jamestown* sailed from Norfolk for the Mediterranean on 9 April 1964. She carried out productive intercepts along the North African coast from Morocco eastward to Egypt, with special tasking to intercept signals from the electronics of Soviet-built, Komar-type missile boats during Soviet premier Nikita Khrushchev's visit to Egypt. That tasking was unsuccessful.

After transiting the Suez Canal southward, the most productive phase of the *Jamestown*'s operation was off the eastern coast of Africa with significant new intercepts of communications in Ethiopia, Somalia, Malagasy, and Portuguese Mozambique. The *Jamestown* then sailed around South Africa and across the Atlantic, returning to Norfolk on 27 August 1964.

The *Jamestown* began her second deployment on 13 October, that time to the western coast of Africa. The primary targets were military and government communications in the Democratic Republic of the Congo, Angola, and South Africa. The assignment was sparked by the ongoing crisis in the Congo. Notable on that deployment were the intercepts of Congolese Morse code nets and the detection of a new means of communications used by the Congolese armed forces. Success in Portuguese Guinea (now Guinea-Bissau) was more significant with the recovery of the Portuguese military network after it had a complete change of call signs and frequencies. And off the coast of Angola, the ship's NSG detachment maintained continuous monitoring of 50 radio-teletype networks while steaming along the coast. The ship returned to Norfolk on 3 February 1965.

Departing port on 23 March 1965, the *Jamestown* had special tasking to monitor events in the Dominican Republic. Her foray into the area discovered a troposcatter communications link between the island state of Dominica and Puerto Rico, and nearly a dozen other multichannel networks. The ship then sailed for the coast of Brazil for intercept operations, after which she traveled northward to transit the Panama Canal and steam along the coast of Ecuador. There she made the initial intercept of an Ecuadorian network carrying military, police, and other government traffic. Farther south, off Chile, the *Jamestown* intercepted a unique network connecting all major Chilean military installations. In June the *Jamestown* visited the port of Valparaíso and on 4 July celebrated U.S. Independence Day in Callao. The ship then sailed north, transited the canal eastbound, and arrived at Norfolk on 23 July.

On 23 October, after an extended overhaul that included the installation of moon-bounce and enhanced high-frequency/direction-finding equipment, the *Jamestown* left Norfolk, sailing for the South China Sea, following the *Oxford* by six months. Unlike the *Oxford*, which had deployed via the Indian Ocean, the *Jamestown* transited the Panama Canal and tracked northward off the western coast of Central America. She stopped for liberty and fuel in Acapulco, then again at Pearl Harbor, and afterward crossed the Pacific to arrive at Subic Bay on 2 January 1966.

From 7 January 1966 to 18 October 1969, the *Jamestown* made 14 excursions of 45 days each into the South China Sea to support the U.S. SIGINT coverage of North Vietnam, Laos, Cambodia, and southern China, areas that already were being covered to some extent by U.S. ground intercept sites in South Vietnam, Thailand, Taiwan, and the Philippines. Both the *Jamestown*'s crew and her NSG detachment were rotated so that no one would serve more than one year on board unless volunteering to do so. Between intercept taskings, the ship underwent maintenance at Subic Bay and enjoyed liberty in Hong Kong, Subic Bay, Bangkok, and Taiwan. A major overhaul was undertaken at Yokosuka from February to April 1967.

The *Jamestown* departed the South China Sea for the last time on 7 October 1969, sailing to Sasebo, Japan, for deactivation. The ship was decommissioned on 19 December 1969 and scrapped.

The *Belmont*

The Navy acquired the former Victory-type World War II-era freighter *Iran Victory* in February 1963. Converted into a technical support ship at the Willamette shipyard in Portland, Oregon, she was commissioned on 2 November 1964 as the USS *Belmont* (AG 167, later AGTR 4). The *Belmont*'s Naval Security Group detachment consisted of six officers and 128 enlisted personnel. (The Navy's other Victory-type AGTR conversion was the *Liberty* [AG 168/AGTR 5].)

From 2 to 21 December, the *Belmont* sailed from Bremerton, Washington, through the Panama Canal, and to her home port of Norfolk. On 20 January 1965, the ship sailed to Guantánamo for a shakedown with her NSG detachment practicing its intercept talents off Havana from 20 to 26 February, after which the ship returned to Norfolk.

The *Belmont* next departed her home port for the western coast of Africa on 26 April. However, two days later the violence in the Dominican Republic resulted in the *Belmont*'s changing course for the Caribbean. The NSA used helicopters to transfer Spanish translators and related technical material to the *Belmont* as she transited westward along the northern coast of Puerto Rico. The ship arrived on station on 29 April.

Off the Dominican Republic, her NSG detachment was able to gain intelligence on the fighting and obtained almost daily intercepts of the communications among the rebel leaders. The United States intervened in the Dominican turmoil on 30 April 1965, with 1,700 Marines flown into the country by helicopter from the carrier *Boxer* (LPH 4, ex-CV 21) and a brigade of the Army's 82nd Airborne Division flown into the San Isidro airfield near the capital. The U.S. ground forces were supported by intercepts from the *Belmont*, which remained in the vicinity of the Dominican Republic for two months, returning to Norfolk on 13 July 1965.

On 15 September, the *Belmont* sailed from Norfolk on her second deployment to the Caribbean and the northern coast of South America. While en route to Venezuela, her NSG detachment was tasked to further develop an understanding of the Haitian and Dominican Republic's military and government communications. Although the major fighting in the Dominican Republic had ended by early May 1965, local unrest continued into 1969.

Subsequently, off the coasts of Venezuela and Colombia, the ship was tasked with monitoring military, shipping, and government communications, primarily because of narco-guerrilla organizations in both countries that were of concern to the United States. The *Belmont* returned to Norfolk on 28 January 1966.

The *Belmont* once more departed Norfolk on 16 March, transiting the Panama Canal for South America's Pacific coast. There the ship targeted communications in Colombia, Ecuador, Peru, Bolivia, and Chile, with her NSG detachment focused on guerrillas, illicit organizations, and dissident groups, as well as those nations' new national military and police communications. The *Belmont* made port visits at Callao and Valparaíso before returning to the Canal Zone on 23 May.

Nice Dog and Chili Pepper

The French government conducted 17 nuclear tests in the southwestern Algerian desert from 1961 to 1966. The French nuclear test program then was shifted to the Moruroa and Fangataufa atolls in French Polynesia in the Southwest Pacific. The French Pacific testing program began on 2 July 1966. There were 193 nuclear tests at the atolls, atmospheric and underground, from 1966 to 1996.

The U.S. National Security Agency needed to develop SIGINT tip-offs that could provide at least a one-day warning of impending French test detonations. That notice would enable monitoring flights by specially equipped aircraft based on Oahu to observe the tests. The *Belmont* was tasked to provide that advance warning because of the unavailability of the missile range instrumentation ship *Richfield* (T-AGM 4) that usually operated in that area.

To gain that advance notice of a test detonation required a sustained close-in effort to intercept and understand the French electronic signals and communications for indications of a forthcoming nuclear test. The NSA provided intelligence material and French linguists to the ship at Panama, and the *Belmont* departed the Canal Zone for the South Pacific on 28 May 1966.

The overall U.S. program to monitor French nuclear testing was called Nice Dog, with each year having a specific codename; in 1966 that was Chili Pepper. The surface ships *Belmont* and/or *Richfield* were given the codenames Underbid, and the surveillance aircraft flying from Oahu were designated Garlic Salt. Operating near the French test area, the *Belmont* developed more than 1,200 ELINT and COMINT "indicators," including closed-circuit television, facsimile, data transmissions, and radio-telephone intercepts, many of which were indicators of impending nuclear test events.

Early in July 1966, the *Belmont* was relieved by the *Richfield*, and the spy ship returned to Norfolk on 21 July. A letter of commendation awarded to the *Belmont* from Admiral Moorer, the commander in chief, Atlantic Fleet, and future chief of naval operations, read:

> For extremely meritorious performance of duty from 26 April 1965 to 13 July 1965 while participating in the Dominican Republic crises, and from 16 March 1966 to 21 July 1966 while participating in two additional operations of national importance . . . *Belmont* distinguished itself in the achievement of complex responsibilities which contributed significantly to the national interest.

Back to the Americas

The *Belmont* departed Norfolk on 8 September 1966, again steaming for the Pacific coast of South America. She transited the Panama Canal on the 19th and proceeded along the coasts of Colombia, Ecuador, Peru, and Chile to a point several hundred miles south of Valparaíso to monitor a Soviet space event. The tasking of the ship's NSG detachment included the intercept of illicit, dissident, and guerrilla activities, and Latin American communications intelligence on paramilitary and other government activities. She returned to the Canal Zone on 4 November, transited, and arrived at Norfolk on the 14th for a two-month maintenance period.

On 1 February 1967, the *Belmont* again departed Norfolk for a unique deployment—circumnavigating the South American continent clockwise. The *Belmont* sailed a relatively direct track to Buenos Aires to provide communications support in countering potential threats to officials of the Organization of American States who were meeting there 15 to 27 February 1967. The NSG team acted in direct support of the security personnel of the U.S. delegation, headed by Secretary of State Dean Rusk. After Rusk's departure, the *Belmont* remained in the Atlantic, targeting Brazil, Uruguay, and Argentina until rounding Cape Horn on 27 April 1967 and proceeding through the Strait of Magellan to Valparaíso.

The *Belmont* then moved slowly up the Pacific coast of South America, monitoring the military and government communications of Chile, Bolivia, Peru, Ecuador, and Colombia. Finally reaching the Panama Canal on 3 June, she transited the canal and arrived at Norfolk on 8 June 1967.

Africa Operations

Following the attack on the *Liberty* in the eastern Mediterranean on 8 June 1967, the NSA considered a quick turnaround in Norfolk for the *Belmont* and a deployment to the Mediterranean to replace the *Liberty*. However, with the recent decision to maintain a 100-n.mile standoff range of the coast for U.S. spy ships, there was little that a technical research ship could intercept in that area. Thus, the *Belmont* remained in Norfolk until 15 August, when she deployed to the Atlantic coast of Africa, south of Luanda, Angola. Again, her NSG detachment was tasked to intercept military and paramilitary communications, both government and oppositional forces, from Angola to South Africa.

On 3 October, the *Belmont* additionally was tasked to cover an impending Soviet space event, requiring her to reach a specific position in the Indian Ocean. That mission was concluded on 10 November, and after a port visit to Mombasa, the *Belmont* was homebound on 15 November. She tracked up the Atlantic coast of Africa from 22 November to 1 December; refueled in Monrovia, Liberia; and arrived in Norfolk in mid-December for a five-month overhaul.

On 14 May 1968, the *Belmont* commenced her seventh deployment with refresher training at Guantánamo from 15 May to 14 June and then departed for the west coast of Africa. Her primary mission was to assist in the development and maintenance of a SIGINT database for government communications of 18 sub-Saharan African countries.

The *Belmont*'s operating orders were changed several times en route to Africa, as the standoff distance to Nigeria was changed to 100 n.miles because of the ongoing civil war there, which also affected the ship's coverage of the Cameroons. After covering Nigeria, the Congo became a second priority, and Gabon third, with lower priorities given to SIGINT coverage of the other African coastal states. The intercept targets for those African nations were military and paramilitary operations, communist activity, anti--U.S. and Western European activities, movements of arms and other military equipment, and government actions to suppress dissident elements. Portuguese colonies such as Guinea, Angola, and Mozambique were assigned special tasking for indications of foreign support of anti-Portuguese activities, especially originating from Tanzania, Congo (Kinshasa), Zambia, China, or Cuba.

On 25–26 September, the *Belmont* rounded the Cape of Good

Hope to begin intercept operations along the eastern coast of Africa. While off Mozambique, the *Belmont* successfully intercepted signals from the Soviet Soyuz spacecraft. After operations along South Africa, Malagasy, Mozambique, Tanzania, and Kenya, the ship departed from Lourenço Marques, Mozambique, on 2 November for home.

After rounding the Cape of Good Hope westbound, the *Belmont* crossed the Atlantic for a refueling call at Recife, Brazil, from 13 to 16 November. She then conducted intercept operations against French Guiana, Suriname, and Guyana before arriving in Norfolk on 28 November 1968.

Back to the Mediterranean

The *Belmont* remained in Norfolk because of maintenance requirements and the installation of new intercept equipment. She departed Norfolk on 19 June 1969 for a twofold mission: intercept operations against North African and Middle Eastern communications, and SIGINT operations against the Soviet Mediterranean squadron. Special tasking of her NSG detachment included collecting Soviet anti-ship cruise missile signals "to assist in developing effective countermeasures" and signals related to Soviet aircraft operating from Egyptian airfields.

Due to the concurrent deployment in the area of the intelligence ship *Palm Beach* (AGER 3), the commander of the Sixth Fleet assumed operational control of both spy ships to avoid mutual interference or conflicts in their tasking. While in the Mediterranean, the *Belmont* conducted several patrols centered on monitoring the activities of the Soviet helicopter carrier *Moskva* and her escorts. That was the first deployment to the Mediterranean of the innovative, 15,280-ton combination missile cruiser–helicopter carrier; she had joined the fleet less than two years earlier.

From 9 July to 2 August, the *Belmont* remained in the vicinity of the Kythira anchorage off the western tip of Crete while awaiting the *Moskva* and escorts. After a port call in Athens, the *Belmont* returned to the anchorage on 11 August and observed the *Moskva* upon her arrival on 20 August. The *Belmont* maintained close surveillance of the *Moskva* task unit until the 28th, when the *Belmont* broke off from the Soviet ships for a port visit to Valletta, Malta.

On 2 September, the *Belmont* reestablished surveillance of the carrier *Moskva* and her escorts. When the *Moskva* repeatedly entered the Gulf of Sallum—Egyptian waters at the extreme western coast of Egypt—the *Belmont* remained 50 n.miles off the coast. On the 11th, the *Moskva* entered the Bosporus to return to the Black Sea and her home port. Two days later, the *Belmont* broke off surveillance and returned to the Kythira anchorage to monitor other Soviet naval ships. On 25 September, the *Belmont* arrived at the island of Rhodes (Greece) for liberty for her crew. From 7 to 20 October, the ship again steamed in the vicinity of Kythira.

The ship then was called back to Norfolk for deactivation. After a port call at Rota, Spain, the ship crossed the Atlantic, arriving at Norfolk on 3 November 1969. The *Belmont* was decommissioned on 16 January 1970 and subsequently sold for scrap. She was the last ship of the U.S. Navy's AGTR spy ship program.

Project Azorian

One other U.S. ship in this period undertook a highly unusual "intelligence collection" effort—the *Hughes Glomar Explorer* operated by the Central Intelligence Agency. A U.S. Air Force seafloor acoustic system had detected the sinking of the Soviet diesel-electric, ballistic missile submarine *K-129* in the North Pacific on the night of 11/12 March 1968. The diesel-electric submarine was lost through the inadvertent ignition of the explosive bolts on the covers of the submarine's three ballistic missile tubes followed by the ignition of the rocket engines of two of the craft's three nuclear missiles. The entire crew of 98 men died instantly.

The Soviets knew that the submarine had sunk in the North Pacific but could not determine precisely when or the location of the wreckage. The location and condition of the wreckage was secretly confirmed and photographed by a sensor platform towed by the U.S. nuclear submarine *Halibut*.[23] Based on that information, the CIA sponsored the construction of the *Glomar Explorer* under the cover story that the ship was a seafloor mining project sponsored by eccentric billionaire Howard Hughes.

Manned by a civilian crew and with considerable commercial publicity, the *Glomar Explorer* sailed to the *K-129* site "to mine manganese nodules on the seafloor" at a depth of 16,400 feet. The massive lift ship—618⅔ feet long with a 39,700 deadweight tonnage—arrived at the location of the submarine's wreckage on 4 July 1974. After delays caused by bad weather, the ship lowered the "capture vehicle" through doors in the bottom of the ship. The ship's cavernous interior could accommodate the 2,000-ton lifting device as well as the salvaged submarine.

As soon as the *Glomar Explorer* reached the site, her activity was brought to the attention of the commander of the Soviet Pacific Fleet, Admiral Nikolay I. Smirnov. He ordered visual surveillance of the American ship. A specialist on board the *Glomar Explorer* recalled that on the morning of 18 July, "the fog burned off and out of the mist came this . . . what looked to me like a white, beautiful ship [with] very odd radomes on top and some funny looking antennas aft."[24] The shadowing ship was the *Chazhma*, a large, civilian-manned, missile range–tracking ship.[25] The ship had departed Petropavlovsk in mid-June to support a Soviet space event and was en route to her base from a position near Johnston Island when she was directed to observe the American "seafloor mining ship." The *Chazhma* was fitted with extensive tracking devices and had a helicopter hangar and flight deck aft. A Kamov Ka-25 (NATO Hormone) helicopter was on board.

The *Chazhma* initially closed to within about two miles of the *Glomar Explorer*. At 1430 the Soviet ship closed to one mile, and her crew began taking photos of the American ship, and the helicopter took off. The Ka-25 circled the *Glomar Explorer* close in while her crew took photographs.

At Soviet fleet headquarters in Vladivostok, Captain 1st Rank Anatolyi Shtyrov, the fleet's deputy head of intelligence, was concerned about the American ship's activities. He later recalled:

> At night, when relative calm set in at the Fleet command post [headquarters] and communications were not loaded down, I went to the communications and called up the commander of the *Chazhma*. I pumped information from him by bits and pieces. He confirmed that all signs were that the Americans were looking for oil.[26]

The heavily censored CIA history of the lift operation—Project Azorian—relates:

> These actions by the *Chazhma* caused a measure of concern that the Soviets had become knowledgeable from other sources of the true mission of the HGE [*Hughes Glomar Explorer*]. The HGE was vulnerable sitting alone in the vast Pacific Ocean, miles from any friendly supporting forces. . . . Accordingly, [deleted] advise the officer in charge [deleted] to be prepared to order emergency destruction of sensitive material which could compromise the mission if the Soviets attempted to board the ship. The team was designated to defend the control room long enough to destroy the material . . . [deleted] was alerted, but guns were not issued.[27]

The *Chazhma* subsequently closed with the *Glomar Explorer*, at one point coming within 1,000 yards, while her helicopter again made passes over the stationary American ship. The *Chazhma* departed the area on the evening of 18 July. Meanwhile, the *Glomar Explorer* continued her clandestine lift efforts.

On the morning of 22 July, the Soviet Navy's oceangoing tug *SB-10* arrived on the scene to keep watch on the American ship's activities. The tug initially maintained a distance of some three to four miles from the lift ship, later closing to within 200 yards. The *Glomar Explorer*'s captain repeatedly warned the tug by radio messages and signal flags to keep her distance.

The Americans estimated that the Soviet ship was manned by a crew of about 40 men and two women. Some of the crew wore fatigue-type outfits; others usually were in swim trunks or shorts. On board the *Glomar Explorer*, some crewmen observing the Soviet ship believed that the two women exchanged their few dresses every day or two.

The *SB-10*'s crew also photographed the American ship, periodically coming close aboard. At 1135 on 6 August, just as the submarine's wreckage was about to be pulled into the bottom of the hull of the *Glomar Explorer*, the *SB-10* came within 75 yards of the American ship and again was signaled to keep clear. As the Soviet ship backed off, she sounded three long blasts on the whistle and sailed off toward the horizon, heading back to her base at Petropavlovsk. At 2230 she disappeared from the *Glomar Explorer*'s radar screen. The salvage ship completed the lift of the submarine's wreckage without being observed.

As the forward third of the *K-129* was being lifted up to the *Glomar Explorer*, some of the grabbers of the lift device broke, and most of the submarine's wreckage fell back to the ocean floor. Thus, only the forward 38 feet of the Soviet missile submarine was pulled up into the ship's cavernous hull. Still, it contained some important finds, including two nuclear torpedoes and documents.

Soviet ships had held close surveillance of the American ship for most of the *Glomar Explorer*'s lift operation. The CIA report noted, "One can only conjecture the reaction and chagrin of Soviet authorities when they later realized that two Soviet Navy ships were on the scene and, in effect, witnessed the recovery operation against their lost submarine."[28]

The CIA had planned to return to the *K-129* wreckage to recover the surviving (third) ballistic missile from the wreckage of the submarine's amidships section. However, having learned of the earlier salvage effort, a Soviet official declared that if the United States made another attempt to recover additional portions of the submarine, it would "mean war."[29]

6

The Attack on the USS *Liberty*

The eighth and last spy ship sponsored by the National Security Agency to enter service in the 1960s was the technical research ship *Liberty* (AGTR 5).[1] In June 1965, with her conversion and training completed, the Navy-manned *Liberty* steamed out of Norfolk en route to Africa.

The *Liberty*'s moon-bounce communications system gave the ship the capability to communicate directly with NSA headquarters at Fort Meade, Maryland, just north of Washington DC, from anywhere on the world's oceans.[2] The ship also had access to the Navy's HICOM emergency radio system that provided instant voice communications to the highest Navy commands. And in compliance with Navy-NSA policy, the ship was minimally armed with four .50-caliber machine guns—two forward and one on either side of the bridge—plus an armory of pistols, rifles, and concussion grenades. That armament possibly could have repelled pirates.

Africa Operations

Throughout her first two years of service, the *Liberty* operated off the western coast of Africa on deployments of eight to 14 weeks, interrupted by maintenance periods in her home port of Norfolk. The *Liberty* primarily monitored the political and military communications of sub-Saharan nations, especially the chaotic conflict in the Congo.[3] The ship carried Spanish, Portuguese, and French translators during those African deployments.

The *Liberty*'s first such deployment was from mid-June 1965 to late October 1965 off the western coast of Africa. That deployment occurred during the Cuban intervention in the Congo cri-

Photo 18. The spy ship *Liberty* (AGTR 5) underway in late 1966, several months before being attacked by Israeli aircraft and torpedo boats in an infamous "blue-on-blue" attack. A series of missed communications and false identifications led to the accidental assault that left 34 Americans dead and another 171 wounded. / U.S. Navy.

ses. Led by the revolutionary Che Guevara, the Cubans operated in the Congo from April to November 1965.

The ship's second African deployment was from mid-January to late March 1966. Upon her return to Norfolk in April, Commander William L. McGonagle took command of the ship, and Lieutenant Commander David E. Lewis became the officer in charge of the ship's Naval Security Group detachment.[4]

The *Liberty*'s third deployment off Africa began in late May; she arrived back in Norfolk in late August 1966. She conducted her fourth African deployment from early November 1966 to late February 1967 and departed Norfolk for her fifth deployment in early May 1967. The *Liberty* was in port in Abidjan on the Ivory Coast on 23 May 1967, when Egypt undertook the blockade of the Gulf of Aqaba, denying transit of that vital waterway to Israeli shipping. That action "crossed a line in the sand" that Israeli prime minister Golda Meir had announced at the United Nations on 1 March 1957:

> Interference by armed force, with ships of Israeli flag exercising free and innocent passage in the Gulf of Aqaba and through the Straits of Tiran will be regarded by Israel as an attack entitling it to exercise its inherent right of self-defense under Article 51 of the [United Nations] Charter and to take all measures as are necessary to ensure the free and innocent passage of its ships in the Gulf and in the Straits.[5]

The Egyptian blockade thus guaranteed that there would be open warfare with Israel. It would be the third Arab-Israeli conflict. (The previous conflicts were in 1948–49 and 1956; the first began on 14 May 1948, when the State of Israel was established.)

Into the War Zone

The U.S. Joints Chiefs of Staff ordered the *Liberty* from the western coast of Africa and into the eastern Mediterranean. Departing Abidjan on the morning of 24 May, the spy ship sailed northward. She reached the Spanish-U.S. naval base at Rota, Spain, on 1 June. There she exchanged translators, received information on intercept targets, and took on fuel and provisions.

At Rota, three civilian and three Marine translators came on board: the civilians were Arabic linguists; the Marines were two Arabic linguists and one Russian linguist. The Russian linguist had undergone 15 weeks of Hebrew language training several years earlier. He was on board due to an error in assignment. In personnel records, Hebrew was recorded as "Special Arabic," and he had erroneously been assigned as the ship's sixth Arabic translator. Thus, there were five bona fide Arabic linguists on board and one translator—assigned in error—with limited Hebrew-language facility.

The *Liberty* departed Rota for the eastern Mediterranean on 2 June. Her intercept targets were *Egyptian* military communications and electronics. There also was concern over possible Soviet intervention. *The ship was not tasked to monitor Israeli communications*. From an official—and practical—perspective, no Hebrew linguists were on board.

The ship was steaming south of Italy on 5 June 1967 when the Six-Day War erupted with Israeli aircraft striking and rapidly destroying the air forces of Egypt, Jordan, and Syria, and the in-area Iraqi Air Force. The *Liberty* was still one day out from the war zone when Israeli ground forces defeated the Egyptian armored divisions in the Sinai and punched through Egyptian lines, moving toward the Suez Canal.

The war was three days old when the *Liberty* arrived on station off the Sinai coast, south of Gaza, on the morning of 8 June. The ship's original orders were to maintain a minimum distance of 6½ n.miles off the coast of Israel and 12½ n.miles from the Egyptian coast. Only hours before her arrival on station the orders were revised: They directed the ship to sail no closer than 15 n.miles off the coast of Israel and 20 n.miles off Egypt. A second message from the Joint Chiefs of Staff belatedly ordered the *Liberty* to a position no closer to Israel and Egypt than 100 n.miles. Both messages were misrouted; the ship *never* received them.[6]

The communications failure would place the *Liberty* in great jeopardy.

Why was the *Liberty* off the coast of the Sinai? Tasking from both the CIA and the Department of Defense had been levied to obtain intelligence on Egyptian naval, air, and ground forces—particularly their capabilities and status. Additionally, the *Liberty* could "plug" the hole caused by the NSA's expected loss of at least three ground intercept sites in Middle East areas that could be exposed to combat. Thus, the NSA needed the *Liberty* to meet its "consumer requirements" concerning the Egyptian military.[7] There were no intercept requirements with respect to Israel because of the special relationship that existed between Israel and the United States.

The Israeli armed forces had moved rapidly and were so effective in destroying Egyptian aircraft, radars, and missile defenses that Egypt's tactical communications and other electronics were almost completely silenced by 8 June. Thus, when the *Liberty* arrived on station, most of the combat in the Sinai had ended, and the opportunity of acquiring significant electronic intelligence on the Egyptians had passed.

About 0545 on 8 June (local Israel time), an Israeli Air Force reconnaissance aircraft, with Navy observer Commander Uri Meretz on board, reported that "apparently a warship" was about 70 n.miles west of the coastal city of Tel Aviv. That message was relayed to the Israeli Navy's command center in Haifa, and the ship was marked as "unidentified" on its plotting table. About 15 minutes later, Meretz identified the *Liberty* as an "American supply ship," and the naval plot marker was changed to indicate a "neutral ship."

The *Liberty* on Station

The *Liberty* arrived on station about 13 n.miles off the southern boundary of the Gaza Strip at 0850 on 8 June. Within one minute of the ship's arrival, two Israeli jet aircraft crossed astern and then circled the ship three times.[8] At 0900 an Israeli pilot, returning from strikes in Egypt, reported to his Air Force controller that an unidentified ship 20 miles north of El-Arish on the Sinai coast had fired on his aircraft as he was trying to identify the ship. Two Israeli destroyers were ordered to investigate but were quickly recalled due to inconsistencies in the pilot's debriefing.

The duty officer at Israeli Navy headquarters in Haifa, Commander Avraham (Rami) Lunz, later testified that at 1055 the naval liaison officer at Air Force headquarters in Tel Aviv informed him that "an electromagnetic audio-surveillance ship of the U.S. Navy named *Liberty*, whose marking was G.T.R. 5," was off the Sinai coast.[9]

However, because that sighting information was several hours old and considered "stale," Lunz had the neutral ship tag marking the *Liberty* removed from the plot at 1100. From that moment forward, the possible presence of the *Liberty* in the area faded from situational awareness at Navy headquarters in Haifa. Because ships "don't linger," the conclusion was that the American ship had moved elsewhere.

Throughout the morning of 8 June, the *Liberty* was on a southwest course at five knots, generally parallel to the Sinai coast.[10] Unknown to the *Liberty*, an Israeli reconnaissance flight at 1126 had not been briefed that an American ship might be in the area, and it was trying to locate an Egyptian warship that was believed to be shelling Israeli positions near the port of El-Arish. Two reports of such a bombardment had reached Israeli military headquarters in Tel Aviv, which ordered the Navy to determine if any Israeli ships were off the coast near El-Arish. At 1145, Tel Aviv received a third report: There were *two* ships approaching the Sinai coast near El-Arish.[11] It also had reports at 1100 of Egyptian submarines off the Israeli coast and that Israeli reconnaissance aircraft were conducting intensive searches for them in the area. Those aircraft were completely unconcerned with the presence of the *Liberty*.

Reports of several other overflights during the morning hours from *Liberty* crewmen apparently were unrelated to Israeli concerns of a ship shelling their positions near El-Arish. Rather, those aircraft appeared to have been Israeli strike and reconnaissance aircraft flying from bases in Israel to and from targets in Egypt.[12] They too gave no attention to the *Liberty*.

In response to orders received at 1205 from Israeli military headquarters, the head of the Navy's operations section in Haifa, Captain Yitzchak (Izzy) Rahav, dispatched three motor torpedo boats under Lieutenant Commander Moshe Oren to investigate the reports of a ship off the coast of Sinai.[13] Ens. Aharon Yifrach on the torpedo boat *T-204*—with Oren embarked—at 1341 reported a radar contact at a distance of 22 miles, almost twice the normal range of the craft's radar. Yifrach reported the target moving toward Egypt's Port Said *at 30 knots!*[14] The *Liberty* was underway at five knots at that time.

The Israeli naval rules of engagement in 1967 stated: "When there are reports of an enemy in the theatre and radar detects one or more ships sailing at a speed above 20 knots, they shall be considered hostile and no further identification shall be carried out."[15]

Several minutes later, Oren reported the target ship making *28 knots*. At Navy headquarters, Rahav twice requested Oren to recalculate the speed, and twice Yifrach confirmed his calculations. As the target was fleeing at 28 knots, Oren's torpedo boats might not overtake the ship before she reached the safety of Egypt's Port Said. At about 1345, Oren reported that the target was 17 miles distant and still making 28 knots.

Meanwhile, neither Oren nor the officers at Navy headquarters in Haifa appear to have noted the range to the target had dropped five miles in less than seven minutes. Obviously, the target was not fleeing at the reported speed. Subsequently, at 1348, Rahav sent a request to Air Force headquarters authorizing aircraft to attack "if it is a warship." At that time, the Israeli Navy had the exclusive responsibility for authorizing attacks on naval targets. When aircraft were requested to assist the torpedo boats, existing procedures *required* the Air Force aircraft to attack if "identified as a warship."

At about 1350, the *Liberty* made radar contact with three small surface craft approaching on her starboard quarter. The *Liberty* also detected an aircraft over the three torpedo boats at 1351. The aircraft then approached and spent about five minutes flying over and around the *Liberty* at an altitude of about 3,000 feet.[16]

The Air Attack

As the *Liberty* was detecting the Israeli torpedo boats and the overflying aircraft, the chief of Israeli Air Force intelligence, Col. Yeshyahu Bareket, in Tel Aviv called the U.S. naval attaché at the American Embassy in Tel Aviv, Commander Ernest C. Castle, asking for information about the *Liberty*. Castle replied that he had no information related to the ship.

Lieutenant Colonel Shmuel Kislev, the chief air controller at Air Force headquarters in Tel Aviv, received the Navy's request for air support at 1348, and the first aircraft that he could direct to the target were two Dassault Mirage III fighters armed with rockets and 30-mm guns. He ordered that "Kursa" flight to identify the ship steaming northwest of El-Arish and authorized an immediate attack "if a warship," as requested by Navy headquarters.

The two aircraft overflew the *Liberty* twice at an altitude of 3,000 feet. The flight leader, Captain Iftach Spector, who had no training in ship identification, reported that the ship appeared to have one stack and one mast, and he thought that she was a small military ship.[17] When asked if he saw a flag, Spector replied that he saw no flag or other identifying markings. The ship was painted gray and appeared to have two guns on her bow. He took photographs to verify his identification.[18]

At 1354, an officer monitoring Kislev's air-control frequency blurted out, "What is this? Americans?" A deputy controller responded on the same circuit: "Where are Americans?" That cross talk was ignored, and Kislev continued his control of the developing engagement, expediting the arrival of another pair of fighter-bombers to relieve Kursa flight when its planes had expended all of their ammunition.

With the Mirage flight leader's visual identification that the target was armed and painted military gray, and with the Navy's report that she was fleeing at 28 knots toward Port Said, the Kursa flight attacked just prior to 1400.[19] The two Mirage fighters strafed the ship with 30-mm cannon and fired rockets for five minutes, making a total of six attack runs.

Kislev improvised a second strike consisting of two Super Mystères armed with napalm canisters—hardly a preferred weapon for attacking a ship—in addition to cannon and rockets.[20] That "Royal" flight arrived over the target at 1404, just as the two Mirages were making their last attack. The newly arrived aircraft each made one attack, dropping napalm and strafing with 30-mm cannon.[21]

During the attack by the Kursa flight, at 1401, Lieutenant Commander Oren on torpedo boat *T-204* notified Navy headquarters that the target had not returned fire and that she could be an *Israeli ship*. Kislev at Air Force headquarters ordered the Mystères to pause their attacks until identification of the target could be confirmed as hostile.

Navy headquarters then contacted all Israeli ships in the area; none reported that she was under attack. However, Kislev felt uneasy by the lack of return fire from the target ship, and after the Royal flight's first firing run, he ordered the Super Mystère flight leader, Captain Yossi Zuk, to attempt to identify the ship.

As the attack continued, Zuk sought ship identification indicators after his next attack run by tracking alongside the *Liberty* at an altitude of 30 feet. He reported at 1411 that the ship's markings were "Charlie Tango Romeo" (CTR) in English and "five" in Hebrew. A few moments later, after repeating the markings, Zuk added: "There is no flag on her."[22]

During that last air attack, the *Liberty* was on fire, with billowing black smoke. As essentially no wind blew over the ship except that generated by the ship's forward motion at five knots, the attacking aircraft, flying from bow to stern at high speed, could not see American colors.

After completing Royal flight's second (and final) strafing run, Zuk's air controller asked: "What country?" Kislev replied: "Apparently American."[23] A third flight—"Nixon" flight—consisting of two Mystères armed with ship-sinking 500-pound bombs was then en route to the *Liberty*'s position. With the realization that the ship could be American, Kislev abruptly canceled further attacks at 1412, ordering: "Leave her; leave her; leave her; leave her!"[24]

In the 13-minute attack, the four aircraft had made a total of ten attack runs, firing rockets and 30-mm cannon, and dropping four napalm canisters. Three of the canisters had missed the ship; one had struck. On board the *Liberty* at that time, probably nine men were dead or dying, and about 75 were wounded. Worse was to come.

Up to that moment, the *Liberty* had been the victim of misidentification in the so-called fog of war. Kislev's instant realization that the target was not Egyptian and immediate decision to call off the air attack no doubt saved the *Liberty* from being sunk within the next few minutes. At 1413, Kislev ordered two rescue helicopters to fly out to the ship and offer assistance.

Conspiracy theories describing the attack as planned to eliminate the American ship with her intercept capabilities are debunked by an examination of Kislev's obviously improvised engagement. If preplanned, the first aircraft would have carried ship-killing "iron bombs." Instead, the first flight had only 30-mm guns and rockets; the second flight was armed with guns, rockets, and napalm. The third flight, which did have such bombs, was canceled immediately when the identity of the target became uncertain. The air attack was not preplanned; it obviously was carried out in response to an unanticipated request from the Israeli Navy.

The *Liberty*'s radio logs show that attempts to transmit reports of the attack were made as early as 1358, but with damage to almost all of the ship's antennas, it was not until an emergency repair was made to a high-frequency, 35-foot whip antenna that a "flash" message reporting the attack could be sent. That message went out by voice just prior to 1425, about 15 minutes after Colonel Kislev halted air attacks and less than 25 minutes before an ensuing torpedo attack.[25]

The *Liberty*'s voice message that she was under attack was received aboard the U.S. aircraft carrier *Saratoga* (CVA 60), then steaming more than 500 n.miles away, south of Crete. The *Saratoga* immediately relayed the message to the U.S. Sixth Fleet commander, who was embarked in the missile cruiser *Little Rock* (CLG 4) in the Mediterranean, and to the commander, U.S. Naval Forces Europe, in London.

The Israeli Navy's liaison officer at Air Force headquarters in Tel Aviv at about 1415 passed the pilot's identification of the target as a non-Egyptian ship with "C.T.R. 5" marking on the hull to Navy headquarters in Haifa. There is evidence that Haifa *did not* pass that identification to Oren.[26] From that moment forward, one man would make a series of tactical decisions that would dwarf the damage of the earlier Israeli mistakes.

Torpedo Attack!

Navy headquarters in Haifa ordered Lieutenant Commander Oren's three torpedo boats to abort their attack at 1420 because of concerns over the target's identity.[27] That order was recorded in the *T-204*'s logbook, and Oren's boat commander later testified that he had personally informed Oren of the order. (Oren testified that he never received that order.[28])

At 1425 the three torpedo boats were four-to-five n.miles off the *Liberty*'s starboard beam and were surprised to find that the target was a "supply ship" rather than the high-speed Egyptian destroyer that they had expected to encounter. The *Liberty* was on fire with vast clouds of black smoke rising almost vertically into the sky. At about that time, her commanding officer, Commander McGonagle, noted that the ship's American flag had been shot away during the air attack, and he ordered a seven-by-13-foot "holiday" flag be hoisted.[29]

Witnessing the sustained air attack from several miles away, Oren on the *T-204* twice requested that the Air Force cease fire and allow him to finish off the target. Then, perhaps in an abundance of caution, Oren decided at 1427 to attempt to contact the target by flashing light. By signal light from about one mile away, Oren queried the *Liberty*: "What ship?" He reported that the smoke was so thick that all he could see was "a portion of the ship's bow, part of her bridge, and the tip of her mast." Oren's signalman on the *T-204* stated that they received a reply from the *Liberty* of "AA," meaning "identify yourself first." But McGonagle later would report that he could not and did not reply by signal lamp.

(That Israeli account seemed to replicate the situation experienced in 1956 when Israeli ships overtook the Egyptian destroyer *Ibrahim el Awal* at night and signaled, "What ship?" They had received "AA" in reply. The Israelis then attacked, boarded, and captured the ship. Oren had been on the scene at the capture of the *Ibrahim el Awal*.)

The *Liberty*'s starboard signal lamp had been destroyed, and McGonagle was unable to read Oren's query through the smoke. Instead, he hoisted the international signal flags for "unable to maneuver"—meaning that the ship was in a desperate situation.[30] Oren misinterpreted the *Liberty*'s efforts to communicate, reporting that the target acted "suspiciously."

With the *Liberty* then underway at about ten knots while accelerating from five to 15 knots, Commander McGonagle recorded that the men at his starboard .50-caliber machine gun opened fire toward the torpedo boats without his authorization. Oren reported sighting flashes of gunfire from the target at 1435.

Minutes later, both Oren and the *T-203* boat commander, using identification guides, independently determined that the *Liberty*'s mast-funnel arrangement was that of the small Egyptian freighter *El-Quseir*.[31] (Oren's initial report of a 28-knot speed for the target was false, given the visual character of both the *Liberty* and the *El-Quseir* as "supply ships," neither of which could attain speeds much above 15 knots.)

Once Oren had identified the target as the *El-Quseir* and saw the target was not responding to his signals and had fired on his torpedo boats, he was convinced the target was hostile. Following up on the Air Force attacks, Oren reported his visual identification of the target as Egyptian to Navy headquarters at 1437. The war log of Oren's torpedo boat division recorded that the identification "seems to be reasonable." Oren then twice forcefully requested permission to attack by torpedoes based on a "reasonable" identification. Why? Oren's division had a 15-to-20-knot speed advantage over the target and had plenty of opportunity to obtain a positive identification rather than a "reasonable" assessment.[32]

While the torpedo boat's war log clearly records the reasonable identification, the Israeli Navy headquarters' war log entry first stated: "Looks like the Egyptian supply ship *El-Quseir*." Then, in the same time entry, at 1436, it stated: "Identification is definite, approval was made for torpedo attack."[33]

Captain Rahav at Navy headquarters in Haifa had failed to transmit to Oren the suspected identity of the target was not Egyptian—as reported by attacking aircraft—thus denying Oren critical information.[34] Worse, the officers at Navy headquarters who recalled that an American ship had been in the area *assumed* Rahav had that information. But he had not been at headquarters when the plot marker showed the presence of the *Liberty* nor had Commander Lunz briefed Rahav of that information at their turnover.

(One of the unanswerable questions of this entire incident is, why did Oren and Rahav want to sink an "Egyptian" cargo ship that was already badly damaged by air attack? Why not call the Israeli destroyers to board and capture her? Why the rush to sink her? A senior Israeli officer had told one of the authors of this book that some naval personnel felt that so far the "war" had been won by the Israeli Army and Air Force, and that the Navy had to make some "contribution.")

Oren's three torpedo boats closed on their target at high speed, commenced firing on the *Liberty* with 40-mm and 20-mm guns, and independently launched torpedoes starting at 1443. The *T-206* fired two torpedoes from one-half-mile distance, both of which ran straight and normal, but neither exploded (one was sighted passing close astern of the *Liberty*, indicating an error in estimating the target's speed). The *T-203* fired two torpedoes from one mile away about one minute later. One torpedo veered off course; the other ran straight and true—striking the target. The *T-204* fired only one torpedo that seemed to sink without activating. Thus, there was one hit from five torpedoes launched against a slow, non-maneuvering target. An officer on the *T-204* called them "lousy Italian torpedoes."

The torpedo hit on the *Liberty* blew a hole 39 feet wide and 24 feet high in the amidships technical spaces, instantly killing more than 20 of the Naval Security Group detachment and four other men. Many more men were injured either by the torpedo explosion or the torpedo boats' gunfire.

Following the torpedo attack, the boats made runs firing their 20-mm and 40-mm cannon, and .50-caliber machine guns, crossing the spy ship's bow and stern. One boat's crew finally noticed the stern markings in non-Arabic script and the attack stopped at 1447. Oren then reported to Navy headquarters his realization that the target was not Egyptian, and he received orders to search for survivors and to positively ascertain the nationality of the target.

At 1451, Oren reported that the target might be Soviet due to the lettering "CTR 5." The chief of the General Staff, General Yitzhak Rabin, wrote in his memoirs that this report raised so much concern at Navy headquarters that it was immediately sent to Prime Minister Levi Eshkol and that a meeting was convened to discuss possible Soviet reactions to such an attack.[35]

At 1514 the two Israeli Air Force helicopters reported seeing an American flag on the target. Oren finally reported to Navy headquarters at 1520 that the ship was American. Naval headquarters ordered the dispatch of two tugs from the port of Ashdod to assist the damaged ship. At 1640, at the direction of Navy headquarters, Oren's torpedo boat approached the *Liberty* and, by megaphone in English, offered assistance. It was rejected.[36] Oren's three torpedo boats remained with the *Liberty* until 1704, when they were ordered to return to port.

The U.S. Sixth Fleet's two-carrier task force at the time was intermingled with Soviet surface ships, intelligence ships, and cruise missile–armed submarines. The Soviets had seen its Middle East client states decisively defeated by Israel, which destroyed Soviet-provided aircraft, tanks, and missile systems in wholesale lots. After the defeat of Egypt, Israel had turned on Syria, which was not only a Soviet client but also provided the only Arab port in the Middle East fully open to Soviet warships. The Soviet government threatened to intervene directly in Syria if Israel did not immediately cease fighting.

"Need Assistance"

The *Liberty* sent a situation report at 1435 by voice radio reporting the approach of three unidentified "gunboats." And at 1452: "Hit by Torpedo; Listing Badly, Need Assistance Immediately."

At that moment the Sixth Fleet aircraft carrier *America* (CVA 66) was engaged in a nuclear weapon–loading exercise, which her commanding officer, Captain Donald D. Engen, immediately halted. The *America* had several aircraft aloft at the time carrying unarmed, nuclear bomb "practice shapes." Engen would not launch aircraft armed with conventional weapons until the faux "nukes" had been landed and lowered to their magazines and properly stored. The second carrier in the Sixth Fleet, the *Saratoga*, began to launch aircraft.

Several popular accounts of the *Liberty* attack inaccurately assert that the U.S. carriers launched aircraft carrying nuclear weapons, especially the F-4B Phantom fighter-attack aircraft. An officer on board the *Liberty* at the time, Lieutenant James Ennes, later wrote: "Two nuclear armed F-4 Phantom jets left *America*'s catapults and headed almost straight up, afterburners roaring. Then two more became airborne to rendezvous with the first two, and together the four powerful jets turned toward *Liberty*, making a noise like thunder."[37]

However, U.S. Navy Phantoms were not wired to carry nuclear weapons nor were their crews trained in nuclear weapons delivery. And it was "unthinkable" for a carrier's commanding officer to launch nuclear-armed aircraft without specific direction from Washington or the theater commander. (While the Navy did test the compatibility of the Phantom with nuclear weapons, neither U.S. Navy nor Marine Phantoms ever were deployed with a nuclear weapons capability.[38])

Some popular accounts also assert that the "Sixth Fleet's immediate response was to launch aircraft against Egypt, the initial suspect for the attack on board the Sixth Fleet flagship *Little Rock*." Sixth Fleet aircraft were recalled just in time, heading toward Egypt."[39]

Photo 19. The *Liberty* on 9 June 1967, heavily damaged and listing to starboard, with a U.S. Navy SH-3 Sea King helicopter taking off wounded crewmen. The *Liberty* was able to sail to Malta for drydocking and temporary repairs. She then sailed for the United States to be taken out of service. / U.S. Navy.

That statement also was incorrect. Sending off a dozen light attack aircraft escorted by fighters to strike (multiple) Egyptian airfields in the midst of a war was too ludicrous to contemplate.

Upon learning of the attack on the *Liberty*, Vice Admiral William I. Martin, Commander, Sixth Fleet, declared the unidentified attacking force "hostile" and ordered the aircraft carriers *Saratoga* and *America* to each launch four attack aircraft *with conventional weapons*, with fighter escorts and aerial tankers, to assist the spy ship. The initial estimated aircraft launch time was 1545 with a flight time of one-and-a-half-to-two hours to the *Liberty*.

In response to Admiral Martin's launch order, the *Saratoga* sent off four conventionally armed A-4 Skyhawk and four A-1 Skyraider attack aircraft with an escort of four F-4B Phantoms. The carrier also launched four Skyhawks with "buddy stores" (fuel tanks) to serve as aerial tankers for the other aircraft. Those 16 aircraft all were launched within ten minutes following eight minutes' notice to launch. After returning the nuclear weapon practice shapes to the carrier's magazines, the *America* launched four A-4C Skyhawks with an F-4B Phantom escort. None carried nuclear weapons although several books and articles contend that they were so armed.

The orders from the Sixth Fleet commander to the carriers were: "You are authorized to use force including destruction as necessary to control the situation. Do not use more force than required. Do not pursue any unit towards land for reprisal purposes. Purpose of counterattack is to protect *Liberty* only."[40]

The aircraft launched from the *Saratoga* and *America* were recalled at 1639, just 25 minutes after the U.S. Embassy in Tel Aviv sent out an alert that the attack was made in error by Israeli forces. None of the aircraft reached the *Liberty* before turning back.[41] All of the aircraft returned safely to their carriers.

Intentional or Inadvertent?

The Israeli Air Force and Navy had made several intentional and deadly attacks on their target—the USS *Liberty*. But were the attacks ordered or conducted knowing that the target was a U.S. naval ship?

At 1429, less than 15 minutes after Colonel Kislev received the news from Captain Zuk that "CTR 5" was painted on the target's bow, the Israeli Air Force responded to reports of men in the water and dispatched the two rescue helicopters from Hatsor airfield to the stricken ship. The helicopters—French-built SA 321 Super Frelons—arrived at the *Liberty*'s position at 1505.

The communications between Hatsor airfield and the two helicopters, and some of the communications between the helicopters and the torpedo boats, were intercepted by a U.S. Navy EC-121M Warning Star electronic intelligence aircraft orbiting about 60 n.miles off the Israeli coast.[42] That aircraft had flown from Athens, Greece, to monitor communications during the Arab-Israeli conflict. On board was an NSG intercept specialist who was a Hebrew linguist—Chief Petty Officer Marvin E. Nowicki. He recorded those radio exchanges between the Israeli ground controller and the senior helicopter pilot:

1430 **Hatsor**: There was a warship there which we attacked. Men jumped from it into the water. You will try to rescue them.

Helo 815: I understand it was hit and unable to fire.

Hatsor: No fire was seen from her and those on board did not fire.

1434 **Hatsor**: The ship is now identified as Egyptian. You can return home now. [The identification of the target by Commander Oren was logged by Navy headquarters at 1437 but reached the Hatsor controller at Israel Defense Forces (IDF) headquarters time 1434. IDF time is the most accurate as it is recorded with time marks every 20 seconds.]

1438 **Hatsor**: The both of you will head toward the ship. [Apparently Air Force authorities did not trust the Navy's identification.]

1459 **Hatsor**: When you start bringing up the men, clarify by the first man that you bring up, what nationality he is. And report to me immediately. It's important to know.

1502 **Hatsor**: I request to receive a report. Tell me the nationality.

1503 **Helo 815**: There is a large ship, smoke isn't rising. At the present time, smoke is a little to the right on its left side. I see . . . three small vessels.

1506 **Hatsor**: If any of them are speaking Egyptian, you take them to El Arish; If they are speaking English, not Egyptian, you take them to Lod [Airport], is this clear?

1509 **Hatsor**: The first matter to clarify is to find out what their nationality is.

1510 **Helo 815**: GTR 5 is written. Does this mean something?

Thorn (in torpedo boat *T-203*): No, it doesn't tell us anything. [That information was not forwarded to Navy headquarters by Oren until 1520. The helicopters made radio contact with the torpedo boats during their approach; most of their conversation was on a different frequency.]

1512 **Hatsor**: Did you clearly see an American flag? We request you make another pass and check once more if this is really an American flag. What is the make of the flag? [The original report of an American flag was on an unmonitored frequency and logged at Israel Defense Forces headquarters at 1512.][43]

Those recordings clearly reveal the confusion that prevailed and documents the time that the helicopter pilot made a visual report confirming that the target had U.S. Navy markings on her bow. The U.S recording is totally in consonance with Israeli documents and recorded tapes that subsequently were released to the U.S. government.[44]

At the highest levels of Israeli military leadership, the nationality of the ship being attacked off El-Arish was known—or strongly suspected—to be American by 1414, when Mystère pilot Yossi Zuk reported to Tel Aviv the "CTR 5" on the *Liberty*'s bow. But that report was not confirmed until about an hour later, relayed from the scene by the helicopters at 1512.[45]

The torpedo attack was made after the first report that the target might be American and 35 minutes before its confirmation. The torpedo boat's attack was more than a case of information not penetrating to the tactical level in time to prevent a disaster. It was caused by the hyperaggressive attitude of a relatively junior officer and exacerbated by errors in command and control at Navy headquarters. The U.S. defense attaché to Israel, Air Force Col. Anthony (Bud) Perna, later evaluated the Israeli Navy's attack as a "result of [the] eagerness of [the] IDF Navy to glean some portion of [the] great victory being won by IDF Army and Air Force."[46]

The entire engagement by the torpedo boats exhibited extreme tunnel vision, and unprofessional behavior, that was exacerbated by a naval headquarters command exhibiting both poor information handling and abysmal tactical awareness. The situation was further confused by the Navy headquarters and its plotting team's being in Haifa while the IDF headquarters and its plotting team were in Tel Aviv.[47]

Commander Oren and his torpedo boats were consistent throughout the engagement—consistently inept and unprofessional. Oren erred from the calculation of the *Liberty*'s being underway at an estimated 28 knots—the underlying element in identifying the target as a hostile warship—to his misidentification of the *Liberty* with her mass of antennas as an Egyptian cargo ship. He failed to properly interpret the *Liberty*'s attempt to reply to his queries and could have remediated the problem by circling to the upwind side of the target. Finally, his three boats launched five torpedoes at close range against a non-maneuvering target and (fortunately) scored only a single hit.

Commander Castle at the U.S. Embassy in Tel Aviv received a call from the headquarters of the Israel Defense Force at approximately 1600 to officially notify the United States of Israel's responsibility for the attack. Subsequently, Castle's urgent message to the White House and to U.S. naval forces in the Mediterranean at 1614 made known to the U.S. national military command structure of the Israeli apology and offer of assistance. The Israeli government did not hesitate in admitting to the error and in issuing immediate apologies.[48] Castle recalled that the Israelis sent "abject apologies and request[ed] info of other U.S. ships near [the] war zone."[49]

Why Was She There?

Why did the NSA place the *Liberty* in international waters immediately adjacent to an ongoing, major conflict? The agency was both factual and evasive in response to that question. NSA officials emphasized that the targeted communications, radars, and other interests required primarily line-of-sight interception: "It is necessary to be as close as possible to the source of transmission in order to maintain adequate coverage." Such statements of fact were intended to deflect an examination of the NSA's original selection of the *Liberty*'s operational areas close to potential combat areas.[50]

The NSA staff had a major blind spot in the initial planning for the *Liberty*'s employment in a war zone. Obviously, the waters adjacent to active combat could involve inadvertent—or possibly intended—attacks on neutral shipping. Neither the NSA nor the

Joint Chiefs of Staff correctly gauged how soon combat between Israel and Egypt would erupt. Neither they nor the Sixth Fleet commander provided contingency plans to the *Liberty* in the event that hostilities started in the area. Then communications errors and delays interfered with the frantic efforts to withdraw the ship to 100 n.miles from the coast; those orders failed to reach the *Liberty*.

In his history of the attack on the *Liberty*, Dr. A. Jay Cristol—a historian, federal judge, and retired U.S. Navy captain—wrote:

> Thus the scene for a tragedy was set. The *Liberty*, following orders issued on June 1, 1967, sailed toward an active war zone without knowledge that on June 7 the U.S. National Security Agency, through the Joint Chiefs of Staff, had ordered her withdrawn from harm's way. What followed was the worst disaster in fifty years of U.S.-Israel relations.[51]

Despite their reputation as intelligent and efficient warriors, Israeli naval forces had a recurring problem in misidentifying shipping both before and after 1967. During the 1956 conflict, the Israelis attacked the British destroyer *Crane*, mistaking her for an Egyptian Z-class destroyer. During the 1967 war, they attacked the *Liberty*, identifying her as an Egyptian transport. On 11 October 1973, Israeli patrol boats sank a Soviet merchant ship during a raid on the Syrian port of Tartus.[52]

Yet, despite the history of Israeli naval errors—and similar errors made in wartime by U.S. and other forces—many officials in the U.S. government strongly believed that the Israelis had acted intentionally and criminally. Initially, practically all senior leaders in the U.S. intelligence community believed that the attacks were intentional. Possibly foremost among those officials was Lieutenant General Marshall S. Carter, the NSA director from 1965 to 1969. He voiced the opinion that the Israelis were so efficient and effective in their war-fighting abilities, and with such outstanding intelligence capabilities, that such a mistake by Israeli forces was less likely than a planned attack. Carter went to his grave harboring that opinion.[53] He could not admit that some of the NSA's early decisions in the *Liberty*'s assignment were mistakes that ultimately led to the Israeli attacks.[54]

On 22 June 1967, the CIA reported to President Johnson:

> The Israelis presumably thought the vessel they were attacking not to be the *Liberty*, for it is also clear that when the initial attack took place the ground controllers and the pilots believed the ship to be a belligerent. In addition, the Israelis have admitted that the jets were ordered to attack the unidentified vessel and, therefore, the *Liberty* was not taken under fire by overzealous pilots, acting on their own. The *Liberty* had been identified prior to the attacks, but the Israelis were apparently not aware that they were attacking the *Liberty*. The attack was not made in malice toward the U.S. and was by mistake, but the failure of the IDF Headquarters and the attacking aircraft to identify the *Liberty* and the subsequent attack by the torpedo boats were both incongruous and indicative of gross negligence.[55]

In a memorandum dated 13 June 1967, the chairman of the Joint Chiefs of Staff and the head of the Defense Intelligence Agency (DIA) came to a similar conclusion but voiced in an oppositional tone: "There is no available information which would conclusively show that the Israelis made a premeditated attack on a ship known to be American. In fact, the best interpretation we can make of the available facts is that Israeli command and control in this instance was defective." On 28 June, the DIA added to that report, stating that further information "had clarified the sequence of events but failed to show that the attack had been premeditated and did not alter the interpretation of the incident."[56]

Subsequently, both the United States and Israel have declassified a large volume of documents relating to the *Liberty* attack. Those documents further reveal that the attack was deliberate and deadly. That remains indisputable. But as the initial evaluations by the CIA and the DIA indicated, and subsequently declassified data confirms without qualification, the attacks were not knowingly made against a U.S. naval ship. The CIA and DIA evaluations were accurate and delivered in a timely manner to the president and to the chairman of the Joint Chiefs in 1967.

Claims that the attack was made knowing that the target was an American ship are thus manifestly false. Conspiracy theories abound, but they are unsupported and mostly have been highly emotional accusations that misconstrue the facts and twist data. Those facets of the conspiracy theories are easy to recognize when reviewing the now-declassified documents and examining the Nowicki tape transcripts.

Still, a decade after the attack, Joseph Lentini, a petty officer first class on the *Liberty* at the time of the attack, wrote in the prominent *Washington Post* newspaper: "The *Liberty*'s logs record both surface craft and aircraft leaving the same Israeli port and heading directly for the *Liberty*."[57] There were no entries in the ship's log about which port the torpedo boats had departed from and, of course, which airfield the aircraft came from (not a port). That information was unknown to the *Liberty*'s crew and beyond the surveillance capabilities of the ship.

Lentini continued, "On the first passes, the unmarked jets shot rockets through each of the *Liberty*'s four machine gun mounts." Another Israeli critic, James Scott, wrote: "The fighters zeroed in on the bridge, strafing the command center with rockets and 30-mm cannons." He added, "The fighters first strafed the *Liberty* from bow to stern, targeting the bridge, machine guns and antennae. With those destroyed or on fire, the attackers crisscrossed the ship to target the engine room."[58]

All Israeli aircraft were clearly marked with the Star of David insignia, in part to avoid "blue-on-blue" encounters, a critical concern with the variety of combat aircraft flown by the Israelis and the Arab states. Those aircraft attacking the *Liberty* at several hundred miles per hour would hardly be able to target such specific objects as the machine guns and antennas.

Lentini concluded his comments: "The infamous attack was calculated, premeditated murder." Such calumny and unfounded accusations have frequently been repeated, despite the obvious fact that the intent and knowledge of the attackers were impossible to ascertain from the deck of the *Liberty* and are simply highly emotional opinions. Still, such claims by *Liberty* survivors and others have continued.

In 2003, 29 years after his retirement as chairman of the Joint Chiefs of Staff, Admiral Moorer and several other notables released the results of their "independent investigation" of the *Liberty* incident. It supported conspiracy theories and voiced such emotion-laden opinions as "Israel committed acts of murder against American servicemen and an act of war against the United States" and that "the White House deliberately covered up the facts of this attack."

The rigor of that investigation was revealed by such counterfactual "findings" as "the Israeli air attack lasted approximately 25 minutes" by "unmarked Israeli aircraft." (The air attack actually lasted 13 minutes, and all aircraft were painted with standard Israeli Air Force markings.) And "30 or more sorties were flown over the ship by a minimum of 12 attacking Israeli planes." (The entire air attack was made by four aircraft in two two-plane attacks.) Admiral Moorer's 2003 investigation was merely a recitation of then-existing conspiracy theories with little attention to then known facts.[59]

The central failure of the conspiracy theories is an answer to the question why: Why would the Israeli government or the Israeli Air Force or Navy wish to attack a U.S. Navy ship at the potential cost of severing the special relationship with the United States that was central to the continuation of the State of Israel? Why, if the Israeli government had made such a decision, was the *Liberty* allowed to survive afloat? And why is it difficult to acknowledge that the Israelis make mistakes and display moments of ineptitude and incompetence—like the rest of the world?

The conspiracy theories defy common sense. Yet they have continued.

Government to Government

Only three and a half hours after the torpedo boat attack that ended the assault on the *Liberty*, U.S. secretary of state Dean Rusk telephoned Israeli ambassador Avraham Harmon in Washington, asking him to convey "at once" to the Israeli prime minister the U.S. government's dismay over the attack on "a U.S. naval vessel by Israeli naval unit(s)." Minutes later, Rusk was on the telephone with the U.S. ambassador to the United Nations, declaring, "If Israeli torpedo boats are attacking international shipping in international waters, that is a very dangerous business; if they were to hit a Soviet vessel that is extremely explosive."[60]

When aircraft from the Sixth Fleet carriers *America* and *Saratoga* were launched to support the *Liberty*, President Johnson immediately sent a message to Moscow on the new U.S.–Soviet "Hot Line" (teletype system) to explain that U.S. naval aircraft were not intervening in the Arab-Israeli conflict but were acting to protect a U.S. Navy "auxiliary." U.S. fears of Soviet intervention in support of Syria against Israel were very acute at that moment.

Secretary Rusk also thanked the Israelis for the speed with which their apology had been made. He later wrote, "This speed of notification in itself may have avoided very serious consequences."[61]

Possibly the most cogent conclusion from an examination of the attack on the *Liberty* is that in the history-changing moment that was the Six-Day War between Israel and several Arab states, the attack on the *Liberty* was of small concern to the American and Israeli leadership once the latter had admitted responsibility. The attack was an *incident*, although many people have spent considerable time and effort in attempting to shape the public's perception of the attack as an intentional, criminal act by Israel. Again, the key question that undermines every conspiracy theory remains: What possible advantage could Israel gain in attacking the *Liberty*?

So-called blue-on-blue incidents, where a nation attacks its own or allied forces, are all too prevalent. In American history those include, among others, the downing of U.S. transport aircraft carrying paratroopers for the invasion of Sicily in 1943 and the sinking of the U.S. submarine *Seawolf* (SS 197) with all her crew in 1944. A later example was U.S. fighter aircraft downing American helicopters over Iraq—*after* hostilities had ceased—in April 1994, killing 26, including representatives from four allied countries. When different states are involved—as were Israel and the United States in the *Liberty* incident—the fog of war, different languages, missed communications, and simple stupidity can exacerbate the situation and the errors leading to the blue-on-blue disasters.

A former U.S. director of Naval Intelligence, Rear Admiral Thomas A. Brooks, astutely observed:

> Conspiracy theories die hard. Americans seem to have a peculiar fondness for the notion of conspiracies. "Who shot JFK?" is still the subject of books and TV programs; there have been several

books on the supposed FDR [Franklin D. Roosevelt] conspiracy to allow the Japanese to attack Pearl Harbor; there even are new theories on who shot Lincoln and why.[62]

Withdrawal

The *Liberty* limped away from the scene of the attack at eight knots as Sixth Fleet forces raced to her support. Carrier air support was more than an hour away, and two U.S. destroyers, steaming at 30 knots, could not rendezvous with her for almost 20 hours. The aircraft were turned back when the Israeli acknowledgment was received. (As the events unfolded in the Mediterranean, the Pentagon watch officers' nightmare was that Israeli and U.S. Navy pilots could become embroiled in combat above the *Liberty*.)

The day after the attack the destroyers *Davis* (DD 937) and *Massey* rendezvoused with the *Liberty* in the early morning, took off the wounded, and provided extra personnel to assist Commander McGonagle in damage control. The *Liberty* was able to reach Malta under her own power, arriving there on 14 June for drydocking. After temporary repairs, the ship departed on 16 July for the United States with an escorting U.S. fleet tug. The two ships reached Little Creek, Virginia, on the 29th. Commander McGonagle was relieved as the commanding officer in October 1967.

Once back in the United States, no further repairs were made to the *Liberty*; she was stricken from the Navy List on 1 June 1970 and subsequently scrapped. McGonagle's actions were applauded by the Navy's court of inquiry. He was promoted to captain and awarded the Medal of Honor in recognition of his "superb professionalism, courageous fighting spirit, and valiant leadership." Subsequently, Captain McGonagle was given command of the new ammunition ship *Kilauea* (AE 26). The *Liberty* was awarded the Presidential Unit Citation for the action with many of the ship's crew and NSG personnel awarded personal decorations.

About one year after the attack, the Israeli government paid humanitarian reparations to the *Liberty*'s wounded and to the families of the deceased. Under international law and most national legal systems, such payments for human suffering are considered humanitarian gestures and not as an admission of guilt or liability.[63] Later, Israel also reimbursed the U.S. Navy for the negotiated value of the ship *Liberty*.

There remains confusion about other U.S. *and* Soviet ships that may have been in the area at the time of the attacks. The U.S. submarine *Amberjack* (SS 522) was in the eastern Mediterranean at the time, and some persons have claimed that she photographed the Israeli attacks. No photos have surfaced, and the submarine's log indicates that she was some 100 n.miles from the area at the time of the attacks. The Soviet merchant ship *Proletrsk* was in the area but not at the scene of the attacks. Similarly, the Soviet destroyer *Neuperzhinyy* was reported by some sources to be in the area, but other sources put her much farther to the west.

Nine hours after the attack on the *Liberty* ended, the U.S. Joint Chiefs of Staff ordered the fleet tug *Atakapa* (ATF 149), fitted with radio intercept equipment and embarking a small NSG detachment, to sail into the eastern Mediterranean. She was ordered to remain at least 100 n.miles off the coasts of Syria, Israel, and Egypt as she monitored military communications in the region.

7

American Spy Ships

Part 2

The considerable success of the *Oxford* in intercepting Cuban microwave communications during the Cuban missile crisis in the fall of 1962 resulted in a boon for the U.S. National Security Agency's technical research ship program.[1] Also, the Navy had developed a separate and an even more grandiose plan to build an "electronics research fleet" from the keel up at a cost of $35 million per ship, each to have a cruising speed of at least 20 knots.

Despite the volatile sensation brought about by the *Oxford*'s successes, the numbers would not add up: It cost $13.5 million to convert a Liberty-type merchant ship into an *Oxford*-type AGTR but only $3.3 million to repurpose a smaller, *Valdez*-type, MSTS-operated ship. The Department of Defense was strapped for funds in the 1960s because of the escalating Vietnam War; thus, the Navy's proposed new-construction SIGINT fleet soon fell victim to the budget axe.[2] Failing in its "big" plan, the Navy opted for a far cheaper option: converting smaller cargo ships at significantly less cost and outfitting them for general intelligence collection including SIGINT. Their *primary* purpose would be to meet *naval* intelligence objectives with a secondary national tasking from the NSA. The ships would be designated as environmental research ships (AGER).

The NSA leadership opposed the AGER program from its beginning. Even when he was the deputy director of Central Intelligence at the CIA, NSA director Lieutenant General Marshall Carter did not work well with Dr. Eugene G. Fubini, the deputy director of defense research and engineering, who helped to inspire the AGER program.[3] Carter's acceptance of the position of director of the NSA was conditional on an agreement that he would report directly to Deputy Secretary of Defense Cyrus Vance and not through Fubini. Carter did not hide his disdain for the brilliant and opinionated Fubini, once calling him "a radar technician beyond his competence." But as Fubini continued to exercise major influence over NSA programs, it did not significantly matter whether Fubini was in Carter's direct line of supervision or not. The two men battled continuously—often to the detriment of NSA programs—until Carter's retirement in 1969. Carter's confrontational relationship with the staff of the Office of the Secretary of Defense in general and with Fubini in particular was more than matched by his almost disastrous relations with the leadership of the military services.

Carter always was on the lookout for service encroachments on the NSA's prerogatives.[4] Some NSA senior officials—including Carter—believed that the Navy's AGER program was impinging upon the NSA's authority to control the nation's SIGINT activities. The Navy had initiated the AGER program over NSA's objections and converted the first AGER in mid-1965, with the light Navy cargo ship *Banner* (AKL 25) becoming the AGER 1. The Navy's long-range ambition was to acquire a dozen such spy ships.

When the Navy went forward in 1965 with a request to convert two additional *Banner*-type SIGINT ships, the NSA officially opposed it. Deputy Secretary of Defense Vance directed the NSA and the Navy to fashion a compromise in which the AGERs would sail sometimes on solely *Navy support* missions (i.e., Navy-generated missions) and sometimes with hybrid *Navy/national* (NSA) tasking. Those ships would be in every respect be Navy owned and manned, and have Naval Support Group intercept personnel embarked. The ships were smaller and less capable than were the *Oxford* or *Valdez*, and their speed was limited to about 12 knots. They would be essentially defenseless, but up to that time, SIGINT ships had not been significantly harassed by hostile forces.[5]

In the flush of enthusiasm from the value of the operations of the *Oxford*, *Valdez*, and other NSA-controlled ships, the latent problems in those programs and potentially in the new AGER program were hidden. However, problems with command and control of the ships had become increasingly evident. The flexibility of the AGTR program had led to those ships being targeted against

Photo 20. The *Banner* (AGER 1) was the first of the U.S. Navy's environmental research ships. This 1968 photo clearly shows the SIGINT Operations Detachment (SOD) "hut" and other spaces fitted forward of the bridge structure. The Navy's three AGERS were converted from light cargo ships (AKL). / U.S. Navy.

areas with exotic language requirements that the Navy could not meet. Also, SIGINT crew training and expertise levels appeared to decline in the face of numerous short-notice deployments to remote locations. Command and control of the spy ships became convoluted, especially in war zones, and at times it appeared that no one in the NSA or in the Defense Department fully understood which agency or office had control of the ships during certain operations. The control issue—as well as other problems—contributed to both the *Liberty* and *Pueblo* disasters.[6]

Further, communications intercept ships had to compete with

the extensive U.S. Air Force *and* Navy electronic reconnaissance aircraft programs. Often the airborne force won out because aircraft could reach target areas faster in a crisis, and they often had better-trained operators and linguists. Finally—and fatally—floating SIGINT platforms proved to be not as immune from attack as had been anticipated. The *Liberty* incident in 1967 shocked the cryptologic community, which had always assumed American SIGINT platforms would be accorded the same considerations and safety that the United States accorded to Soviet spy ships. The *Liberty*'s vulnerability was replicated—with variations—just seven months later when North Korea seized the *Pueblo*.

Environmental Research Ships

Lieutenant Robert P. Bishop took command of the light cargo ship *Banner* in October 1964. The former Army freight and supply ship FS-345 was built in 1944 and manned by a crew of 42. As a light cargo ship (AKL 25), she operated with the U.S. Pacific Fleet, transporting supplies, diesel fuel oil, ammunition, and passengers between Guam and Yokosuka.

In July 1965, Bishop was ordered to sail without delay to the Puget Sound Naval Shipyard near Seattle, Washington, for the *Banner*'s conversion into an intelligence collection ship. That was the Navy's first significant action in executing the Integrated Naval Surveillance and Intelligence Ship Program, which the chief of naval operations had established in May 1965. The program's name itself at that time was classified. In unclassified correspondence, the program was referred to as the "AGER program"—the new Navy designation for miscellaneous auxiliary, environmental research ship.[7]

The *Banner* entered the shipyard for conversion of her number 2 hold into an auxiliary engine room (for the ship's increased electrical needs), storerooms, and a ship's office. Installed above the number 2 hold on the main deck were the SIGINT operational space—called the "SOD Hut" (SOD being an acronym for SIGINT Operations Department)—and additional berthing space for a Naval Security Group detachment of one officer and 28 enlisted technicians. Additional ship's crew would be added, bringing the total naval personnel on board to 83. After conversion, the ship sailed as the AKL 25, being redesignated AGER 1 a year and a half later on 1 June 1967.

Navy planners originally intended for those SIGINT ships to be unarmed, except that for the physical security of the crew the ship would be provided ten Thompson .45-caliber submachine guns, seven M1911A1 .45-caliber pistols, one M14 .30-caliber rifle, and hand grenades. Subsequently, in August 1967, after the attack on the *Liberty*, the decision was made to install defensive armament of at least two 40-mm cannon on board all Navy ships not otherwise armed. Rear Admiral Frank L. Johnson, the commander, Naval Forces Japan, later testified before Congress that he did not receive that directive. Because of the AGER's size, construction, and weight distribution, the Office of the Chief of Naval Operations made the decision not to install the cannon on the AGERS.

At the end of her shipyard conversion in October 1965, the *Banner* retained her previous hull number as a cargo ship—AKL 25. The shipyard conversion was accomplished in the exceptionally short period of six weeks, compared to the 18-month conversions of her later sister ships. The high-priority attention that Washington paid to the AGER program was evident in a message from the chief of naval operations to the *Banner* upon completion of her conversion:

> The enthusiastic response of the Commanding Officer and ship's company of *Banner* to this new, unexpected and sudden requirement for shipyard work nearly five thousand miles from their home port was one of two major factors which made possible such dramatic foreshortening of the expected time requirement. . . . The performance . . . in the successful accomplishment of this evolution has in all respects earned our traditional "Well Done."[8]

The *Banner* departed the shipyard in early October, transited to Midway Island for a brief refueling stop, and arrived at Yokosuka on 24 October—a three-week transpacific crossing. The ship's listing in the Navy's organization of the Western Pacific was a complex of administrative and operational commanders: Upon crossing 160 degrees East longitude, the *Banner* sent a message announcing her arrival to the Seventh Fleet commander, who would be the *Banner*'s operational commander when she was not under the direct control of the commander, Naval Forces Japan, at Yokosuka.

The Yokosuka command would plan and manage almost all of

the *Banner*'s operational missions in response to the advice and requirements of the commander in chief, Pacific Fleet, as well as the Joint Chiefs of Staff and the National Security Agency. The *Banner*'s administrative commander was the commander, Service Squadron 3, which was headquartered in Sasebo, Japan, and would provide direct support, such as personnel, payroll, and postal services.

The newly added operating and berthing spaces on the *Banner*—the so-called SOD Hut—was intended to support a permanent NSG detachment with five or six operating positions, or about one-fourth of the positions in the larger AGTRS. The first officer in charge of the detachment was Lieutenant William T. Durocher. For each mission, NSG personnel from the communications station at Kami Seya, Japan, would augment the detachment with appropriate linguists and other technicians, usually another two or three men.[9]

Against the Soviets

The *Banner* sailed on her first SIGINT mission—codename Clickbeetle One—on 29 October 1965, five days after arriving at Yokosuka. She sailed without having conducted emergency destruction drills for classified material and equipment, and without having the means to scuttle the ship in the event of an attack or boarding. The AGER program had extraordinary priority from Washington-level entities, but several administrative and material requirements never were implemented during the first two years of the ship's operations.

The AGER program initially employed the *Banner* in "freedom of navigation" missions, testing the Soviet Union's sensitivity and reactions to an unarmed, U.S. Navy auxiliary ship engaged in overt intelligence collection in Soviet home waters, albeit outside of the 12-n.mile territorial limit. That mission would later be expanded to testing the sensitivity and reactions of China and North Korea to U.S. spy ships sailing in their areas.

Phase II of the AGER program would be completed with the conversion of two additional small cargo ships that would join the *Banner* in late 1967. The code words for those ships' operations were Breeder for AGER operations worldwide, Clickbeetle for Phase I operations by the *Banner*, Ichthyic for Phase II operations by the first two AGERS operating out of Yokosuka in 1968, and Gravyboat for the unclassified oceanographic research conducted aboard the AGERS while on classified missions.[10]

A seven-month program was scheduled for the first two AGERS (see table 5). Phase III was to expand the AGER program with *an additional 15 ships!*

Clickbeetle One was intended by the Joint Chiefs of Staff to generate Soviet communications and radar emissions to discern Soviet coastal defense systems and capabilities. The *Banner*'s sailing instructions included guidance to remain outside the Soviet Union's claimed 12-n.mile territorial waters. At that time, the United States claimed three-n.mile territorial waters and occasionally penetrated other nations' claimed territorial waters to four n.miles as a demonstration of the U.S. government's displeasure with claims greater than three miles; however, the U.S. Navy treated the Soviet 12-n.mile claim with respect to avoid an international confrontation.

The *Banner* initially was directed to the waters south and east of the major Far Eastern port of Vladivostok, where the Soviets not only claimed 12 n.miles as their territorial waters but also drew a line from the mouth of the Tumen River on the Korean Peninsula, across the Peter the Great Bay, to Cape Povorotny. They then drew a parallel line 12 n.miles south of the Tumen–Povorotny line and claimed that line as the boundary of their territorial waters. The United States did not recognize that Soviet claim.

On 12 November, after more than a week of the *Banner*'s quietly tracking south of the Soviet coast in the vicinity of Vladivostok, the Soviet Navy sent out the minesweeper *MSF-146* to investigate the American ship. The *Banner* then crossed the Soviet-claimed 12-n.mile line with the Soviet minesweeper in company. On 13 November, the destroyer *Gnevnyy* joined the *MSF-146* and signaled to the *Banner* in international code:

> **Gnevnyy**: From 5-to-11 PM the territorial waters of the Soviet Union were violated. What is your name? What is the port of your registry? What is the name of your captain? Signed Captain.
>
> **Banner**: Your territorial waters not violated by this ship. Name U.S. Navy Ship *Banner*, Research Ship.

The *Banner* then moved from the area. A short time later the Soviet AGI *GS-34* intercepted the *Banner*. The two ships "gave each other a thorough intelligence inspection."

On 24 November, the *Banner* again penetrated the 12-n.mile line south of the Tumen–Povorotny line with the *GS-34* in company; the Soviet ship did not challenge the *Banner*. The U.S. Navy had provoked an incident that would be handled by senior-level Soviet authorities and not by local authorities. The Americans' unspoken intention was to demonstrate the U.S. right to employ small, unarmed ships in international waters for intelligence collection in reciprocation of the Soviet fleet of intelligence ships being used extensively against Western targets. That message was received "loud and clear," and the lack of reaction by the *GS-34* to the *Banner*'s movements on the 24th demonstrated that Soviet officials understood the "message."

The *Banner* departed the area on the 24th and arrived in Yokosuka four days later. The Clickbeetle One mission was completed.

On 6 December 1965, after a week of debriefings, fueling, provisioning, and some liberty for her crew, the *Banner* departed Yokosuka for Clickbeetle Two. That mission's objectives were similar to those of the previous deployment. Between 10 and 19 December, the *Banner*'s operating area was within an arc extending 100 to 175 n.miles from Vladivostok. To exploit targets of opportunity, the *Banner* was to penetrate the Tumen–Povorotny line but to sail no closer than one mile from the U.S.-recognized Soviet territorial 12-n.mile limit. The *Banner* experienced no significant harassment from Soviet naval ships during that operation.

The *Banner* returned to Yokosuka on 20 December for debriefing and a Christmas stand-down. In early January 1966, the *Banner* transited to her home port of Apra Harbor, Guam, for additional modifications and equipment installation to enhance her spy ship capabilities. She returned to Japan in early March.

The *Banner* departed Sasebo for Clickbeetle Three on 12 March, entering the Sea of Japan via the Tsushima Strait, and loitered about 20 n.miles off Tongjoson Bay, North Korea, from 14 to 16 March. There was no reaction from North Korean forces. Departing from the coast of North Korea on the 16th, the *Banner* arrived south of Vladivostok the next day. She conducted surveillance activities until 21 March, when she attracted the attentions of a Riga-class frigate and a Petya-class frigate. Both Soviet warships took great umbrage at the *Banner*'s presence in the area and engaged in harassment and intimidation tactics to encourage the U.S. ship to leave.

The Riga trained her 100-mm guns at the *Banner*, illuminated the U.S. ship with gunfire control radar, and signaled demands that she depart the area. The Petya also made a close approach to the *Banner* and trained her 76-mm guns and torpedo tubes on the U.S. ship. After several signal exchanges with flashing lights, the two Soviet warships departed the area.

The *Banner* continued to operate south of Vladivostok until 6 April without further incident. While at sea, on 1 April the *Banner*'s home port was changed from Guam to Yokosuka, and the crew's families made their way to their new home port. The ship arrived at Yokosuka on the ninth.

For Clickbeetle Four, the *Banner* departed Yokosuka on 16 April 1966 and transited up the eastern coast of Honshu for the Sea of Japan. The *Banner*'s orders called for her to enter the Vladivostok area from the north after sailing along the coast and some of the Soviet Union's most sensitive naval facilities in the Far East. The Soviet reaction was predicted to be energetic. It was:

> 23 April: The Yurka-class minesweeper *MSF-385* made a close approach, activated her fire control radars, and trained her guns on the *Banner*.
>
> 29 April: The small naval tanker *Oka* rendezvoused with the *Banner* and began a lengthy period of close surveillance.
>
> 1 May: The *Banner* observed the Soviet May Day Parade in Vladivostok by means of the crew's recreational television, modified by NSG technicians for Russian TV encoding.
>
> 11 May: The *Oka* closed to within a few yards off the *Banner*'s starboard bow, then executed a turn to starboard, swinging her stern to within five feet of *Banner*. Also on 11 May, the *Banner* observed a Soviet anti-submarine exercise at a distance of three miles.

The *Banner* returned to Yokosuka on 16 May without further harassment. The *Banner*'s commanding officer in 1969, Lieutenant Commander D. L. Pfister, offered his opinion:

> By the end of Clickbeetle Four, *Banner* was becoming highly proficient at her task as a unique intelligence collector. The amount and quality of intelligence collected during Clickbeetle operations, plus the unprecedented close-up pictures and descriptions of Soviet Naval activities in their home waters, caused the U.S. intelligence community to realize the value of the program.[11]

Increasing Soviet Sensitivity

For Clickbeetle Five the *Banner* departed Yokosuka on 31 May 1966, sailing on a northward track east of Honshu. She entered the Sea of Japan at night, giving the ship the opportunity to work the Soviet coast from north of Hokkaido southward to Vladivostok before being detected by Soviet patrols. In doing so, the *Banner* transited past the massive submarine base at Bukhta Vrangelya (just north of Cape Povorotny), the torpedo test ranges south of Fokino, the nuclear support complex at Nakhodka, the shipyards at Bolshoy Kamen, and the fleet complex at Vladivostok. Once discovered, the U.S. ship was "attended" by the usual assortment of naval auxiliaries, warships, and, on occasion, aircraft.

That fifth Clickbeetle operation proceeded normally until just shortly before the planned termination. On 24 June, the Soviet intelligence ship *Anemometr* initiated what appeared to be an intentional incident and collided with the *Banner*. Sam Tooma, a civilian oceanographer with the Naval Oceanographic Office, was one of the first oceanographers to participate in the AGER program. He related his observations of the collision between the U.S. and Soviet Navy ships:

> [A]bout one day before we were scheduled to return to port, I was on the bridge arguing with the Captain. Some of the watch standers started to act quite excited and began yelling about the "crazy Russians." I looked around, and this rust bucket was coming straight at us. The Captain ordered the helmsman to maintain course. According to international rules of the road, we had

> the right of way. Meanwhile, the distance between them and us was closing quite rapidly. We continued to maintain course, until I thought that we were all doomed. At the last second, the Captain ordered the helmsman to go hard right rudder. I'm glad that he didn't wait any longer, because all we got was a glancing blow. We had a fairly nice "dent" in our port bow.
>
> When we arrived in port a few days later, I was taken aside by some guys dressed in black uniforms and instructed to never say anything about this incident.[12]

The U.S. State Department generated an official diplomatic protest to the Soviet Union.[13] However, the incident was not publicized until the collisions involving the U.S. destroyer *Walker* (DD 517) in the Sea of Japan the following summer.[14] Three U.S.-Soviet collisions in the Sea of Japan in 1966–67 did not "reflect any deliberate intention to worsen U.S.-Soviet relations," according to the U.S. State Department. And the Soviet ambassador to the United States was quoted as stating that the Soviet Union had no intentions "to harass deliberately" the U.S. ships.[15] Aggressive tactics and incidents by both U.S. and Soviet naval ships multiplied as the Vietnam War intersected with expanding Soviet naval out-of-area operations.

The *Banner* dodged Typhoon Kit while returning to Japan. With a stopover at the Japanese naval base at Ominato to refuel, she arrived at Yokosuka on 2 July. The spy ship remained in port until the 16th.

For Clickbeetle Six, the *Banner* departed her home port on 16 July, entering the Sea of Japan via the Tsushima Strait, and sailed directly to her operating areas south and east of Vladivostok. The Soviets undertook no significant harassment. During that mission, the *Banner* was tasked to collect SIGINT on the Soviet naval response to the annual anti-submarine exercise in the Sea of Japan south of Vladivostok. That was a tri-national exercise with U.S., Japanese, and South Korean ships and aircraft. Intelligence collection efforts by the *Banner* were effective, providing an abundance of operational intelligence.

After a week in Yokosuka, the *Banner* departed for Clickbeetle

Seven on 15 August, through the Tsugaru Strait, for her normal patrol area south of Vladivostok. During that transit, she picked up a new tattletale—the Soviet spy ship *Gidrolog*.

Neither Clickbeetle Six nor Seven generated harassment by Soviet ships or aircraft. The *Banner* returned to Yokosuka on 7 September. She departed Yokosuka for Clickbeetle Eight on the 27th, once again sailing into the waters south of Vladivostok. On 9 October, her old adversary, the Soviet intelligence ship *Anemometr* rendezvoused and warned the *Banner* to depart the area because of naval gunfire exercises. The *Banner* ignored the warning and continued operations in the area without incident.

The *Banner*'s instructions for that mission were to await the annual Soviet Pacific Fleet's autumn exercise and to monitor the operation. When the Soviet exercise failed to materialize, the *Banner* was released on 21 October to return to Japan. She stopped for fuel at the Japanese base at Ominato and arrived back at Yokosuka on the 26th.

Spying on China

The *Banner* departed Yokosuka on 7 November 1966 on Clickbeetle Nine for the first mission beyond her normal operations off the Vladivostok area. The new mission would be the first test of China's reaction to an unarmed U.S. naval auxiliary ship operating near its territorial waters on an overt intelligence collection mission. The mission was undertaken at the behest of the National Security Agency.

U.S. authorities were considerably uncertain as to how vigorously the Chinese would react. In the Korean War (1950–53), China was believed to have lost more than a million men fighting against American-led United Nations forces. Further, the United States supported the Nationalist government on Taiwan, some 100 miles from the mainland, providing political support and military assistance to that regime after the Communist takeover of the mainland in 1949.

Thus, U.S. forces were prepared to support the *Banner* should the Chinese take action against the ship while she was operating close to China's territorial waters. At the time, the United States was deeply engaged in the Vietnam War, and China was providing direct support to North Vietnam.

The U.S. Air Force prepared a dozen fighter aircraft on Okinawa to respond to any Chinese actions against the *Banner*.[16] The Seventh Fleet placed a destroyer on alert with orders to respond if required from her patrol area in the Taiwan Strait, some 400 n.miles south of the *Banner*'s operating area. It would take the Air Force fighters about two hours to arrive on the scene in response to a call for help, and the destroyer could take up to 16 hours. Departing Yokosuka on 7 November, the *Banner* fueled at Sasebo before proceeding to her operating area off the major Chinese port city of Shanghai.

The *Banner*'s reception off the Chinese coast was unlike her experiences off the Soviet Union. Instead of the generally professional decorum of Navy-to-Navy interactions with the Soviets, the Chinese reacted to the *Banner* vigorously and aggressively with a "mob" of armed, steel-hull fishing craft. An enlisted member of the *Banner*'s crew, Rex Catron, recalled, "I remember us being surrounded by junks and other vessels off the coast. . . . The captain set 'repel boarders' and called for help. At dawn the next morning you could see the top mast of a destroyer on the horizon, then the boats all scattered."[17]

Eleven fishing trawlers had surrounded the *Banner*, using harassment and intimidation tactics. Lieutenant Bishop radioed for support, and the Seventh Fleet destroyer in the Taiwan Strait, the *Everett F. Larson* (DD 830), arrived on the *Banner*'s horizon in 15 hours. By that time, the *Banner* had escaped encirclement and was departing the area. The *Larson* remained just over the horizon in support of the *Banner* for the next week.

The *Banner* completed her patrol without further incident, returning to Yokosuka on 11 December. On the 20th, Lieutenant Commander Charles R. Clark relieved Lieutenant Bishop as commanding officer of the *Banner*. A message from the commander, Seventh Fleet, was read at the change of command ceremony: "I view with pride the outstanding achievements and performance of the officers, crew and research department of *Banner* during the first eight [*sic*] missions. Your pioneering of a new concept in naval research operations have been conducted in a manner in keeping with the highest traditions of the naval service. Well done."

Off North Korea

The *Banner* departed Yokosuka on Clickbeetle Ten on 31 January 1967, first proceeding to Sasebo for fueling. She sailed from Sasebo on 4 February and entered the Sea of Japan via the Tsushima Strait. Commander Clark had orders to linger off the North Korean port of Wonsan on this, his first mission. The commander, Naval Forces Japan, had made no arrangements to support the *Banner* should North Korea react aggressively to this second AGER spy ship visit off the country's eastern coast.

On that mission, the *Banner* was fitted with the innovative and top-secret BRIGAND system, which was able to display an image from an intercepted target radar and develop an electronic map or radar scope picture.[18] It enabled the BRIGAND operator to "peak over the shoulder" of the enemy's radar operator and reveal the precise location of the emitting radar.

There was little response to the *Banner*'s presence off the North Korean coast from 5 to 7 February. The spy ship was approached by North Korean patrol boats that passed about three n.miles away, but they appeared to be uninterested in the *Banner*. Still trying to elicit reactions from the North Koreans, Commander Clark opened the range to the coast to 40 n.miles and then made a two-hour, ten-knot run directly toward the coast. Still no reaction.

Subsequently, Clark moved a few miles north, into an area populated by numerous North Korean fishing boats, where he conducted man overboard drills. Again he aroused no apparent interest. After two days off Wonsan, the *Banner* proceeded to her normal operating area south of Vladivostok, arriving on station on 7 February.

Soviet Anti-Submarine Exercise

Within hours of arriving south of Vladivostok, lying dead in the water while casting a Nansen bottle for oceanographic data, the *Banner* observed a Soviet Echo-class guided missile, nuclear-propelled submarine surfacing close aboard. The submarine slowly opened the range to the *Banner*, while a column of three Soviet destroyers steamed directly toward the U.S. ship. At a distance of 4,000 yards, the column turned toward the submarine. The submarine submerged, and the three destroyers commenced an exercise with the submarine. A Kashin-class destroyer illuminated the *Banner* with her signal lamps, while another passed ahead and tracked down the *Banner*'s starboard side at a distance of only 100 yards.

The Kashin came to a stop close alongside and commenced a high-powered twist, swinging her bow toward the *Banner*, which had remained dead in the water throughout the interaction. Commander Clark got underway and came hard to starboard to remain within the Kashin's turning circle. A Krupny-class destroyer then eased ahead on the *Banner*'s port bow, thus forcing Clark to continue his turn. Later, in a letter to a fellow AGER commanding officer, Clark wrote that it felt as if he was "on a freeway in a go-cart with a Greyhound bus roaring up" from behind.[19]

The following morning the *Banner* was joined by a Riga-class frigate that took up "escort" duties on the American ship. On the ninth, the Riga signaled: "You are in territorial waters, heave-to or I will open fire." The *Banner* moved from the area at slow speed with the Riga in trail. There was no additional harassment during the remainder of that operation.

The *Banner* departed her operating area on 20 February, arriving in Yokosuka on the 23rd. She had gained new information on Soviet anti-submarine techniques and valuable, close-up photography of the Echo-class submarine.

After three weeks in port, the *Banner* departed Yokosuka on 16 March on Clickbeetle Eleven, again sailing for her normal operating area south of Vladivostok. While that mission lacked the excitement of the harassment of her previous foray, the *Banner* was met with a strange pair of escorts: a guided missile support ship and a nuclear, biological, and chemical warfare training ship. The poor seamanship demonstrated by both ships indicated that they seldom went to sea, and there were several minor collisions between the two. Upon completing her mission, the *Banner* arrived at Yokosuka on 14 April. She spent the next three weeks in port.

For Clickbeetle Twelve, the *Banner* departed from Yokosuka on 1 May to monitor and provide direct intelligence support to the multinational anti-submarine exercise that again involved a U.S. aircraft carrier. The spy ship's involvement was considered normal, and her participation ended on 14 May. The *Banner* then made her third pass along North Korea's eastern coast, southbound, on 15–16 May without incident. She arrived at Sasebo on the 18th for fueling and departed three days later for a second mission off the Chinese coast. However, due to "tenseness in the world situation," the Joint Chiefs of Staff canceled that mission.

On 1 June 1967, the *Banner* was redesignated as an environmental research ship—AGER 1. She arrived at Yokosuka on 13 June for a five-week maintenance period.

For Clickbeetle Fourteen, the *Banner* was to sail into the Sea of Japan via the Tsugaru Strait, then proceed between Sakhalin Island and the Soviet mainland before coasting southward to Vladivostok. The ship's orders restricted her penetration of the Tartary Gulf. The ship departed Yokosuka on 15 July, and as she approached her target area, the ship picked up Soviet escorts. The *Banner*'s arrival at Yokosuka on 10 August ended the mission, during which a navigation error had taken the ship into Soviet territorial waters, an event that apparently was not observed by her escorts.

Back to Shanghai

The *Banner*'s second mission into Chinese waters—Clickbeetle Fifteen—began on 17 August 1967. The NSA-directed mission would again have the *Banner* operating off Shanghai. The Air Force would have quick-reaction aircraft ready on Okinawa, and again a destroyer on patrol in the Taiwan Strait was alerted to respond if required.

On 31 August, after the *Banner* had been on station for ten days, the Chinese belatedly reacted to her presence. Two Chinese Navy patrol boats circled the ship at close range with weapons trained on her. The Chinese appeared to want the *Banner* to stop, and attempted to communicate with flag signals, but they did not use international codes. Commander Clark chose to temporize by misunderstanding their signals. Lieutenant Robert Richard (Dick) Fredlund Jr., the *Banner*'s executive officer, recalled: "They were flying all kinds of signals that we had reason to believe meant it was going to be serious. They kept signaling us and we kept signaling back: 'We don't know what you're saying; would you please repeat that!'"[20]

High-ranking uniformed officers were visible on the two patrol boats, apparently evaluating the *Banner* and her purpose. Frustrated by their inability to communicate with the *Banner*, the patrol boats departed after a couple hours, and the remainder of *Banner*'s patrol off Shanghai continued without incident.

Fredlund recalled:

> I was the General Quarters officer-of-the-deck. . . . Over a period of almost two hours of purposefully failing to communicate with the Chinese gunboats, Captain Clark quietly and skillfully maneuvered the *Banner* away from the coast. By the time the Chinese officers' patience was exhausted, we were well off the coast and well outside the Chinese 12-mile territorial waters. So, we withdrew from the area without having to call for support. Captain Clark was always calm and in total control in an emergency or in a confrontation.[21]

Into the Philippine Sea

On 15 September, the *Banner* was ordered to Naha, Okinawa, to fuel, provision, and prepare for special operations in the Philippine Sea. The *Banner* arrived at Naha on the 17th and departed the following day.

The ship was tasked to locate and attempt to trail two Soviet destroyers operating in the Philippine Sea. As the destroyers were capable of 30-plus knots and the *Banner* only 12 knots, there appears to have been a serious disparity between mission tasking and platform capability. The target destroyers were seldom seen and only intermittently emitted radio or radar signals. Eventually Commander Clark discerned a movement pattern from those signals that could be intercepted and found the destroyers on 25 September. The *Banner* remained in trail for most of another day until the Soviets declined to further limit their speed to the *Banner*'s "slow crawl," and they disappeared over the horizon.

The *Banner* returned to Yokosuka on 29 September.

The ship departed Yokosuka for Clickbeetle Sixteen on 23 October, again sailing for her familiar operating area south of Vladivostok. The Soviet reaction was muted, except the minesweeper escort was aggressive and approached the *Banner* to close range. Commander Clark was able to record the Soviet skipper's expletives on a voice recorder on the *Banner*'s bridge. Air surveillance of the *Banner* included a Tu-16 Badger, a twin-jet bomber that "buzzed" the American ship at less than 100 feet. The *Banner* returned to Yokosuka on 15 November without further incident.

The Final China Mission

The *Banner* departed Yokosuka for Clickbeetle Seventeen—her final Clickbeetle mission and her third foray into Chinese waters off Shanghai—on 22 November 1967. The staff at U.S. Naval Forces Japan advised the Air Force of the *Banner*'s schedule but did not request that aircraft be placed on alert status to respond should the ship encounter difficulties with Chinese forces.[22]

The *Banner* carried out her activities without untoward Chinese reactions until the night of 12 December, when six armed fishing trawlers surrounded the ship. In the morning, they made threatening gestures with weapons manned and pointed at the U.S. ship. Ralph Clarke, a quartermaster petty officer 3rd class on the *Banner*, recalled the event:

> Each of these boats had a machine-gun mounted on the forward deck—about the size of a .50-caliber or somewhat larger. And they were all manned and pointed at us—one gunner and another person holding the ammo belt. There was a portrait on Chairman Mao on the pilothouse bulkhead of each of these boats. An inscription read: (as interpreted from one of our foreign language guys) "Chairman Mao is the envy of our hearts."[23]

As with the two previous missions off Shanghai, on alert in the Taiwan Strait was a Seventh Fleet warship—the less-capable radar picket escort *Wilhoite* (DER 397), which had a maximum speed of only 21 knots. She was dispatched in response to the *Banner*'s call for help. Upon arrival on scene, the *Wilhoite* remained over the horizon as the *Banner* retired from the "engagement" with the fishing trawlers and without needing assistance.

The three missions off the Chinese coast had revealed armed and swarm reactions. There appeared to be no similarities between the Soviet and Chinese reactions.

Ichthyic Operations

The Clickbeetle missions ceased at the end of 1967, and Ichthyic operations were planned for 1968 out of Yokosuka with two AGERS:

the *Banner* and the *Pueblo*. They would relieve each other with operations going as far north as Petropavlovsk and as far south as the Taiwan Strait.

Table 5. Phase II AGER operating schedule, 1968

Ship	Dates	Operational area
Pueblo	5 January–4 February	North Korea
Banner	21 January–22 February	Petropavlovsk
Pueblo	19 February–20 March	Sea of Japan
Banner	6 March–6 April	East China Sea
Pueblo	3 April–3 May	Petropavlovsk
Banner	21 April–21 May	East China Sea
Pueblo	17 May–16 June	Sea of Japan
Banner	12 June–1 July	Sea of Japan
Pueblo	27 June–27 July	Sea of Japan

On 5 January 1968, the *Pueblo* departed Yokosuka under Commander Lloyd M. Bucher for Ichthyic One en route to the North Korean coast. The *Banner* sailed from Sasebo on 21 January toward Vladivostok for Ichthyic Two. She was well within the Sea of Japan when the foundation of all the U.S. spy ship programs—the *assumption* that no nation would purposely attack a U.S. naval ship in international waters—disintegrated in an act of premeditated violence against the USS *Pueblo* (see chapter 8).

After the *Pueblo*

The *Banner* immediately returned to Yokosuka after the North Korean seizure of the *Pueblo*. The *Banner* then departed on 26 January 1968 to join the three U.S. aircraft carriers and their escorts operating in the Sea of Japan in a response to the *Pueblo* situation. The spy ship remained at sea until returning to Yokosuka on 11 March.

The *Banner* was at Yokosuka until 30 May, conducting training, removing excess classified material, installing emergency destruction devices, mounting two twin 20-mm cannon, and making ready for her next deployment. On 3 June, the *Banner* sailed on her third assignment to monitor Soviet reactions to the annual allied trinational, anti-submarine operations in the Sea of Japan. For what had been a routine cruise twice in the past, the *Banner* now conducted it with a fully available destroyer on call.

The *Banner* returned to Yokosuka on 14 June. She sailed again on 2 July with tasking to monitor the unusual operations of the Soviet AGI *Gidrograf* and the ocean-going tug *MB-16*, which were sailing south of Honshu. On the fourth, the *Banner* made contact with the *MB-16*, but the following day the sea conditions necessitated that she break contact and return to her home port.

A major overhaul of the *Banner* began at Yokosuka on 10 August. One of the items added to the ship was an explosive scuttling system intended to sink the ship in three-to-five minutes. During the overhaul, Lieutenant Commander Pfister relieved Lieutenant Commander Clark as her commanding officer.

Then, despite her lengthy and expensive overhaul from August to December 1968, the *Banner* was defunded, and her intelligence equipment was removed. She was decommissioned on 14 November 1969 and sold for scrap.

The U.S. Navy converted two small ex-Army freight and supply (FS)/Navy cargo (AKL) ships into additional AGERS: the *Pueblo* (to become AGER 2) and the *Palm Beach* (AGER 3). The latter ship was reactivated from the Reserve Fleet in 1966 and sent to the Puget Sound Naval Shipyard for conversion into a spy ship. Her first commanding officer was Lieutenant Commander Albert D. Raper, who took command at her commissioning on 13 May 1967.

The *Palm Beach* arrived at her home port of Little Creek (Norfolk) in December 1967. Her first deployment was delayed because of the seizure of the *Pueblo* off North Korea. In response, the Navy made several modifications to the *Palm Beach* prior to the first mission, including replacing the two .50-caliber machine guns with two twin 20-mm cannon, fitting explosive scuttling charges, and conducting extensive crew training in the emergency destruction of classified equipment and documents.

Her first deployment as a spy ship began on 20 May 1968, sailing to the submarine base at Holy Loch, Scotland, and then "working" the Norwegian Sea area while monitoring Soviet naval activities. The ship visited several Norwegian ports and at the end of the deployment again called at Holy Loch as well as Belfast, Ireland, before returning to the United States in October. Significantly, the *Palm Beach* monitored major Soviet Northern Fleet sorties into the Atlantic. On 14 August 1968, Lieutenant Commander Donald L. Burson relieved Raper as the ship's commanding officer.

The *Palm Beach* departed for the Mediterranean on 19 April 1969, her second—and last—intelligence mission, sailing in company with the tug-cum-spy-ship *Atakapa*. From April through June, the U.S. Sixth Fleet had two spy ships available: the *Belmont* and *Palm Beach* (the *Atakapa* was operating in the Norwegian Sea). The *Palm Beach*'s operations in the central sea were routine but restricted to sailing no closer than 100 n.miles to the Egyptian-Israeli-Syrian coasts, thus severely limiting her intercept capabilities.

The *Palm Beach* returned to Little Creek in company with the *Atakapa* and was decommissioned and stricken from the Navy List on 1 December 1969. (The *Palm Beach* later was employed in commercial service, renamed *Oro Verde*.)

Auxiliary Spy Ships

All of the technical research ships (AGTR) were under the control of the Joint Chiefs of Staff for national tasking, and the *Banner* and *Pueblo* were in the Pacific to satisfy both national and Navy collection requirements. The Navy decided to employ several small auxiliary ships with NSG personnel as additional intelligence collection ships for the Atlantic area.

In the summer of 1965, the submarine rescue ship *Tringa* (ASR 16) was fitted with communications intercept equipment, a small NSG detachment came aboard, and she sailed for the northern Norwegian Sea and Barents Sea areas. In the northern latitudes, she observed extensive Soviet air activity and was overflown almost every day by Soviet naval aircraft and at times was escorted by a Soviet destroyer. The *Tringa* returned to Norfolk in the early fall, and the intercept equipment was removed.

As noted earlier, in 1966 the fleet tug *Atakapa* was equipped for communications and electronic intelligence intercepts, and an NSG detachment joined the ship. She sailed in June 1966, first for the coast of Norway to monitor a Soviet fleet exercise. While awaiting the start of the exercise, she sighted and trailed two Zulu-class diesel-electric submarines sailing on the surface en route to the Mediterranean. During the subsequent Soviet exercise, the *Atakapa* collected valuable intelligence; however, her slow speed (17 knots) proved inadequate for the surveillance of fleet operations.[24]

The *Atakapa* then entered the Baltic Sea for SIGINT collection, where her speed would not be a significant problem. However, the Baltic area was very well covered by NATO land intercept sites and the *Atakapa* collected little of interest there. She returned to Norfolk in mid-September 1966.[25] After similar deployments to the Norwegian Sea in the spring–summer of 1967—during which time she was ordered to the Mediterranean in response to the attack on the *Liberty*—and again in 1968, the *Atakapa* returned to Norfolk for a major security overhaul. Emergency destruction devices were installed, and explosive scuttling devices were provided.

In April 1969, the *Atakapa* departed Norfolk in company with the *Palm Beach*, sailing for the Azores. The fleet tug then sailed to Rosyth, Scotland, while the *Palm Beach* proceeded to the Mediterranean. The *Atakapa* set course for a "holding area" near Norway's North Cape, awaiting the periodic transit of naval ships from Murmansk to the Mediterranean. Unexpectedly, the Soviet ships failed to appear. After a couple port visits, the *Atakapa* sat in Portsmouth Harbor, England, for six weeks before sailing for the Spanish-U.S. naval base at Rota. There she rendezvoused with the *Palm Beach*, and the pair sailed for home. Thus, the tug's 1969 deployment was unproductive from the perspective of intelligence collection.

Upon arrival at Little Creek in July, the *Palm Beach* was decommissioned, and on 1 December 1969, she was stricken from the Navy List. The *Atakapa* was stripped of her special equipment and returned to fleet tug assignments. She was decommissioned on 1 July 1974 and assigned to the Navy's Military Sea Transportation Service. With a civilian crew, she served for another dozen years.

Program Termination

During 1966, while the *Pueblo* and *Palm Beach* were in the shipyard at Bremerton, Washington, preparing for Phase II of the Navy's AGER program, the additional ships planned for Phase III and others ships to support the NSA's objectives were unfunded.[26] Phase III of the Navy's AGER program at that time called for the construction of 15 additional spy ships, each of which would be larger and faster—and more expensive—than the three AGER conversions. Those 15 ships were intended for specific operating areas:

Sea of Japan/Sea of Okhotsk	3
Black Sea/Mediterranean	2
Barents/Baltic/North Sea	4
Mid-Pacific area	3
East and South China Seas	3

The Navy's estimate for the construction cost of those 15 ships was $151 million over five years. However, the Office of the Secretary of Defense blocked every attempt by the Navy from 1965 to 1968 to fund Phase III. The NSA's alternative five-year program was much more modest, requiring only four ships similar to the *Banner* in size and configuration to replace the oldest and least effective of the technical research ships. Still, the Department of Defense was unenthusiastic and would not approve the NSA program unless the ships were solely directed toward intelligence collection in support of the Vietnam War. As the *Oxford* and *Jamestown* were adequately fulfilling that mission, the NSA decided to defer its program indefinitely.

From 1965 to 1968, the NSA evaluated the Navy's small "trawler" (AGER) program as a possible successor to its technical research ships. The final version of the NSA's "SIGINT Trawler (AGER) Study" was forwarded to the Navy and the Department of Defense in March 1968, just six weeks after the seizure of the *Pueblo*. While the NSA study indicated a requirement for spy ships larger than trawlers in certain situations, it acknowledged and supported the smaller design as able to meet the majority of the NSA's requirements and encouraged the Navy to submit its AGER Phase III program for funding. But the NSA did caution that a joint Navy-NSA program for AGER-type ships would need to harmonize with a future, large-ship AGTR program, and both ship efforts should be designed to complement other mobile intelligence collection requirements. Thus, even after the *Liberty* and *Pueblo* attacks, the NSA strongly supported the need for a fleet of small intelligence collection ships under Navy control and for the later acquisition of several larger AGTRS under only NSA operational and technical control.

However, the secretary of defense was unwilling to support the Navy's Phase III program for building additional trawler-type AGERS. When the NSA completed its trawler study, the Defense Department's opposition to new construction AGERS had not changed; rather, it had been hardened by the rapidly increasing costs of the Vietnam War.

In 1966–67 the NSA had focused considerable intellectual energy on developing a proposal for trawler-type AGER ships to replace the larger AGTR fleet. When that proposal failed, there was no viable alternative. As the NSA's existing AGTRS were aging, and new construction was deferred, the possibility of additional conversions was investigated. However, no additional World War II–era light cargo ships (FS/AKL) were readily available. The concept of converting mothballed World War II minesweepers into AGERS was investigated, but the costs of converting them proved to be prohibitive. Four ex-Liberty ships, active as missile range instrumentation ships and scheduled for their termination in that role, were available. Also, converting the USNS *Kingsport* (T-AG 164), a satellite communications ship, into an AGTR was considered for the relief of the *Oxford* or *Jamestown*. Those proposals never progressed to funding.

After returning to Norfolk in July 1967, the damaged *Liberty* was considered for repairs and rehabilitation. Also, the concept of converting the *Liberty* and the other AGTRS to civilian/MSTS manning was examined. However, funds could not be obtained to convert the AGTRS to civilian operation by the MSTS or for rehabilitating the *Liberty*. Accordingly, the Navy initiated the first deactivation of an AGTR ship, the *Liberty*, in January 1968.

In early 1968, the Navy's *operational* support for an afloat SIGINT intelligence capability started to crumble. The Navy's doubts were generated by the *Liberty* attack, the *Pueblo*'s capture, and the costs and disruption caused when AGTRS and AGERS in potentially hostile waters required surface warship and/or combat aircraft support. The continuing shift in the Navy's operating funds and warship assignments to the Vietnam War was making the escorting of intelligence ships less acceptable to fleet commanders.

In the 12 months between March 1968 and March 1969, the AGTR/AGER problem had morphed from determining what types and numbers of ships should be acquired to what existing platforms, *if any*, should remain in service.

On 30 July 1969, Melvin R. Laird, the new secretary of defense in the Richard M. Nixon administration, signed off on a series of major defense budget reductions.[27] The Navy's share of those reductions—among other actions—would eliminate five SIGINT ships: the AGTRS *Valdez*, *Muller*, and *Georgetown*; and the two remaining AGERS, the *Banner* and *Palm Beach*. The *Oxford* and *Jamestown* would remain in service for operations off South Vietnam, while the *Belmont* would assume the *Muller*'s station off Havana.

The Nixon administration demanded still more reductions in the defense budget. The Navy offered to drop the *Oxford* and *Jamestown*, leaving only the *Belmont* as an active, dedicated surface ship intelligence collector. The Navy-nominated ships to be discarded were aging, slow, and costly to operate in comparison to their capabilities. The recent decision to operate them 50- or 100-n.mile distant from target coasts also had rendered their intercept capabilities considerably less effective than earlier, when they could move in close enough to intercept low-powered, very-high-frequency, and microwave signals.

Defense officials sought the opinions of the military area commanders. The heads of the Atlantic and European commands both considered the intelligence value of the existing intelligence collection ships was more than offset by the costs and the burden of escorting them and that they were too old to retain. The commander in chief, Pacific Command, did favor retaining one or more technical research ships for contingencies. The Central Intelligence Agency had no objections to terminating the TRS program completely but also concurred that one TRS should be kept available for contingencies.

The NSA stood out as the only organization to protest the complete axing of the TRS program. NSA officials noted that the loss of four of the total fleet of five ships could hardly be construed as the "withdrawal of contingency capabilities" and that the proposed cuts would adversely affect NSA's SIGINT mission. The NSA reclama was that the absolute minimum requirement for national shipboard SIGINT collection was three technical research ships—

one each for Cuba, the Mediterranean, and Southeast Asia. However, without the support of the military area commanders, the CIA, or the Navy, the NSA stood alone in its defense of a fleet of dedicated SIGINT collection ships.

Upon receiving the recommendations of the commanders in chief, the CIA, and the NSA, the new secretary of the Navy, John H. Chafee, favored terminating *all* shipboard SIGINT programs. On 1 October 1969, the Department of Defense announced that it had accepted the recommendation of the secretary of the Navy to eliminate all AGTRs. For contingencies, when shipboard collection capabilities might be needed in the future, a plan was to be prepared for using available warships and auxiliary ships.

The AGTRs and AGERs were ordered into ports and stripped of their electronic equipment, and their NSG detachments were closed down.

With the *Belmont*'s deactivation, the era of dedicated U.S. SIGINT surface ships came to an end. However, subsequently the NSA and the Navy would find methods of employing other ships for SIGINT collection (see chapter 9).

Table 6. U.S. intelligence ship deactivations

Number	Name	Deactivated[a]	Stricken[b]
T-AG 169	*Valdez*	7 November 1969	15 August 1976
T-AG 171	*Muller*	16 September 1969	same date
AGER 1	*Banner*	14 November 1969	same date
AGER 3	*Palm Beach*	1 December 1969	same date
AGTR 1	*Oxford*	19 December 1969	14 January 1970
AGTR 2	*Georgetown*	19 December 1969	same date
AGTR 3	*Jamestown*	19 December 1969	14 January 1970
AGTR 4	*Belmont*	16 January 1970	same date
AGTR 5	*Liberty*	28 June 1968	same date

a. Military Sea Transportation Service (USNS) ships were deactivated; commissioned Navy ships (USS) were decommissioned.

b. Stricken from the Naval Vessel Register—that is, the Navy List.

8

The Seizure of the USS *Pueblo*

> At that particular point in history, the common confidence in the historic inviolability of a sovereign ship on the high seas in peacetime was shown to have been misplaced. The consequences must in fairness be borne by all, rather than by one or two individuals whom circumstances had placed closer to the crucial event.
>
> —Secretary of the Navy John H. Chafee, 6 May 1969

The second AGER that was converted from an ex-Army FS/Navy AKL light cargo ship was the USS *Pueblo* (AGER 2). After brief Navy service as the AKL 44, she entered the Puget Sound Naval Shipyard and, in July 1966, began her conversion to a spy ship. Lieutenant Commander Lloyd W. Bucher was ordered to serve as the officer in charge of the *Pueblo* until she was placed in commission; then he would become her commanding officer.

But the conversion process for the *Pueblo*—like that for the *Palm Beach*—was very slow and complex, in part because of differences in the FS/AKL ships' construction that required specific modifications. Lieutenant Commander John Arnold, then with the Naval Security Group, related:

> Lt. Dick Yeck of the [NSG] G-50 staff came to me and asked if I would look over the . . . proposal for the SIGINT system for *Pueblo/Palm Beach*. I looked it over and returned it to his desk with a note attached saying "I would NOT buy this for all the tea in China," not knowing that the work was [already] underway.[1]

Arnold had discerned that the layout of the equipment would violate the standard work pattern of the communications technicians operating that equipment. Electronics that had to be within arm's reach of a particular operator might be under his knee level or require his standing on tiptoes to operate. That layout problem alone added almost two months to the conversion. Arnold continued:

> One memorable problem I saw was the back-yard garbage incinerator installed in the open on the signal bridge. [The Naval Ship Systems Command representative] had personally selected the incinerator from a local hardware store. I made the observation that it was inappropriate for even routine destruction/burning of classified material let alone emergency destruction.[2]

After 15 months of work on each ship, the *Pueblo* and the *Palm Beach* were placed in commission together at the Puget Sound yard on 13 May 1967. After their commissioning, both the *Pueblo* and *Palm Beach* remained under the care of the shipyard for several more months as problems and issues were corrected.

Before the *Pueblo* departed the yard, the chief of naval operations had responded to the attack on the *Liberty* with a fleet-wide dictate that all U.S. Navy ships be fitted with increased self-defense weapons. The original requirement levied on the AGERS was to mount two 3-inch/50-caliber dual-purpose guns. The *Pueblo*'s captain, Lloyd Bucher, brought to the attention of the Pentagon that those guns were too heavy for the *Pueblo* and recommended that 20-mm cannon be mounted instead of the larger weapons. That armament was approved, but the guns were not readily available prior to the *Pueblo*'s completion. Thus, the *Pueblo* was granted an exception and sailed from the shipyard without armament.

The *Pueblo* sailed from Bremerton to San Diego in September 1967 for refresher training and a pre-deployment workup. She departed San Diego for Pearl Harbor on 6 November. At Pacific Fleet headquarters in Pearl Harbor, Bucher met with Lieutenant Commander Ervin R. Easton, an intelligence officer on the Pacific Fleet staff. He informed Bucher that the *Pueblo*'s "initial operation would be off the coast of North Korea," where the *Banner*

Photo 21. The intelligence ship *Pueblo* (AGER 2) off the California coast in late 1967. Four months later—on 23 January 1968—North Korean forces boarded and captured her. Less the one fatality, her crew eventually was returned to the United States; the ship remains a "trophy" in North Korea. / U.S. Navy.

had operated "on a couple of occasions and been totally ignored by the Koreans."

Easton provided all of the *Banner*'s patrol reports for Bucher's examination.[3] Easton continued:

> From *Banner*'s experience, you can expect harassment, but actual violence is considered highly unlikely to occur. They can be recklessly aggressive, but still smart enough not to challenge American seapower with a handful of subchasers and PT boats. That would be quite different from a few infiltrations and firefights along the [Demilitarized Zone]. But you might as well hear what the thinking about it is from higher echelon.[4]

Easton escorted Bucher to meet with Rear Admiral George L. Cassell, the assistant chief of staff for operations at Pacific Fleet headquarters. Cassell added,

> In the unexpected event of a serious attack against *Pueblo*, it would probably happen beyond the range of immediate assistance. You can count on everything being done as quickly as possible to come to your assistance and that in any case a retaliation would be mounted within twenty-four hours. We consider the risk to be nominal if not nonexistent.[5]

After three days in Pearl Harbor, the *Pueblo* sailed for Japan, arriving on 1 December 1967—eight months behind her original schedule.[6] On the 19th, the *Banner* also arrived at Yokosuka, having completed her final Clickbeetle mission. She joined the *Pueblo* at pier side, and Bucher met with the *Banner*'s commanding officer, Commander Charles Clark, to discuss the North Korean mission area, patrol history, and operating procedures for the next sortie.

Clark's briefings addressed the three *Banner* missions off North Korea, where he always kept 13 to 20 n.miles from the Korean coast and offshore islands (see chapter 7). Unlike the *Banner*'s experiences off the Soviet Union and China, the North Koreans had never harassed or even physically reacted to the AGERS steaming off their coast. Clark's briefings seemed to corroborate the evaluation of the Pacific Fleet's intelligence staff that the *Pueblo*'s first mission would have "minimal" risk.

The armament issue arose again at Yokosuka, and that time the requirement was met with the mounting of two .50-caliber machine guns on the *Pueblo*, but they were placed on the open weather deck, without protection for the gunners. Small arms also were provided. Prior to the *Pueblo*'s departure, the commander, Naval Forces Japan, Rear Admiral Frank L. Johnson, declared,

> I am against arming your ships. It could lead to trouble for you which you are not prepared for. . . . I suggest you keep your guns covered and pointed down, or better yet, stow them below decks. . . . Remember you are not going out there to start a war. . . . Make sure you keep them covered and don't use them in any provocative way at all. It doesn't take much to set those damned Com-

munists off and start an international incident. That's the last thing we want![7]

On 5 January 1968, the *Pueblo* sailed for Sasebo, Japan, to fuel and to send ashore excess classified codes and publications. At 0600 on 11 January, the *Pueblo* cast off lines en route to the ship's first intelligence mission.[8]

Ichthyic One

The Clickbeetle codename for the Navy's AGER program in 1966–67 was changed to Pinkroot in December 1967, when the commander, Naval Forces Japan, transmitted the *Pueblo*'s initial operation order.[9] That specific mission, codenamed Ichthyic One, was intended primarily to monitor naval activity off several North Korean ports and to "sample" the electronic signals being generated along the eastern coast of North Korea. Second, the *Pueblo* was to determine the Korean Communist and Soviet "reaction to an overt intelligence collector operating near [the] Korcom periphery." Other objectives included observing the Soviet naval forces that the ship might encounter.

The U.S. Navy sponsored the *Pueblo*'s mission to meet *naval* intelligence objectives. The NSA was not a mission cosponsor, and any national intelligence objectives met during the cruise would be incidental. Despite that fact, the NSA sent a message to the Joint Chiefs of Staff and to the Navy's Pacific commands urging caution in the vicinity of North Korea due to a surge in Pyongyang's recent hyperbole and military actions against South Korean targets.[10]

The *Pueblo* was ordered to sail from Sasebo via the Tsushima Strait and the Sea of Japan, and to operate off the North Korean coast in areas designated Mars, Venus, and Pluto, "concentrating in areas which appear most lucrative."[11] The final paragraph of the ship's sailing order stated: "Installed defensive armament should be stowed or covered in such a manner as to not elicit unusual interest from surveying/surveyed unit(s). Employ only in cases where threat to survival is obvious."[12]

Bucher described his plan of action: "I planned to work my way north through the assigned operation areas, respectively, Mars, Venus, and Pluto, remaining 30–40 miles offshore, then closing to the coast to within 15 miles and working south through the operating areas."[13] The *Pueblo* had 83 officers and enlisted men on board, including two Marine Corps Korean linguists, and two civilian Navy oceanographers.[14]

No U.S. naval air or surface units were placed on alert to react to a *Pueblo* emergency. The Air Force "was neither required nor requested to provide any preplanned support for the *Pueblo*'s mission."[15]

Area Pluto Southbound

Tracking 30 to 40 n.miles off the Korean coast northbound in a winter storm-wracked sea, the *Pueblo* entered her northernmost operating area—Pluto—on 15 January 1968. She laid to that morning as the crew chipped excessive ice off the superstructure and exercised the ship's two .50-caliber machine guns. It took 20 minutes until the first round could be fired.

Then Bucher sailed the *Pueblo* into a position about 15 n.miles off the North Korean port of Chongjin and laid to for the rest of the day. No Korean reaction was observed. With the coming of nightfall, Bucher moved 20 to 25 n.miles offshore for the hours of darkness; in the morning he moved back to a position 15 n.miles offshore.[16]

On the evening of the 17th, Bucher transited south to a position about 25 n.miles off the coast of the port of Song-Jin (now Kimchaek). The operating pattern continued: laying to about 15 n.miles off the port during the day and widening the distance to 20 to 25 n.miles at night. The *Pueblo* operated under total radio and radar silence, and during the night she steamed without normal running lights.

Song-Jin also was a disappointment. Very little intelligence was obtained either visually or electronically. On the evening of the 19th, the *Pueblo* transited southbound to a position about 20 n.miles off the island of Mayang Do (in the vicinity of Sinpo), in the area labeled Venus. Moving in to some 15 n.miles of the coast at about 0800, Bucher ordered the ship's radar activated briefly to confirm a navigation fix.

Possibly in response to the interception of a U.S. ship's radar emissions, a North Korean SO-1-class patrol craft approached the *Pueblo*, coming as close as one mile as night was falling. The patrol craft continued south toward Wonsan, not changing her course or speed. Bucher concluded the *Pueblo* had not been identified, and he did not break radio silence to report the event. From 19 to 21 January, a North Korean fire control radar periodically locked onto the ship.[17]

Off Wonsan

On the night of 21/22 January, the *Pueblo* transited south to the Wonsan operating area Mars, arriving about dawn. Shortly after noon, two trawlers, painted gray and with fishing gear, approached the *Pueblo* and circled at about 500 yards. They then moved some two to three miles away, converged apparently for their commanders to talk, and then returned to the *Pueblo*'s position. When the two trawlers closed to about 30 yards and again circled the *Pueblo*, Bucher got underway and sailed at slow speed away from the coast.

Bucher broke radio silence to send his first mission report, describing the situation. At about 1600, the two trawlers departed, and Bucher intended to resume radio silence. However, communications problems required his radios to remain active throughout the night while attempting to deliver the 22 January report and the intercept information accumulated by the ship's NSG detachment.

Once the *Pueblo* reached a position 20 to 25 n.miles off the coast, as determined by bearings to coastal lights and the fathometer depth, she loitered until dawn. Bucher then proceeded to a point 15.5 n.miles off the coast—determined by visual bearings to landmarks—and went dead in the water at 1000.

Unbeknownst to the *Pueblo*, the North Korean radar station at Kukchi-bong (to the south of the *Pueblo*'s location, near the South Korean border) during the night and early morning of 22/23 January had marked the *Pueblo* as an "enemy ship" and had directed North Korean ships toward the target. Significantly, Kukchi-bong referenced an element of the country's Ministry of National Defense during its vectoring of ships out to intercept the *Pueblo*, indicating that the ministry probably was directing an event of major significance.[18]

At 1100, *Pueblo* radio operators finally had acknowledgments for the messages that they had transmitted the previous day. After obtaining a receipt at 1150 for the ship's second report stating that all was calm and that the *Pueblo* was returning to radio silence,

Bucher requested that the U.S. Navy facility at Kami Seya, Japan, keep the radio circuit open due to new developments.

At about 1145, the SO-1-class patrol craft *SC-35* was observed closing at high speed. Bucher recorded in his book *Bucher: My Story* that at that time the *Pueblo* was 15.9 n.miles from the closest land, the island of Hung Do (now Ung-do), as confirmed by radar at about 1205.[19] (Many of the event times were estimated due to the unavailability of the *Pueblo*'s logs.)

The *SC-35* reported to Wonsan by radio at 1210 that "G.E.R. 2" was 18.3 n.miles from "Ung-do."[20] The *SC-35*'s radio reports to Wonsan included: "Judge it to be a reconnaissance search ship." After the *SC-35* circled the *Pueblo*, she signaled by flag: "What nationality?" Bucher responded at about 1215 by raising the American flag and a signal flag indicating the ship was conducting hydrographic operations.[21]

After Bucher raised the flags, the *SC-35* reported by radio, "It is American; a hydrographic mapping ship; weapons are not visible." Ten minutes later, the North Korean ship reported, "The ship has a lot of antennas on it; radar-type antennas and radio antennas; think it is a ship for detecting something."[22] The *Pueblo* was specifically tasked with intercepting VHF radio, and much if not all of this information should have been available to Bucher, had his on-board Korean "linguists" been proficient in the Korean language. They were not, and Bucher was not cognizant of that deficiency.[23]

A short time later, three P-4 torpedo boats were sighted at a distance of five n.miles and closing. Bucher had the quartermaster of the watch double-check the range to the nearest North Korean land—15.8 n.miles. As the *SC-35* was circling, she signaled by flags: "Heave to or I will fire." The *Pueblo* was already dead in the water. Bucher again checked the ship's location—15.8 n.miles offshore.

Bucher attempted to signal "I am in international waters" at about 1220, but his signalman could not find such a signal in the International Code of Signals. He then attempted to send that message to the *SC-35* by flashing light. The Korean patrol craft refused to acknowledge the flashing light signal.

A fourth torpedo boat arrived, and they surrounded the *Pueblo*.[24] Two MiG-type turbojet fighters circled overhead, and a second SO-1 patrol craft was approaching at high speed.

Attack and Capture

Bucher sent his first situation report to Kami Seya at 1252 by "flash" priority. Heavily armed soldiers were seen transferring from the SC-35 to a torpedo boat, and they began efforts to board the *Pueblo* at about 1255. He ordered two-thirds speed—about ten knots—and maneuvered to avoid the torpedo boat's efforts to put troops on the *Pueblo*. At the same time, he steamed almost due east to open the range from the coast. The SC-35 fell behind, probably awaiting orders on how to proceed.

Intercepted North Korean communications—not available until after the attack—between the SC-35 and the torpedo boats revealed that their plan was to transfer a boarding party of five soldiers and their commander from the SC-35 to a torpedo boat and for them to board the *Pueblo*. The Koreans initially intended to tow the *Pueblo* into Wonsan harbor.

After another North Korean craft pulled alongside the SC-35 and one or two men boarded, the SC-35 increased speed and closed on the *Pueblo*, again with signal flags indicating: "Heave to or I will fire." Bucher continued steaming eastward, increasing speed to 12 knots and maneuvering to deny the patrol craft a firing position on his beam. He dispatched what might have been the first use of the new critical intelligence (CRITIC) message reporting system at about 1315; the alert was received in the White House Situation Room at 1343 Korean time.

(CRITIC was designed to flash to the U.S. president and a few other senior officials an intelligence alert and warning of the highest priority—for example, of an imminent coup, or the assassination of a world leader, or an attack on an American embassy or *on a U.S. naval ship*. The system's goal was to have the message on the president's desk within ten minutes of the actual event.)

At about 1325, the SC-35 opened fire with her 57-mm cannon. The fire was aimed high, into the masts, antennas, and the flying bridge. The torpedo boats added their machine gun fire. The gunfire barrage lasted only five or six seconds. Bucher ordered the emergency destruction of classified documents and equipment.

Also in response to the attack, Bucher ordered full speed eastward as the MiGs "buzzed" the ship for a second time. That time the lead aircraft launched a rocket that struck the water well ahead of the *Pueblo*.[25] The SC-35 and the torpedo boats again opened fire at about 1330. Again, the fire was aimed high, into the masts, funnel, and superstructure. Now the North Korean naval and air force units launched a coordinated attack, and it was obvious that they wanted to *capture* the spy ship, not sink her.[26]

Still refusing to yield, Bucher drove the *Pueblo* to the southeast, accelerating to full speed—approximately 15 knots, faster than the ship's rated 12-knot speed. The SC-35 then fired a third barrage, still aimed high and apparently primarily at the pilothouse to disable the ship's command personnel. That third barrage of gunfire induced Bucher to accept the inevitable. The *Pueblo*'s engines were stopped, and she drifted to a halt at about 1335. North Korean communications intercepted at 1336 from the SC-35 stated that the target had come to a stop because of the "warning shots." There had been no warning shots; the initial salvo was aimed directly into the *Pueblo*'s superstructure.

"Follow Me"

The North Koreans did not immediately board the *Pueblo*; rather, the U.S. ship was ordered to follow the SC-35 into Wonsan harbor. Bucher steered astern of the SC-35 at one-third speed to allow the crew more time for the emergency destructions to continue. He ordered "all stop" at about 1340 when he realized the chaotic condition of the destruction effort.

The SC-35 radioed to Wonsan that she intended to fire a few more rounds to make the target "come in." The SC-35 then poured 57-mm rounds into the *Pueblo*'s starboard side, aft of the bridge, causing one fatal and two minor casualties. Bucher immediately got underway again, at one-third speed. Communications intercepts at 1408 from Wonsan to the SC-35 ordered that the *Pueblo* was to "go in farther before boarding." The North Korean did not want to board the *Pueblo* while she was in international waters.

The delay enabled the emergency destruction of classified documents and equipment to continue for more than 45 additional minutes. However, Bucher and his NSG officer in charge, Lieutenant Stephen R. Harris, had never conducted an emergency destruction drill; thus, those efforts were haphazard and largely ineffectual.[27] The delay in boarding also allowed extra time for the *Pueblo* to make additional radio transmissions describing her situation. At about 1450, the North Koreans boarded the *Pueblo*, probably at or near the 12-n.mile limit. She took more than one hour to get underway again with armed Koreans overseeing the American helmsman and enginemen.

The *Pueblo* entered Wonsan harbor at about 1700 with the crew at gunpoint, blindfolded, and their hands on their heads. By about 1900, they were pier side. The *Pueblo*'s casualties were one crewman killed and three wounded, including Bucher. Should there have been any doubt that the *Pueblo* was assaulted with authorization at the highest government level, the North Korean Air Force had established an airborne screen of some 30 MiG fighter aircraft defending Wonsan by 1640 that afternoon.

As with the Western prisoners held during the Korean War, North Korea did not accord the *Pueblo* crew the minimal humane treatment required under international law. The *Pueblo* crewmen received the same threatening behavior, physical abuse, and torture as did American prisoners held by China and North Korea during the 1950–53 conflict.

Bucher later related that their incarceration began with routine beatings and with psychological torture, including death threats. The treatment became harsher after the Koreans learned—from a *Time* magazine article—that the Americans' "middle-finger salute," which the crew told their captors was a Hawaiian good luck sign, was actually a signal of defiance and disrespect. Prior to the crew's release after almost year in captivity, the physical abuse lightened during the final months and then ended.

Commander Bucher, as the commanding officer, was targeted for special attention. When he refused to write and sign a "confession," he was threatened with the execution of his crew one by one until he did. After he then signed the confession, the level of physical torture, beatings, and mishandling was reduced. His so-called confession was a masterpiece of nonsense and malapropisms—with a ridiculous selection of nouns, verbs, and adjectives—and an obvious construct signaling that it was elicited under duress. It ended with: "So help me, Hanna. s/L.M. Bucher."[28]

The NSG technicians primarily were interrogated for their knowledge of the workings of the cryptographic equipment, both that on board the *Pueblo* and other devices that were mentioned in documents found on the *Pueblo*. Because the Koreans seized the operations and maintenance manuals, and the actual encoding machines nearly intact, there was little real harm in minimizing the beatings by responding accurately in those interrogations.

The North Koreans used the *Pueblo*'s crewmen as political pawns for 11 months, until they were released after a theatrical U.S. apology and "admission" that the *Pueblo* had transgressed into North Korean territorial waters. That statement was verbally disavowed moments before its delivery at the Korean-U.S. negotiation site at Panmunjom on the North–South Korean border.

Even if the *Pueblo* had violated North Korea's 12-n.mile territorial waters—which the available evidence shows she did not—the international law of the sea states that a foreign warship "enjoys immunity, even when it is in the territorial waters of a foreign nation. It can't be boarded, although it can be required to leave."[29] North Korea's attack and seizure of the *Pueblo* was in blatant disregard of international law.

The "Response"

In response to the radio messages from the *Pueblo* that she was being forced into the port of Wonsan, the U.S. Air Force attempted to find fighter aircraft in South Korea or Japan that could quickly react—without success. The U.S. aircraft in Japan could not respond because of questions concerning the country's status of forces agreement; U.S. Air Force fighter-type aircraft in South Korea on ready alert were armed with nuclear weapons and had no air-to-air capability. Air Force fighters were scrambled from Okinawa but had to land in South Korea to refuel, and by the time they were ready for takeoff, it was nearly sunset, and the *Pueblo* was entering Wonsan. The U.S. Navy had no forces outside of Japan that could react other than the carrier *Enterprise* (CVAN 65), which at the time was some 500 n.miles southeast of Wonsan. It was several hours before the *Enterprise* received instructions to respond to the developing situation.[30]

As the *Pueblo* incident unfolded, the commander in chief, U.S. Pacific Fleet, and the Joint Chiefs of Staff rushed to prepare a spectrum of potential military responses to the North Korean capture of the spy ship. There was no debate on the seriousness of the event; it was a casus belli, a national embarrassment, and a major U.S. military failure.

Senior officials at every operational level in the Navy responded with incredulity that the North Koreans would risk reopening the Korean War by attacking a clearly identified U.S. Navy ship. The term "international waters" seemed to hold a kind hypnotic spell over Navy planners and operational staffs. But as with the *Liberty* incident only six and a half months earlier, the mystical power of the term "international waters" had failed to protect a U.S. Navy ship. Unlike the *Liberty* incident, however, the capture of the *Pueblo* had been sanctioned at the highest levels of the offending government.

After the seizure of the *Pueblo*, the U.S. military undertook several responses including sending additional troops to South Korea, conducting SR-71 Blackbird reconnaissance flights over the Korean Peninsula, moving additional B-52 Stratofortress bombers into the region, and increasing U.S. fighter aircraft strength in South Korea. Operation Formation Star was the surge deployment of a massive U.S. naval force into the Sea of Japan: two attack aircraft carriers and one anti-submarine carrier, three cruisers, 12 destroyers, and support ships. They operated in the area from 21 January to 22 March 1968. Sixteen U.S. submarines—nine nuclear propelled and seven diesel-electric—also were deployed into the area.

Several direct actions against North Korea were considered, some involving the spy ship *Banner*, which cruised in the center of the carrier task group from 31 January to 11 March. The Johnson administration eventually rejected all retaliation options as counterproductive to the safety of the *Pueblo*'s crew and as too laden with the risk of initiating a pattern of escalation and counter-escalation with North Korea.

At the time the United States also was deeply involved in the Vietnam War. That conflict was then entering a critical phase as

North Vietnam's Tet Offensive had begun one week after the *Pueblo*'s capture. The CIA later evaluated the *Pueblo* incident as "probably aimed primarily at generating diversionary pressures on the U.S."[31]

Thus, the military responses to the *Pueblo*'s capture were limited, as political and military officials in Washington realized the United States could not open a second conflict on the Asian mainland. It was militarily infeasible and politically poisonous.

The Critical Losses

The loss of the *Pueblo* compromised a trove of COMINT and other special intelligence documents that identified U.S. national intelligence objectives and targets, and intelligence organizations, priorities, and methods. Also lost were classified manuals and equipment for four cryptologic systems. Especially severe was the loss of about 8,000 special intelligence messages transmitted during the period 1 to 24 January. Not until the *Pueblo*'s crew was released after 11 months did the government learn that the crew had not destroyed the monthly "code cards" for November and December 1967, thus adding another 20,000 or so to the number of encoded messages compromised.[32]

There were other effects of the North Korean capture of a U.S. spy ship: The ship's personnel records identified the intelligence clearances of the crewmen and the Naval Security Group personnel. That information enabled the North Korean interrogations to be focused and more productive. The NSG detachment personnel and the *Pueblo*'s commanding and executive officers had their career histories in their personal service jackets, information that also could guide their captors' questions about former assignments.

After lengthy negotiations, the North Korean regime released the *Pueblo*'s crew on 23 December 1968. The men were flown to the United States by military aircraft. In the United States, there was considerable sympathy for their incarceration and the torture that they had suffered from a savage and brutal regime. But simultaneously many Americans felt the crew had failed to resist with the rigor and honor expected of American warriors. Many Americans—in and out of uniform—believed, even with one dead and three wounded from a crew of 83 men, that with the ship still able to navigate and armed with two machine guns and small arms, surrendering without a fight was "dishonorable."

Commander Bucher and his officers were brought before a naval court of inquiry to explain their actions—or lack thereof. After 26 days of hearings, the court recommended general courts-martial for Bucher for five counts of dereliction of duty and for Lieutenant Harris, the NSG detachment officer in charge, for three counts of dereliction of duty. Nonjudicial punishment in the form of letters of reprimand were recommended for the *Pueblo*'s executive officer; the commander, Naval Forces Japan; and for the director, Naval Security Group Pacific.[33]

The commander in chief, U.S. Pacific Fleet, Admiral John J. Hyland, who had convened the court of inquiry, rejected the recommendations for courts-martial for Bucher and Harris, and instead recommended letters of reprimand. Hyland approved the recommended letters of reprimand for the *Pueblo*'s executive officer and the commander, Naval Forces Japan, but disapproved the recommendation of a letter of reprimand for the director, Naval Security Group Pacific.[34] The dereliction of duty charges mostly involved the failure to establish, train, and conduct an effective emergency destruction of classified material.[35]

Upon receipt of Admiral Hyland's endorsement, Secretary of the Navy John Chafee ordered that all charges against Bucher and Harris be dismissed, and he disapproved all nonjudicial punishment or letters of censure. Chafee stated: "I make no judgment regarding the guilt or innocence of any of the officers . . . [but] it is my opinion that they have suffered enough. . . . I have determined that the charges against all of the officers concerned will be dismissed."[36]

Commander Bucher continued his naval career without penalty until his retirement in 1970, after 27 years of naval service. Unlike Captain McGonagle of the *Liberty*, Bucher received no personal award for the incident or for his 11 months in captivity, although he was widely recognized as holding his crew together in good spirits throughout that ordeal. Nine of his crew received personal awards and honors for their resistance during incarceration; all crewmen did receive the Navy Commendation Medal and the Purple Heart in recognition of their arduous confinement and torture. Later, all were awarded the military ribbon for having been prisoners of war.

As a postscript to the *Pueblo* saga, in February 2021, a U.S. federal judge ruled that the 61 surviving crew members and 110 surviving family members of the *Pueblo* were entitled to $2.3 *billion* in compensation for the crew's captivity and torture in North Korea. (The money was to be paid from the U.S. Victims of State Sponsored Terrorism Fund, which is supported by fines levied and sanctions placed on individuals and corporations that conduct or support terrorist activities.)

The *Pueblo* was never released by the North Koreans. She was displayed as a prize of war at Wonsan until October 1999. Then she was towed from Wonsan on the Korean east coast and around the peninsula to the port of Nampo on the west coast. The United States made no effort to interfere with the transfer.

After some restoration work at a Nampo shipyard, the *Pueblo* was moved to Pyongyang and moored in the Taedong River. Later she was moved to the Pothong River, becoming a museum ship. The *Pueblo* remains there as this volume went to press. She also still is listed in the U.S. Naval Vessel Register with the status of "Active, in commission."[37]

In the wake of the *Liberty* attack and the capture of the *Pueblo*, the U.S. Navy considered providing warship escorts for the specialized spy ships. That was not believed to be a cost-effective option given the high costs of maintaining the AGER/AGTRS in service and the potential alternative means of intelligence collection. In July 1969, the chief of naval operations, Admiral Moorer, recommended that all spy ships be taken out of service.

The EC-121M Shootdown

The *Pueblo* incident was not the last military action that the North Korean regime took against U.S. surveillance and intelligence collection efforts.[38] On 15 April 1969, a U.S. Navy reconnaissance aircraft flying from Atsugi, Japan, was on a routine COMINT/SIGINT flight over the northern Sea of Japan, targeting North Korean and Soviet military communications. Previously the Soviet Union and

Photo 22. A U.S. Navy EC-121M Warning Star electronic reconnaissance aircraft being escorted by American aircraft. North Korean fighters shot down a similar aircraft over international waters 90 n.miles from the Korean coast on 15 April 1969, with the death of all 31 men on board. / U.S. Navy.

China both had shot down U.S. reconnaissance aircraft flying over international waters.

The reconnaissance aircraft was a modified version of the four-piston-engine Lockheed Constellation—a Navy EC-121M Warning Star. The aircraft had 31 crewmen on board—nine of whom were NSG technicians—flying a normal reconnaissance flight profile with the radio call sign "Deep Sea 129." U.S. Navy and Air Force aircraft had flown more than 200 such reconnaissance flights off the North Korean east coast during the previous three months alone. Deep Sea 129's flight was no different and was considered a minimal risk.

Two North Korean MiG-21 Fishbed turbojet fighters flying from the Wonsan area attacked the U.S. aircraft at 1337 on 15 April, approximately 90 n.miles east of the Korean coast (and about 150 n.miles south of Vladivostok). The MiGs were armed with 23-mm cannon and AA-2 Atoll air-to-air missiles. The North Korean government later reported that a "single shot" brought down the aircraft; it was probably a missile. The EC-121M was unarmed. Only three minutes prior to the shootdown, it had received a warning of approaching aircraft, provided by land-based intercept sites monitoring the North Korean fighter aircraft communications.

There were no EC-121 survivors. Soviet destroyers were sent to the scene to assist U.S. ships and aircraft in the search for debris. The Soviet destroyer *Vdokhnovennyi* reported recovering a rubber life raft, cigarette packs, an aircraft seat, a man's coat, and aircraft parts from the downed EC-121. Another Soviet ship recovered two bodies. The debris and bodies were transferred to U.S. Navy ships in an instance of close collaboration between the Soviet Union and United States.[39]

In reaction to the EC-121 shootdown, the U.S. Navy again sent a multi-carrier task force into the Sea of Japan as a "show of force," but it was quickly stood down. Newly installed president Richard Nixon and his national security adviser, Henry Kissinger, were frustrated by their inability to control the situation. Kissinger later admitted, "Our conduct in the EC-121 crisis was weak, indecisive and disorganized." And Nixon promised that "they'll never get away with it again."[40] Normal U.S. surveillance flights were reinstituted soon after the shootdown.

The question of why the North Koreans once again chose to test U.S. resolve with direct military action against a U.S. Navy intelligence platform in international airspace remains unanswered.

9

Unusual Spy Ships

Beyond the traditional, AGI-type spy ships, two exceptional ship types have been involved in intelligence collection on a large scale: tank landing ships (LST) and ocean surveillance ships (AGOS).

The original LST concept was developed as a joint British-U.S. effort during World War II to provide an effective means of bringing ashore tanks and other vehicles in amphibious landings. The U.S. Navy built 1,052 tank landing ships during World War II, with postwar programs producing another 44 LSTs through 1972. Many of those war-built ships were converted to specialized roles, primarily to repair ships, but they also became mine countermeasures and landing craft support ships, motor torpedo boat tenders, stores-issue ships, casualty evacuation ships, aviation support ships, and "mini" aircraft carriers for operating light aircraft.[1]

The AGOS concept evolved as a multipurpose ship towing lengthy sonar arrays, primarily for anti-submarine operations. However, the ships soon became valuable as a "strategic" intelligence collection tool for the U.S., Soviet/Russian, Japanese, and Chinese Navies.

Tank Landing Ships

At least seven U.S. Navy LST-type landing ships were specifically equipped and employed as spy ships during the Cold War.[2] In their intelligence collection role, William D. O'Neil wrote, the post–World War II *Newport* (LST 1179)-class LSTs have

> good seakeeping qualities and, without troops on board, can carry provisions and spares for long voyages. Their spacious weather and tank decks provide ample room for any necessary special equip-

ment, and there is adequate extra berthing for operators and observers. But most important, perhaps, the . . . propulsion system—six diesel engines driving two shafts—is simple, rugged, and reliable.[3]

In retrospect, it seemed incongruous that the AGTR/AGER ships—when sighted in limited light, as at dawn and dusk, or by an aircraft making a quick overflight—easily could be mistaken for merchant ships, while an LST presented a silhouette that was unmistakable for anything but a naval amphibious ship. Still, the U.S. Navy used at least six LST-type ships in the intelligence collection role against Soviet naval activities plus one off Central America. The first such LST mission probably was that of the *Newport*, the Navy's first 20-knot landing ship, in 1972. Subsequent LST forays into Arctic waters to observe Soviet activities that are publicly known are listed in table 7.

Table 7. U.S. LST intelligence collection operations

Number	Name	Commissioned	Intelligence role
LST 1179	*Newport*	1969	1972, 1980, 1983
LST 1181	*Sumter*	1970	1979, 1983, 1984
LST 1193	*Fairfax County*	1971	1978, 1981
LST 1194	*La Moure County*	1971	1978, 1984
LST 1196	*Harlan County*	1972	1983
LST 1197	*Barnstable County*	1972	1982
ARL 24	*Sphinx*	1945	1985–89

Note: ARL: Built as *LST* 963 and completed as the ARL 24.

Except for the *Sphinx*, all of these ships were employed in the Barents Sea area to collect intelligence on Soviet naval activities. Relatively few details of their operations are publicly available. Also, there are indications that the *Fairfax County*'s 1978 mission was followed by an LST foray on an annual basis, at least into the 1980s, although specific details are lacking.

The LST spy ships were of the *Newport* class built in the 1960s and 1970s, were provided with vans for both COMINT and ELINT interception, and, on occasion, were fitted with acoustic collection capabilities. Each LST embarked a Naval Security Group team numbering some 100 cryptographic technicians plus 20 or more Russian-language translators. They also embarked swimmers trained for small boat operations in hazardous seas to locate and recover floating items of possible intelligence value. While on those intelligence missions, the LSTs were rigged with sufficient explosives to blow out the bottom of the ship should the Soviets attempt to board the ship while she was beyond the range of armed U.S. or allied support.

The *Newport* apparently was the first of her class to operate in the northern area, making her first Arctic cruise in August–October 1972. Details of her special equipment, technical personnel, and mission have not been made public. The *Newport* again made a cruise above the Arctic Circle in March 1980, for the NATO Teamwork 80 exercise, and into the North Atlantic in April 1983, with indications that those sailings most likely included intelligence collection.

The *La Moure County* was at Little Creek (Norfolk), Virginia, being fitted as an intelligence collector in Operation Undercover Ambush in January 1978. She sailed on 2 February to the Caribbean for training and returned to Little Creek on the 25th for loading supplies, provisions, and equipment. The *La Moure County* departed Little Creek on 10 March, encountering bad weather along the track that forced the ship into St. John's, Newfoundland, from 14 to 19 March. The LST then sailed for Reykjavík, Iceland. After the Easter weekend, when 2,400 visitors toured *parts* of the ship, she sailed for the Arctic on the 26th.

The *La Moure County* was at sea observing Soviet naval operations until late April and then conducted a brief fueling stop at Tromsø, Norway, on 28 April. After a liberty call to Bergen, the ship arrived at Little Creek on 17 May.

The great interest in that maiden voyage in an intelligence role was manifested by two vice admirals greeting the return of the lowly LST after a relatively short, two-month deployment. Her commanding officer, Commander Edward L. Schneider, was presented the Legion of Merit, and the Navy Unit Commendation was awarded to the ship for the mission. In addition, several individual awards went to members of the crew and the NSG detachment.

In 1978 the LST *Sumter* was fitted with the BQR-22 passive sonar system and was provided with 500 sonobuoys and 300 bathyther-

Photo 23. The *Sumter* (LST 1181) was one of several LSTs employed for intelligence collection operations in the Barents Sea area. Their large tank decks, open main decks, and troop accommodations facilitated their employment in that role. In this 1978 photo, while refueling from the oiler *Truckee* (AO 147), the *Sumter* (*left*) is loaded with Marine equipment and has pontoons lashed to her sides. / U.S. Navy.

mographs to obtain acoustic intelligence during her forthcoming intelligence collection mission—Operation Smokewatch. The *Sumter* also was equipped with radio fingerprinting equipment and sensors for recording electromagnetic, acoustic, and photographic characteristics of submarines that she could encounter.

The ship set sail for the Barents Sea and Soviet naval home waters in March 1979. On board were more than 120 NSG cryptologic technicians, 23 Russian-language translators, and an explosive ordnance disposal team that was embarked to disarm any weapons that the ship might "acquire." In Arctic waters, she observed Soviet surface ships and submarines, and monitored missile firings. The *Sumter* returned to her home port in June. The operation was considered highly successful, with the *Sumter*'s commanding officer, Commander Frederick A. Olds, being awarded the Legion of Merit and the ship awarded the Meritorious Unit Citation.

The *Sumter* returned to areas north of the Arctic Circle in June and July 1983, and for the third time in April and May 1984.

Details of the *Fairfax County*'s spy ship operations still are clouded in secrecy. Sailing from Norfolk, she is known to have made cruises above the Arctic Circle—possibly into Soviet operating areas—in March and April 1978, and again in March and April 1981. It was well documented that when the *Fairfax County* was in the Barents Sea in 1978, she was trailed and occasionally harassed by Soviet ships. On occasion Soviet frigates sailed close aboard, retrieved bathythermographs launched by the LST, and fired at the weather balloons that she released. Still, according to the commander in chief, Atlantic Fleet, the *Fairfax County* "delivered huge quantities of data," including much information on radio and sonar propagation, "like previous LSTs voyaging to the Barents."

In 1983 the *Harlan County* crossed the Arctic Circle and entered the Barents Sea for close observation of the Soviet Northern Fleet's operations off Murmansk. Admiral Vladen Smirnoff, the fleet's deputy commander, called the LST's deployment "unexpected" and noted the presence of "American, French, and British" ships in the Barents in 1983. Smirnoff mentioned those deployments by NATO ships and the "provocation by the Americans" as the background for Moscow's misreading of the NATO command post exercise Able Archer in November 1983: Moscow believed it was a possible indication that the West was planning an actual nuclear attack on the Soviet Union.[4]

While the *Barnstable County* first penetrated Arctic waters in February 1980, it was not until early 1982 that the ship was fitted for intelligence collection and was assigned an NSG detachment. She departed her home port for Operation Smokey Topaz on 7 May 1982. After a port call in Glasgow to refuel on 18 May, the ship rounded Norway's North Cape on the 25th and proceeded to the vicinity of Kildin Island off the Soviet coast.

The *Barnstable County* spent the next five weeks observing Soviet surface ships and submarines during their spring workup exercises and weapons launches. She put into Tromsø on 1 July to refuel. Then, after additional European port calls, the LST returned to her home port of Little Creek on 24 July, apparently ending the role of LSTs as spy ships.

Spying off Central America

The USS *Sphinx* had been laid down as the *LST 963* in 1944 and was converted during construction to a landing craft repair ship. Large numbers of those modified LSTs were required to support the massive flotillas of small landing craft used in the Army, Navy, and Marine Corps amphibious landings in the Western Pacific in 1943–45 and for the planned invasion of the Japanese home islands in 1946–47.

The *Sphinx* was placed in commission in May 1945 as the ARL 24. After her service in Japanese waters immediately after the war and at the Bikini atoll atomic bomb tests in 1946, she was decommissioned and placed in reserve ("mothballs") from 1947 to 1950. The ship was placed back in commission from 1950 to 1956 for service in the Korean War. Again decommissioned, after a decade in reserve she was reactivated in 1967 as a small craft repair ship for the Vietnam War. She was decommissioned for a third time in 1974 and three years later was stricken from the Navy List.

The Navy reacquired the *Sphinx* in 1985, and that year she was converted into an intelligence collection ship at the Puget Sound Naval Shipyard. After being recommissioned again on 26 July 1985, she conducted patrols off the Pacific coasts of Guatemala and El Salvador, monitoring communications related to the activity of communist guerrillas. The ship used Rodman in the Panama Canal Zone as her base during those missions.

Once again, she was decommissioned in 1989 and subsequently sold for scrap.

Towing Very Long Arrays

In the early 1980s, the U.S. Navy initiated the Surveillance Towed Array Sensor System (SURTASS) with long acoustic arrays towed by slow surface ships. The program was initiated to supplement

Photo 24. The *Sphinx* (ARL 24) was typical of the 1,052 tank landing ships built in U.S. shipyards during World War II. She was completed as a landing craft repair ship and, with minimal modification, was employed for intelligence collection off the coast of Central America in the 1980s. / U.S. Navy.

the Sound Surveillance System in areas where that network of seafloor sensors was inadequate or where the sensors were damaged or destroyed. The SURTASS data would be sent from the towing ships via satellite link to shore facilities at a data rate of about 32 kilobits per second for processing and further transmission to anti-submarine forces. Significantly, the SURTASS data also was of great intelligence value, providing information on foreign submarine operations and characteristics, as well as environmental conditions. The surface ships—designated AGOS for miscellaneous auxiliary, ocean surveillance—also could provide "raw" acoustic data directly to anti-submarine ships in their area. Patrol missions of 60–74 days originally were planned for those ships.

The SURTASS/AGOS concept differed from the tactical towed arrays streamed by warships and submarines, with hydrophone arrays being employed to supplement the ships' hull-mounted sonars. The UQQ-2 SURTASS array is a flexible, tube-like structure some 2,600 feet long that contains numerous hydrophones and is towed with a 6,000-foot cable. It is neutrally buoyant when at depth, which varies with environmental conditions; the typical array operating depths are 500 to 1,500 feet.

A high degree of habitability is provided in the AGOS ships with single staterooms for the civilian crew members and three single and four double staterooms for technicians in ships of the *Stalwart* (T-AGOS 1) class. They normally carry about 20 civilian crewmen and ten Navy technicians. The AGOS ships are not armed.

The initial U.S. Navy planning was for 18 SURTASS/AGOS ships that would be operated by the Navy's Military Sealift Command with civilian crews and carry Navy technicians. The first ocean surveillance ship was the USNS *Stalwart*, which was placed in service on 12 April 1984. She displaced 2,535 tons full load and was 224 feet long. During the next six years, 17 additional monohull ships of that class entered naval service.

Those ships served in many ocean areas, providing valuable data on foreign submarine operations and acoustic conditions. As newer ocean surveillance ships became available, and the Soviet regime collapsed, those ships were retired beginning in the early 1990s. In 1993 the *Stalwart* and her sister ships *Indomitable* (T-AGOS 7) and *Capable* (T-AGOS 16) were converted to serve in the U.S. "war on drugs"; their SURTASS arrays were replaced by SPS-49 long-range, air search radars. Other ships subsequently were transferred to other U.S. government agencies as well as to educational institutions.

Because of the success of the early ships and the then-increasing Soviet submarine threat, in the 1980s the U.S. Navy sought a much larger AGOS program. The 18 monohull ships of the *Stalwart* class plus at least nine ships of the Small Waterplane-Area Twin Hull (SWATH) configuration were planned. The SWATH ships have twin, submerged catamaran hulls.

The first SWATH ship, the *Victorious* (T-AGOS 19), was placed in service on 13 August 1991. She displaces 3,438 tons with a length of 234½ feet. Four SWATH ships were completed in 1991–92. In addition to the UQQ-2 towed array, they have hull-mounted, low-frequency active sonars. The ships were the world's first operational military ships of the SWATH configuration.[5]

Those four ships were immediately followed by larger SWATH ships, led by the *Impeccable* (T-AGOS 23), which entered service on 20 March 2001. She is a 5,468-ton ship with a length of 278 feet. Her larger size would enable operations in rougher sea states, especially in northern latitudes. The SWATH ships also have excellent crew accommodations and, like their predecessors, are unarmed.

The second ship of that design, the *Integrity* (T-AGOS 24), was canceled in late 1991 because of shipyard problems; and with the end of the Cold War that year, additional T-AGOS construction was canceled. The Navy's 30-year shipbuilding plan presented to Congress in 2003 had indicated the construction of eight advanced ocean surveillance ships to be authorized in Fiscal Years 2013–23; however, no characteristics for those ships were revealed. Subsequently, they were deleted from Navy planning. Into the 2020s, the U.S. Navy operated five civilian-manned SURTASS ships, all in the Pacific area:

T-AGOS 19 *Victorious*
T-AGOS 20 *Able*
T-AGOS 21 *Effective*
T-AGOS 22 *Loyal*
T-AGOS 23 *Impeccable*

The U.S. ocean surveillance ships generally have operated without interference. However, on 8 March 2009, five Chinese ships and fishing trawlers surrounded the *Impeccable* as she was operating 75 n.miles south of Hainan Island in the South China Sea. It was reported that at the time she was conducting hydrographic surveys related to China's ballistic submarine base at Yulin. After the Chinese ordered the ship to leave the area or "suffer the consequences," for several days Chinese ships and aircraft hounded the *Impeccable* and the *Victorious*, which was operating in the Yellow Sea some 170 n.miles off the Chinese coast. On 12 March the

Photo 25. The *Victorious* (T-AGOS 19), a civilian-manned U.S. Navy ocean surveillance ship, was configured to deploy very long acoustic arrays to collect intelligence on foreign submarines. The United States, Japan, and China have built small waterplane-area twin hull (SWATH)–configured ships for that role. / U.S. Navy.

U.S. destroyer *Chung-Hoon* (DDG 93) was dispatched to the South China Sea to support the surveillance ship operations.

All of the U.S. ships safely departed the area. A Chinese official responded to an American protest of the Chinese actions, stating that the complaint that Chinese vessels had harassed the *Impeccable* was "totally inaccurate."

The Soviet Navy also developed towed acoustic arrays both tactical for warships and for area surveillance. Little has been revealed about the latter's characteristics or towing ships. However, in 1982 the British submarine *Conqueror* "snipped" and retrieved a Soviet array towed by a Polish ship (see chapter 2).

10

Some Bottom Lines

Ships and small craft have collected intelligence about enemies, afloat and ashore, for thousands of years. In the last century, intelligence collection has increasingly been gained from electronic emissions: radio, radar, telemetry, and sonar. Exploiting electronic phenomena has led to the development of specialized intercept equipment that at first was provided in existing ships—naval and, in a few instances, commercial—and then installed in specialized spy ships and to a limited extent in submarines.

Although the subsequent development of aircraft and satellites have become highly effective spy platforms, surface ships and submarines have continued to prove valuable in intelligence collection roles. The specialized surface ships as well as the submarines employed to collect intelligence have varied in size, shape, configuration, and capabilities. Significantly, after disposing of the specialized AGER and AGTR platforms, the U.S. Navy continued to use surface ships—primarily destroyers—fitted for electronic surveillance. For example, in the early 1980s, the Navy deployed the destroyers *Caron* (DD 970) and *Deyo* (DD 989) as intelligence collectors off the Pacific coasts of El Salvador and Nicaragua. Their principal role was to monitor radio traffic with a special effort to glean information on arms shipments to anti-government guerrillas.[1]

During the 45 years of the Cold War (1945–91), the Soviet Union and the United States sent large numbers of spy ships to sea. Those surface ships and submarines often penetrated the other nation's territorial waters to bring back intelligence and, at times, artifacts

Photo 26. The Bal'zam-class AGI *Lira* underway in the Mediterranean in 1985. Soviet/ Russian intelligence collection ships have sailed in almost all ocean areas but particularly near NATO naval bases and in their naval operating areas. Some ships were fitted with short-range, air-defense missiles and rapid-fire Gatling guns. / U.S. Navy.

from the opponent's weapons tests. On several occasions, both nations harassed their opponents' spy ships and submarines; however, neither of the two superpowers carried out "significant attacks."

Of note, during that period the Soviet Union also was able to employ its large, state-run fishing, merchant, and research fleets for intelligence collection. Those ships sailed on all the world's seas in their peaceful roles but always were on the alert for information of possible value to the state's intelligence organs. At times they embarked intelligence specialists. Further, a principal mission of the research fleet has been to provide direct support to submarine operations with oceanographic and environmental data, and with seafloor mapping.

In that same period, the United States used surface ship intelligence operations to a large degree in Third World areas. Those ships sought information on communist states, especially North Korea and North Vietnam, and on communist, guerrilla, and other anti-government activities in Central and South America, the Middle East, and Africa.

Both the Soviet Union and the United States also have operated large numbers of space events support ships as part of their respective space programs. Those ships have spied on foreign space operations and, on occasion, have been able to collect military-related intelligence because of their comprehensive electronic suites and far-ranging operations. Of course, dedicated spy ships—such as the American AGTR types—periodically have been tasked with monitoring foreign space activities.

Several other nations have operated intelligence ships; especially notable have been those of China, Norway, and Japan—all of which border Russian territory. A few other countries have operated "ones and twos." The single Argentine ship in that role, the fishing trawler *Narwal*, was noteworthy for being the only spy ship sunk in combat when she became a victim of British forces during the 1982 Falklands conflict.

Submarines have been effective as spy ships because of their ability to operate clandestinely in foreign seas. However, the submarines' limited antenna arrays, their need to remain submerged to avoid detection, and other factors have limited their effectiveness in that role. On the plus side of the ledger, submarines have been able to carry out missions that were not possible with surface ships, such as the USS *Halibut* locating and photographing the wreckage of the Soviet submarine *K-129* and HMS *Conqueror*'s snagging a towed acoustic array from a Polish trawler.

The United States and Soviet Union/Russia also have employed several specialized submersibles in the intelligence role. Those craft have been supported and launched at sea from surface ships and from submarines. While the early U.S. craft and some of the later Soviet/Russian craft were manned, there has been increasing interest in unmanned submersibles. Although unmanned "vehicles" are limited in their collection capabilities, they do have valuable attributes such as being able to operate in areas too dangerous or not otherwise suitable for manned undersea craft. In some situations, the launching (manned) submarine can communicate with the deployed "drone," receiving data and issuing new instructions. This opens a new concept of intelligence collection, especially for submarines.[2]

Following the Israeli attack on the *Liberty* and the North Korean seizure of the *Pueblo*, the United States discarded its specialized intelligence collection ships except for the towed-array SURTASS ships (T-AGOS). Beyond relying on aircraft, satellites, submarines, and ground intercept stations for intelligence collection, the United States uses surface warships with SLQ-32 electronic warfare systems and other electronic intercept equipment manned by specialized personnel for collection efforts.

In contrast, Russia still operates dedicated AGIs as do several other countries, albeit in small numbers. From a Cold War peak of possibly 65 dedicated intelligence collection ships when the Soviet regime collapsed in 1991, by the 2020s just over a dozen Russian ships—all purpose-built ships with on-board analysis as well as collection capabilities—were sailing in the AGI role. All of those ships were fitted with minimal self-defense weapons—light guns and point-defense missiles.

Several other nations continue to operate small numbers of specialized intelligence collection ships of both the AGI and AGOS types. Of course, many nations—including Russia and the United States—also continue to employ submarines on spy missions. However, the sobriquet "spy ships" is most accurately applied to the specialized intelligence collection ships sent to sea by the Soviet Union/Russia and the United States during the Cold War and after.

APPENDIX A
Soviet/Russian Spy Ships

6 Miscellaneous Ships: Temporary Service

Name	Completed	Converted	Deactivated
Pchela	1936	1951	after 1958
Irtek	1942	1951	1956
Rulevaya	1945	1952	1955
Bystraya	1932	1953	1958
Kerzhinets	1945	1953	1960
GS-236		1972	1977

These craft were converted for service as intelligence collection ships in the Far East, assigned to the Pacific Fleet, and based at Vladivostok.

Pchela: Small sailing craft with a crew of three plus a warrant officer commanding.

Irtek: U.S.-built Lend-Lease, wood-hull submarine chaser; launched in 1942 as the *PC-646* and reclassified as the *SC-646* in 1943. She displaced 148 tons, was 110 feet long, and had a crew of 23.

She was transferred to the Soviet Union in May 1945, designated *BO-310*, and participated in the conquest of Japanese-occupied South Sakhalin Island in August 1945. The Soviet Navy reclassified her as *Rkk-1483* in July 1950. She was converted into an AGI in 1951 and named *Irtek*. She made one deployment outside the Sea of Japan prior to deactivation.

Rulevaya: A 120-ton ship that made one out-of-area deployment as an intelligence collector.

Bystraya: Japanese-built, 52-ton fishing boat that was transferred to the Soviet Union in 1945 as war reparations. She made one out-of-area deployment prior to deactivation in 1958.

Kerzhinets: Japanese-built, 70-ton fishing boat also was transferred to the Soviet Union as war reparations. She made one out-of-area deployment prior to deactivation in 1960.

GS-236: A 152-ton Japanese fishing trawler that was confiscated in 1971 for fishing in waters claimed by the Soviet Union. She was converted into a SIGINT collection ship and made one out-of-area operational deployment before being discarded.

13 Ships: SRT-400-Type Loggers

Number	Name	Commissioned	Converted	Deactivated
	Argun	16 September 1952	24 November 1975	
	Krab	1953		
	Giroskop (ex-*Neyva*)	1953	1955	1969
	Bui (ex-*Saiga*)	1953	1956	
GS-42	*Andoma*	April 1954		
GS-46	*Kerchum*			1973
	Ritsa	1954		December 1961
	Ugor	1954		
GS-34	*Ungo*	9 May 1955	1955	1972
GS-36	*Atlas*	17 December 1956	1958	October 1972
GS-1		December 1956		1980
GS-2		December 1956		1980
GS-59		17 December 1956	1957	

Builders: Stralsund VEB; Neptun, Rostock; and Rosslauer, Rosslau (all East Germany)
Displacement: 380 tons full load
Length: 129 ft (39.35 m)
Beam: 24 ft (7.3 m)
Draft: 10 ft 3 in (3.1 m)
Propulsion: diesel; 400 horsepower; 1 shaft
Endurance: 30 days
Speed: 9 knots
Complement: 33

East German shipyards constructed more than 200 of these small, steel-hull loggers/trawlers in the early 1950s. Grouped under the category "loggers," at least 13 of these small ships were converted into intelligence collection ships. They were the first major class of dedicated Soviet AGIs.

Up to July 1956, the ships were identified as general naval auxiliaries and thereafter as "messenger ships." With a normal endurance measured in days, the availability of logistics support from fishing fleet ships off the U.S. coasts (Grand Banks and Alaska), in the Mediterranean, and in other areas enabled deployments measured in months.

Design: Their design was marginal in speed, endurance, and space for the intelligence role. Their dimensions, tonnage, machinery, and speed varied by building yard.

They were fitted with masts and sails to augment their diesel propulsion.

Operational: The *Ungo* was taken under fire by a North Korean patrol craft when 30 n.miles off the Korean coast on the night of 28/29 December 1959. One sailor was killed and two injured. The attacker was an SO-1 anti-submarine craft that the Soviet Union had transferred to North Korea in the mid-1950s.

1 Ship: Dry Cargo Type (Project 229)

Number	Name	Commissioned	Converted	Deactivated
	Anemometr (ex-*Kerby*)	20 November 1953	1953–54	July 1967

Builders: Shipyard No. 368, Khabarovsk
Displacement: 228 tons standard
Length: 152 ft (46.36 m) overall
Beam: 26 ft 6 in (8.07 m)
Draft: 10 ft 7 in (3.24 m)
Propulsion: diesel; 1 shaft
Speed: 9.8 knots
Complement: 16
Guns: 2 14.5-mm or 12.7-mm machine guns (twin)

From her completion until 20 November 1953, this small dry cargo ship went by the name *Akademik Bakh*. On that date, she was commissioned into the Pacific Fleet as the AGI *Kerby* and later renamed *Anemometr*.

In July 1967, the *Kerby/Anemometr* was decommissioned and subsequently employed as a training ship at Vladivostok.

Operational: On 24 June 1966, the *Anemometr* collided with the USS *Banner* (AKL 25, later AGER 1) in international waters south of Vladivostok. That was one of the first collisions on record between U.S. and Soviet naval ships (see chapter 7).

The *Kerby/Anemometr* made six out-of-area deployments prior to July 1967.

2 Ships: Belek-Type Seal Hunters (Project 220)

Number	Name	Commissioned	Converted	Deactivated
	Bulak	June 1957	1958	October 1964
	Vazuza	June 1957	1958	1964

Builders: Oy Laivateollisuus, Turku (Finland)
Displacement: 659 tons full load
Length: 133 ft (40.5 m) overall
Beam: 30 ft 6 in (9.3 m)
Draft: 12 ft 8 in (3.9 m)
Propulsion: diesel; 320 horsepower; 1 shaft
Speed: 8 knots
Complement: 37
Guns: none

Two of the 72 wooden-hull Belek-type seal hunters built in Finland from 1953 to 1957 were converted into Soviet intelligence collection ships. As AGIs they were underpowered with limited autonomy.

Both ships were assigned to the Baltic Fleet and operated in the North Sea and Mediterranean. The *Bulak* was transferred to the reserve fleet in 1964; she then was reactivated in 1969 as a degaussing ship. In the latter role, she was renamed *Vizier* and remained in service until at least 1980. The *Vazuza* was transferred to Algeria in 1964.

Design: These ships had small sails that could be used in an emergency and on long transits to marginally increase their speed.

5 Ships: Ermine-Type Pilot Ships (Project 391A)

Number	Name	Commissioned	Converted	Deactivated
GS-4		1958		
	Vekha	1958	ca. 1960	1971
GS-47	*Usash*	16 August 1958	ca. 1961	1973
GS-41		1958	1963	
GS-50		1958	1963	1980

Builders: Sudomekh, Leningrad, and Khabarovsk
Displacement: 430 tons full load
Length: 128 ft 5 in (39.15 m) overall
Beam: 24 ft 2 in (7.36 m)

Draft: 9 ft 8 in (3.0 m)
Propulsion: diesel; 300 horsepower; 1 shaft
Endurance: 30 days
Speed: 9.6 knots
Range: 3,000 n.miles at 7 knots
Complement: 40
Guns: none

The Soviet Navy ordered ten Project 391A ships from the Sudomekh and Khabarovsk Shipyards. All originally were employed as small survey ships, but in the early 1960s, five were converted into AGIs. Very similar to the loggers, these five ships were classified as messenger ships until 8 August 1959, then as small hydrographic survey ships until 1977, and subsequently as reconnaissance/intelligence ships.

About 1980 the *GS-50* was removed from intelligence service and thereafter was employed as a small hydrographic survey ship.

From conversion to deactivation, all ten ships flew the hydrographic ensign and officially were designated as hydrographic ships.

These ships carried sails and occasionally were able to increase their speed by up to two knots by hoisting them.

2 Ships: Bologoe-Type Refrigerated Trawlers (Project 395)

Number	Name	Commissioned	Converted	Deactivated
GS-55	*Nalim* (*Burbot*)	September 1958	ca. 1963	1991
GS-43	*Okeanograf*	ca. 1957	1965	ca. 1995

Builders: Leninskaya Kuznitsa No. 302, Kiev
Displacement: 532 tons full load
Length: 143 ft (43.6 m) overall
Beam: 25 ft (7.6 m)
Draft: 9 ft 8 in (2.96 m)
Propulsion: diesel; 400 horsepower; 1 shaft
Speed: 10.4 knots
Range: 7,500 n.miles at 8 knots
Complement: 40
Guns: none

The Bologoe-class fishing trawlers offered refrigerated holds for electronic equipment. The *Okeanograf* served as a hydrographic ship until about 1965, when she was converted to the AGI role. She was decommissioned after 1985 and subsequently became a youth training ship.

Photo 27. The *Protraktor* (*pictured*) and her sister ship, *Izmeritel'*, were converted from tuna fishing ships to serve as AGIs. Such conversions from commercial, trawler-type designs were common for the Soviets, in part because of the ready availability of such hulls, their seakeeping characteristics, and, in some, their refrigerated holds that were suitable for electronic equipment. / Authors' collection.

2 Ships: Converted Tuna Fishing Ships

Number	Name	Completed	Decommissioned
	Izmeritel' (ex-*Dnepr*)	1958	7 February 1983
	Protraktor (ex-*Dnester*)	1959	7 February 1983

Builders: Ominachi, Osaka (Japan)
Displacement: 750 tons deadweight; 1,050 tons full load
Length: 171 ft (52.1 m) overall
Beam: 29 ft 6 in (9.0 m)
Draft: 12 ft 8 in (3.9 m)
Propulsion: diesel; 1,000 horsepower; 1 shaft
Speed: 15 knots
Complement: 40
Guns: 2 machine guns

Built as tuna fishing ships, both were converted into AGIs at Vladivostok and operated in the Pacific.

15 Ships: Okean-Class Trawlers

Number	Name	Completed	Converted	Decommissioned
	Teodolit (ex-*Tunets*)	31 July 1959	1959	July 1984
	Krenometr (ex-*Nelma*)	10 August 1959	1959	1984
	Barograf (ex-*Vitim*)	1959	1959	1983
G-165	*Alidada* (ex-*Servruga*)	ca. 1959 ca.	1960	1986
	Repiter (ex-*Forel*)	31 December 1959	1960	1988
	Barometr (ex-*Minoga*)	1960 ca.	1960	1992
	Traverz (ex-*Katun*)	20 April 1960	1960	1986
GS-319	*Lotlin* (ex-*Taymen*)	30 June 1960	1960	30 June 1993
GS-514	*Zond* (ex-*Treska*)		ca. 1960	
	Deflektor (ex-*Golavl*)	31 August 1960	1961	1983
	Reduktor (ex-*Suzan*)	31 August 1960	1960	19 March 1992
	Linza (ex-*Yaz*)	29 December 1960	1960	19 April 1990
	Ampermetr (ex-*Syomga*)	31 January 1961	1961	1983
	Gidrofon (ex-*Gorbusha*)	23 February 1961	1961	ca. 1979
G-199	*Ekholot* (ex-*Nerpa*)	10 August 1959	1963	1989

Builders: Volkswerdt, Stralsund (East Germany)
Displacement: 726 tons full load
Length: 166 ft 8 in (50.8 m) overall
Beam: 28 ft 10 in (8.8 m)
Draft: 11 ft 1 in (3.4 m)
Propulsion: diesel; 540 horsepower; 1 shaft
Speed: 11 knots
Complement: 65
Missiles: 2 quad SA-N-5 or SA-N-8 anti-air launchers [16 missiles]
Guns: 4 14.5-mm machine guns (2 twin)

The Okean class was the largest and thus probably most observed class of early Soviet AGIS.

Photo 28. The AGI *Gidrofon* was employed in the 1960s to track U.S. carrier operations in the Gulf of Tonkin during the Vietnam War. The Okean class was the most numerous type of Soviet intelligence collection ships, with 15 derived from a side-trawler design constructed in East German shipyards. / U.S. Navy.

Design: The ships were converted side trawlers. Their details differ. They retained their trawler arrangement of a tripod mast well forward and a pole mast well aft. Like the loggers, they carried auxiliary sailing gear—staysail and mizzen.

Class: With the demise of the Soviet Union in 1991, the *Barometr* was transferred to Azerbaijan.

Names: Okean is the NATO class name. A Moma-class hydrographic survey ship carried the name *Okean*; she was converted in 1989 into an AGI.

1 Ship: Former Transport

Number	Name	Built	Converted	Decommissioned
	Magnit	1947	1960	1977

Builders: Ganz Hajógyári, Budapest (Hungary)
Displacement: 3,340 tons full load
Length: 270 feet (82.35 m) overall
Beam: 43 ft 7 in (13.3 m)
Draft: 14 ft 3 in (4.35 m)
Propulsion: diesel/electric: 2 diesel engines, 1,210 horsepower/2 electric motors, 1,300 horsepower; 2 shafts
Speed: 11 knots
Complement: 150
Guns: none

This ship was laid down in 1947 as a dry cargo ship for Hungarian service and named *Hungaria*. After her transfer to the Soviet Union, she was renamed *Chiaturi* and employed in the Arctic area.

Converted for intelligence collection in 1960, she was renamed *Magnit* and assigned to the Black Sea Fleet.

5 Ships: Mirnyy-Class Whalers (Project 393A)

Number	Name	Commissioned	Deactivated
CCB-405	*Vertikal* (ex-*Shchuka*)	30 September 1964	1989
CCB-403	*Val* (ex-*Skumbrija*)	27 February 1965	1989
CCB-404	*Lotsman* (ex-*Kasatka*)	9 May 1965	19 April 1990
CCB-402	*Bakan* (ex-*Beluga*)	31 July 1965	19 April 1990

Builders: 61 Kommuna, Nikolayev
Displacement: 1,278 tons full load
Length: 208 ft 8 in (63.6 m) overall
Beam: 31 ft 2 in (9.5 m)
Draft: 14 ft 5 in (4.4 m)
Propulsion: diesel/electric: 4 diesel engines/2 electric motors; 3,100 horsepower; 1 shaft
Speed: 17 knots
Complement: 80
Missiles: 2 quad SA-N-5 or SA-N-8 anti-air launchers [16 missiles]
Guns: none

These converted whalers were easily identified by their high "notched" bows (for a harpoon gun). Their details varied.

A system for receiving signals from hydroacoustic buoys (MG-

409) and equipment for detecting a submarine's thermal wake (MI-110K) were installed on the *Vertikal* in 1967.

Design: New deckhouses were fitted between the superstructure and foremast in the early 1970s to provide additional intelligence equipment and working spaces.

Names: Before their conversion for reconnaissance missions, these ships carried "fish" names but were renamed with "technical" ones upon conversion.

3 Ships: Zubov-Class Survey Ships (Project 850M)

Number	Name	Commissioned	Deactivated
CCB-468	*Gavril Sarychev* (ex-*Losos'*)	30 June 1965	19 March 1992
CCB-503	*Khariton Laptev*	26 December 1965	1989
CCB-469	*Semyen Chelyushkin*	31 October 1966	30 June 1993

Builders: Adolf Warski, Szczecin (Poland)
Displacement: 2,460 tons standard; 3,240 tons full load
Length: 294 ft 3 in (89.7 m) overall
Beam: 42 ft 11 in (13.0 m)
Draft: 15 ft 9 in (4.8 m)
Propulsion: 2 diesels; 4,800 horsepower; 2 shafts
Speed: 16.5 knots
Range: 13,500 n.miles at 14 knots
Complement: 127
Missiles: 3 quad SA-N-5 or SA-N-8 anti-air launchers [24 missiles]
Guns: none

These ships were purpose-built as AGIs although they originally were labeled as oceanographic ships as an operational disguise, first being called expeditionary oceanographic ships and after 1977 labeled as oceanographic research ships.

Class: Eight additional ships of this class served as oceanographic research ships in the Soviet Navy.

Design: The Zubov-class ships were notable for their seakeeping abilities and the comfort of their accommodations.

The *Gavril Sarychev* was extensively reconstructed with her forecastle deck extended to the stern and an additional level added to her superstructure. The others had a small, raised platform aft, which was not a helicopter deck.

Electronics: Fitted with Pamyat' and Bronza sonars.

Photo 29. The *Khariton Laptev* loitering off the coast of Florida in July 1970, awaiting the test launch of a Poseidon missile by a U.S. submarine. Soviet/Russian AGIs performed intelligence collection against Western naval bases and missile tests, as well as operational forces. / U.S. Navy.

8 Ships: Mayak-Class Trawlers (Project 502)

Number	Name	Commissioned	Deactivated
CCB-415	*Kurs*	25 November 1965	1993
	Aneroyd (ex-*Sudak*)	1966	1989
	Kursograf (ex-*Kit*)	1966	1988
GS-536	*Girorulevoy* (ex-*Anadyr*)	9 January 1967	12 July 1994
GS-242	(ex-*Karas*)	10 January 1968	30 June 1993
CCB-408	*GS-239*	12 January 1968	1995
CCB-411	*Ladoga*	10 January 1969	24 October 1993
	Khersones	30 October 1969	17 July 1997

Builders: Leninskaya Kuznitsa, Kiev, Yaroslavl
Displacement: 912 tons full load
Length: 177 ft 9 in (54.2 m) overall
Beam: 30 ft 6 in (9.3 m)
Draft: 11 ft 9 in (3.6 m)
Propulsion: diesel; 800 horsepower; 1 shaft
Speed: 12 knots
Complement: 75
Missiles: 2 quad SA-N-5 or SA-N-8 anti-air launchers [16 missiles]
Guns: 4 14.5-mm machine guns in *Kursograf* (twin)

These ships were former side trawlers converted to AGIs. The Mayak class was a reversion to the concept of a small intelligence ship with limited speed and of marginal utility for open-ocean missions.

Armament: The *Kursograf* was fitted with two 14.5 mm twin gun mounts in 1980; they later were removed.

Class: More than 100 Mayak-class trawlers were built in the 1960s. In addition to AGIs, several were converted to naval supply ships and to anti-submarine training ships.

Design: Details vary. The *Girorulevoy* had a flat-topped radome fitted above the bridge, the *Khersones* had a wider main deckhouse, the *Ladoga* had a separate structure forward of the bridge and a third lattice mast, and the *Kurs* had a tall deckhouse on the stern. The deckhouse forward of the bridge varied in length as did their mast configurations.

Names: Mayak is the NATO class name for this design. The Soviet ship named *Mayak* was a naval hydrographic survey ship of the Melitopol class.

Operational: The *Kursograf* was decommissioned in 1988 and became a training ship; the *Kurs* became a refrigerated transport, renamed *Alaska*; and the *Girorulevoy* became the dry cargo ship *Viking*.

2 Ships: Converted Salvage Tugs (Project 2030)

Number	Name	Commissioned	Converted	Deactivated
CCB-477	*Peleng* (ex-*Pamir*)	1958	1966	1985
CCB-480	*Gidrograf* (ex-*Arban*)	1958	1966	1984

Builders: Gävle (Sweden)
Displacement: 2,050 tons
Length: 255 ft 11 in (78.0 m) overall

Photo 30. The *Gidrograf* was one of two AGIs converted from ocean-going tugs. Their amidships structure was built up to provide space for intercept specialists and equipment. Their 17-knot speeds made them viable for tracking naval forces. In various official documents, they often were listed as both survey ships and tugs. / U.S. Navy.

Beam: 42 ft (12.8 m)
Draft: 13 ft 2 in (4.0 m)
Propulsion: 2 diesels; 4,200 horsepower; 2 shafts
Speed: 17 knots
Range: 15,000 n.miles
Complement: 77
Missiles: 3 quad SA-N-5 or SA-N-8 anti-air launchers [24 missiles]
Guns: none

These salvage tugs were converted to AGI configurations with their superstructures enlarged. After their conversion, they were labeled hydrographic ships as a deception.

With their great range and the ability to support as many as 120 personnel, these ships represented the first iteration of the second generation of Soviet spy ships. A speed of 17 knots also differentiated these ships from earlier AGIs, enabling them to keep pace with foreign warships under cruising conditions.

1 Ship: Valdai-Class Rescue Ship (Project 532)

Number	Name	Commissioned	Deactivated
	Gidrolog (ex-*Zubatka*)	1966	1977

Builders: Srednevsky, Leningrad
Displacement: 852 full load
Length: 235 ft 5 in (71.75 m) overall
Beam: 31 ft 10 in (9.7 m)
Draft: 8 ft 3 in (2.52 m)
Propulsion: diesel; 4,000 horsepower; 2 shafts
Speed: 18 knots
Complement: 66
Guns: none

Of ten Project 532 "rescue ships" built from 1960 to 1963, one was converted into an intelligence ship; she originally was commissioned on 12 May 1961 as the *SS-51* and later named the *Zubatka*. In 1966 she was renamed the *Gidrolog* and modified into an intelligence collection ship; she flew the hydrographic ensign as deception.

6 Ships: Primor'ye Class (Projects 394B/994)

Number	Name	Commissioned	Deactivated
CCB-465	*Primor'ye*	13 December 1969	17 December 1994
CCB-590	*Krym*	December 1969	21 February 1997
CCB-591	*Kavkaz*	30 June 1970	9 October 1997
CCB-464	*Zabaykal'ye*	March 1971	30 June 1993
CCB-501	*Zaporozh'ye* (Proj. 994)	9 December 1971	8 September 1997
CCB-502	*Zakarpat'ye* (Proj. 994)	8 May 1972	30 June 1993

Builders: Chernomorsky, Nikolayev
Displacement: 2,900 tons standard; 4,340 tons full load
Length: 277 ft 6 in (84.6 m) overall
Beam: 46 ft 8 in (14.2 m)
Draft: 23 ft 7 in (7.2 m)
Propulsion: diesel; 2,000 horsepower; 1 shaft
Speed: 12.5 knots
Range: 13,000 n.miles at 10 knots
Complement: 150
Missiles: 2 quad SA-N-5 Grail anti-air launchers [16 missiles] on the *Zabaykal'ye*, *Zaporozh'ye*, and *Kavkaz*; 1 quad SA-N-10 Grouse anti-air launcher [8 missiles] after 1983 on the *Krym*
Guns: none

The design of this class was directed by the Soviet military intelligence organization (GRU), not the Navy, and incorporated capabilities to meet national intelligence requirements as well as naval requirements. The ships had large, distinctive "box" deckhouses to house electronic equipment forward and aft on their main superstructure.

Design: These ships were based on a highly successful, Soviet-built, Mayakovskiy-class, stern trawler–factory ships. More than 200 ships of that design were built, with several being modified to civilian research ships.

In their AGI configuration, the ships had distinctive superstructures with up to three antenna masts, while some ships retained the trawler kingpost aft (i.e., a total of four masts).

The first four ships were Project 394B; the latter two were Project 994.

Electronics: The CCB-501 had a large, three-face, phased-array radar mounted on a small, tall deckhouse in the after position (similar to the U.S. AN/SPQ-11 Cobra Judy radar). The ship was employed to monitor U.S. missile tests.

Fitted with Bronza sonar.

12 Ships: Moma-Class Trawlers (Project 861M)

Number	Name	Commissioned	Converted	Decommissioned
CCB-512	*Arkhipelag*	30 June 1968	1968	5 July 1994
CCB-509	*Pelorus*	31 May 1969	1969	30 June 1993
CCB-406	*Kildin*	23 May 1970	1970	Active
CCB-506	*Nakhodka*	10 August 1970	1970	3 March 1998
CCB-514	*Selinger*	31 March 1971	1971	30 June 1993 (sunk)
CCB-472	*Il'men* (ex-GS-117)	31 March 1972	1972	30 June 1993
CCB-474	*Vega*	18 August 1973	1975	August 1995
CCB-418	*Ekvator*	31 October 1968	1976	Active
CCB-416	*Jupiter*	28 June 1973	1976	to Ukraine 1995
	Rybachiy	30 August 1969	1989	17 July 1997
CCB-409	*Okean*	16 September 1970	1989	2 January 2000
CCB-413	*Liman*	23 December 1970	1989	27 April 2017 (sunk)

Photo 31. The Moma-class intelligence collector *Selinger* looking clean and pristine in this 1986 photo. The configurations of these ships differed, with some having cranes forward of the bridge and their forward mast positions varying. The antennas of AGIS differed, depending upon their size, configuration, and mission. /U.S. Navy.

Builders: Stocznia Polnocny, Gdansk (Poland)
Displacement: 1,080 tons standard; 1,560 tons full load
Length: 240 ft 5 in (73.3 m) overall
Beam: 35 ft 4 in (11.2 m)
Draft: 12 ft 9½ in (3.9 m)
Propulsion: 2 diesels; 3,600 horsepower; 2 shafts
Speed: 17 knots
Complement: 85
Missiles: 2 quad SA-N-5 or SA-N-8 [16 missiles] in some ships
Guns: none

This design was developed for hydrographic survey ships and buoy tenders. About 30 ships were built to this design, with 12 converted into intelligence ships. This class of two-shaft trawler AGIS largely replaced the single-shaft, logger-type AGIS.

All but two ships were decommissioned by 2000. One ship was transferred to the newly independent Ukraine in 1995.

The *Selinger* sank beside the pier in Kola Bay in 1996 due to neglect.

Design: The ships varied considerably in details. Some retained their buoy-handling cranes forward. Others had a low deckhouse of varying length between the superstructure and the forward mast, whose positions differed in height and configuration.

Electronics: Provided with Bronza sonar. The *Jupiter* was refitted with a large radome on her fantail.

4 Ships: Bal'zam-Class (Project 1826)

Number	Name	Completed	Deactivated
CCB-516	*Lira*	18 February 1980	8 September 1997
CCB-493	*Aziya*	13 February 1981	30 May 1998
CCB-80	*Pribaltika*	July 1984	Active
CCB-463	*Belomor'ye*	7 February 1987	Active

Builders: Yantar, Kaliningrad
Displacement: 3,250 tons standard; 5,400 tons full load
Length: 346 ft 2 in (105.5 m) overall
Beam: 50 ft 10 in (15.5 m)
Draft: 18 ft 4 in (5.6 m)
Propulsion: 2 diesels; 9,000 horsepower; 2 shafts
Speed: 18.5 knots
Range: 10,000 n.miles at 14 knots
Complement: 188
Missiles: 2 quad SA-N-5 or SA-N-8 anti-air launchers [16 missiles]
Guns: 1 30-mm/65-cal. AK-630 (multibarrel)

These ships were among the largest and most capable AGIs in Soviet service. Two ships remained in commission when this book went to press. Work to recommission and update the electronics suite of the *Belomor'ye* was ongoing in 2020.

Design: The Bal'zam class was the first Soviet ship type designed specifically for the intelligence collection role from the keel up. They were fitted with two large, spherical radomes housing satellite communication antennas. They also had significant at-sea replenishment facilities to permit them to provide supplies and fuel to other ships.

Electronics: Fitted with Pamyat' and Uzh sonars.

Engineering: This design originally provided for gas-turbine-electric drive, which would have provided a maximum speed of 30 knots. As the turbines were not available, diesel engines were provided with a reduction in speed.

Photo 32. The Al'pinist-class *Syzran*, shown in her earlier configuration as the GS-39. This modified stern trawler class was readily identified by the large, amidships bipod mast laden with antennas. This ship later was modified to provide improved intelligence collection facilities and seakeeping. / Royal Netherlands Navy.

4 Ships: Al'pinist-Class Trawlers (Project 503R)

Number	Name	Commissioned	Deactivated
CCB-317	*Syzran* (ex-*GS-39*)	3 February 1981	Active
CCB-739	*GS-7*	16 August 1981	3 December 2005
	GS-8	26 December 1981	5 July 1994
CCB-314	*Zhigulevsk* (ex-*GS-19*)	8 January 1983	Active

Builders: Yaroslavl, Kiev (*GS-8*, *GS-19*, *GS-39*); Volgograd (*GS-7*)
Displacement: 1,238 tons full load
Length: 176 ft 2 in (53.7 m) overall
Beam: 35 ft 2 in (10.72 m)
Draft: 14 ft 1 in (4.3 m)
Propulsion: diesel; 1,320 horsepower; 1 shaft

Speed: 12.6 knots
Complement: 24
Missiles: 1 quad SA-N-5 or SA-N-8 anti-air launcher [8 missiles]
Guns: none

These ships are modified stern trawlers fitted with a bow thruster and configured for the AGI role. The *GS-39*, first seen in 1981, was rebuilt in 1986–87; her forecastle was extended and new electronic intercept equipment installed.

Class: Several hundred stern trawlers of this type were built for the Soviet fishing fleet. Five ships were completed as civilian research ships for operation by the Ministry of Fisheries, and at least one served as a naval trials ship (designated *OS-104*).

Names: The *GS-39* was renamed *Syzran* in 2001, and the *GS-19* was renamed *Zhigulevsk* in 2004.

7 Ships: Vishnaya Class (Project 864/864b)

Number	Name	Commissioned	Status
CCB-520	*Fedor Golovin* (ex-*Meridian*)	14 November 1985	Active
CCB-535	*Kareliya*	24 May 1986	Active
CCB-169	*Tavriya*	17 January 1987	Reserve 2000
CCB-201	*Priazov'ye*	12 June 1987	Active
CCB-208	*Kurily*	16 October 1987	Active
CCB-231	*Vasiliy Tatishchev* (ex-*Pelengator*)	23 July 1988	Active
CCB-175	*Viktor Leonov* (ex-*Odograf*)	1988	Active

Builders: Stocznia Polnocny, Gdansk (Poland)
Displacement: 3,100 tons standard; 3,470 tons full load
Length: 300 ft (91.4 m) overall
Beam: 47 ft 11 in (14.6 m)
Draft: 14 ft 9 in (4.5 m)
Propulsion: 2 diesels; 4,400 horsepower; 2 shafts
Speed: 16 knots
Range: 7,000 n.miles at 12.5 knots
Complement: 146
Missiles: 2 quad SA-N-8 or SA-N-10 anti-air launchers [16 missiles]
Guns: 2 30-mm/65-cal. AK-630 (multibarrel)

These ships were among the largest AGIs in Soviet service.

Photo 33. The large AGI *Kurily* underway in the Pacific. Subsequently she was fitted with two large radomes atop her bridge structure (note the two circular base structures in this photo taken in 1988, shortly after her completion). Most ships of the Vishnaya class were believed to still be in service when this volume went to press. / Japan Maritime Self-Defense Force.

Design: This class has a hull that bears resemblance to the similar-size Bal'zam class, but the antenna, mast, and funnel arrangements differ considerably.

Electronics: The early ships began operations with empty mountings for two radomes atop the bridge structure.

Fitted with Pamyat' sonar.

1 Ship: Sorum-Class Seagoing Tug (Project 07452)

Number	Name	Commissioned	Status
	Chusovoy (ex-GS-31)	1987	Active

Builders: Yaroslavl, Yarolsavsky
Displacement: 1,620 tons
Length: 185 ft 4 in (56.5 m) overall

Beam: 41 ft 6 in (12.64 m)
Draft: 14 ft 8 in (4.47 m)
Propulsion: diesel/electric: 2 diesel engines; 2 electric motors, 3,000 horsepower; 2 shafts
Speed: 13 knots
Complement: 36
Guns: none

This tug initially was an experimental ship (designated *OS-572*) designed for testing towed acoustic sensor arrays. Eventually, the ship was transferred to the Black Sea Fleet, designated *GS-31*, and employed as an AGI.

In 2002, after almost ten years of general AGI employment, the *GS-31* completed her first operational deployment as an acoustic intelligence collector in the Norwegian and Barents Seas, and was involved in testing towed acoustic arrays.

Names: Named the *OS-572* from 1987 to May 1998, and *GS-31* from May 1998 to July 2007, she was renamed *Chusovoy* on 29 July 2007.

2 Ships: Bambuk Class (Projects 10221/12884)

Number	Name	Commissioned	Decommissioned
SSV-391	*Kamchatka*	1986	2014
CCB-189	*Slavutich* (ex-*Pridneprov'ye*)	1992	Inactive

Builders: Chernomorsky, Nikolaev
Displacement: 4,460 tons standard; 5,700 tons full load
Length: 347 ft 10 in (106.0 m) overall
Beam: 52 ft 6 in (16.0 m)
Draft: 19 ft 8 in (6.0 m)
Propulsion: diesel; 6,800 horsepower; 2 shafts
Speed: 16.5 knots
Range: 10,000 n.miles at 14 knots
Complement: 140
Helicopters: 2 Ka-27 Helix
Missiles: 2 quad SA-N-8 or SA-N-10 anti-air launchers [16 missiles]
Guns: 2 30-mm/65-cal. AK-630 (multibarrel)

These ships primarily were outfitted for acoustic intelligence. The *Kamchatka* operated in the Pacific Fleet and was considered an intelligence ship by Western intelligence; however, she lacked the large array of intelligence collection antennas seen on other AGIs.

Class: The *Pridneprov'ye* was constructed for Ukraine in 1992–93 and renamed *Slavutich*. The Ukrainian Navy operated her until

Photo 34. The *Kamchatka* was one of two similar AGIs, the only ones to normally embark helicopters (except for the never-operational *Ural*). The ships had an unusual superstructure configuration. The *Kamchatka* and her sister ship, *Slavutich*, were configured primarily for acoustic intelligence collection. / Japan Maritime Self-Defense Force.

1984. With the Russians' seizure of Crimea in March 2014, she came under the control of the Russian Black Sea Fleet. The ship was inactive when this volume went to press.

Design: The *Kamchatka* had an unusual design with a tall, flat-sided pylon mast aft of the bridge and sponsons on the mast support electronic intercept equipment. A large helicopter deck was provided.

Electronics: Fitted with Dnestr sonar.

2 Ships: Yug-Class Hydroacoustics Ships (Project 862)

Number	Name	Commissioned	Converted	Decommissioned
CCB-328	*Yug*	30 September 1977	1985	1998
CCB-704	*Temryuk* (ex-*Mangyshlak*)	7 November 1983	1990	Active

Builders: Stocznia Polnocny, Gdansk (Poland)
Displacement: 1,960 tons standard; 2,500 tons full load
Length: 270 ft 8 in (82.5 m) overall
Beam: 44 ft 4 in (13.5 m)
Draft: 12 ft 9½ in (3.9 m)
Propulsion: 2 diesels; 4,400 horsepower; 2 shafts
Speed: 15.5 knots
Range: 10,000 n.miles at 14 knots
Complement: 70
Guns: 4 12.7-mm machine guns (2 twin)

These ships were converted from two of the 18 similar ships built for oceanographic research. They were configured for employing towed acoustic arrays.

In December 1995, the *Yug* was taken in tow to Severodvinsk for renovation, but it was never begun. In 2000 she was dismantled, and the hulk was converted into an entertainment barge on the Moscow River.

Conversion: The AGI conversion included extending the ships' superstructure aft to provide more berthing and equipment spaces. Positions for two anti-air missile launchers may have been fitted amidships.

Design: Each ship had two 100-kilowatt electric motors for quiet, slow-speed operations and a 300-horsepower bow thruster for precise station keeping.

1 Ship: Titan Class (Project 1941)

Number	Name	Completed	Decommissioned
CCB-33	*Ural*	1990	2005

Builders: Baltic, Leningrad
Displacement: 35,200 tons full load
Length: 869 ft (265.0 m) overall
Beam: 98 ft 5 in (30.0 m)
Draft: 24 ft 7 in (7.5 m)
Propulsion: CONSAS: 4 steam turbines; 46,800 horsepower; 2 shafts
Reactors: 2 pressurized-water type
Boilers: 2
Speed: 21.5 knots
Complement: 925
Helicopters: 1 Ka-27 Helix
Missiles: 4 quad SA-N-10 anti-air launchers
Guns: 2 76.2-mm/59-cal. dual-purpose (single); 4 30-mm/65-cal. close-in AK-630 (multi-barrel); 8 14.5-mm machine guns (4 twin)

Photo 35. The *Yug* was one of two hydroacoustic intelligence ships based on Polish-built oceanographic research ships. She had been scheduled for renovation, but funding was not available in the post-Soviet period. The ship was stripped, and her hulk was converted into an entertainment barge on the Moscow River. / U.S. Navy.

This was the world's largest ship constructed primarily for the intelligence collection role and was the only AGI with nuclear propulsion. A second ship was proposed but not funded.

The *Ural* was laid down in May 1981; she began trials in the Baltic in 1987 and transited to the Far East in 1989. The *Ural* was assigned to the Pacific Fleet and was moored in Vladivostok just prior to the fall of the Soviet Union. She fell into disrepair due to limited maintenance budgets and the need to keep power supplied while anchored in the channel (no piers were suitable for the ship). She never conducted an operational mission, was decommissioned in 2003, and was scrapped in 2008.

Classification: During construction, the ship was given the NATO designation BALAUX-2 (Baltic Auxiliary). Her NATO codename Kapusta means "cabbage" in Russian.

Electronics: In addition to her extensive tracking and communications antennas, the *Ural* had three flat-faced, octagonal antennas that appeared to have been for a phased-array, three-dimensional tracking radar. A fourth, upward-looking array was on the ship's 02 level, starboard side, just forward of the three ship's boats. (Other than AGIs, the only Soviet ships known to have fixed, phased-array radar antennas were the aircraft carrier *Baku* and the carriers of the *Tbilisi* class.)

She also was fitted with Tayfun-2S and Kristall-BK sonars.

Propulsion: The ship had a Combined Nuclear and Steam (CONAS) propulsion plant similar to that of the *Kirov*-class battle cruisers, which were also built by the Baltic Shipyard. The Baltic yard also built the *Arktika*-class nuclear icebreakers.

2+ Ships: *Yuriy Ivanov* Class (Project 18280)

Number	Name	Commissioned	Status
CCB-175	*Yuriy Ivanov*	25 July 2015	Active
	Ivan Khurs	18 June 2018	Active

Builders: Severnaya, St. Petersburg
Displacement: 4,000 tons full load
Length: 315 ft (96.0 m)
Beam: 52 ft 6 in (16.0 m)
Draft: 13 ft 2 in (4.0 m)
Propulsion: 2 diesels; 5,440 horsepower; 2 shafts
Speed: 20 knots
Complement: 120
Missiles: 6 Igla SA-N-10 anti-air launchers [32 missiles]
Guns: 2 14.5-mm machine guns (single)

The *Yuriy Ivanov* was the first intelligence ship built in Russia following the demise of the Soviet Union. The *Ivan Khurs* replaced the *Liman*, which was lost in a collision in 2017.

Additional ships of this design were planned.

APPENDIX B
U.S. Spy Ships

3 Ships: Ex-Liberty Cargo Ships

Number	Name	Commissioned	Converted	Decommissioned
AG 159/ AGTR 1	*Oxford* (ex–*Samuel R. Aitken*)	8 July 1961	1961	19 December 1969
AG 165/ AGTR 2	*Georgetown* (ex–*Robert W. Hart*)	9 November 1963	1963	19 December 1969
AG 166/ AGTR 3	*Jamestown* (ex–*J. Howland Gardner*)	13 December 1963	1963	19 December 1969

Builders: New England Shipbuilding, South Portland, Maine
Displacement: 11,365 tons full load
Length: 441 ft (134.0 m) overall
Beam: 59 ft (18.8 m)
Draft: 22 ft (6.7 m)
Propulsion: triple-expansion reciprocating; 2,500 horsepower; 1 shaft
Boilers: 2
Speed: 11 knots
Complement: 254
Guns: 4 .50-cal. machine guns (single)

These ships were built as cargo ships during World War II. Placed in reserve after the war, they were reactivated in 1960–63 for conversion to technical research ships and renamed. All three ships were decommissioned and stricken from the Navy List on the above date.

Design: Built as ZEC2-S-C5 type Liberty ships.

Designation: Designated as miscellaneous auxiliary (AG) upon conversion to intelligence collection ships; changed to technical research ship (AGTR) on 1 April 1964.

2 Ships: Ex-Victory Cargo Ships

Number	Name	Commissioned	Converted	Decommissioned
AG 167/ AGTR 4	*Belmont* (ex–*Iran Victory*)	2 November 1964	1963–64	16 January 1970
AG 168/ AGTR 5	*Liberty* (ex–*Simmons Victory*)	1 April 1964	1963–64	28 June 1968

Builders: Oregon Shipbuilding, Portland
Displacement: 15,200 tons full load
Length: 455 ft 3 in (138.8 m) overall
Beam: 62 ft (18.9 m)
Draft: 23 ft (7.0 m)
Propulsion: steam turbine; 8,500 horsepower; 1 shaft
Boilers: 2
Speed: 16 knots
Complement: 358
Armament: 4 .50-cal. machine guns (single)

These former World War II–built cargo ships were operated by commercial shipping lines for the government after the war and were laid up in reserve in 1954 and 1958, respectively. The Navy acquired them in February 1963 for conversion to the intelligence collection role.

Design: Built as VC2-S-AP3–type Victory ships.

Designation: Designated as miscellaneous auxiliary (AG), upon conversion to intelligence collection ships; both were changed to technical research ships (AGTR) on 1 April 1964.

2 Ships: Converted Cargo Ships

Number	Name	Converted	Deactivated
T-APC 119/ T-AG 169	*Pvt. Jose F. Valdez*	1961	7 November 1969
T-APC 118/ T-AG 171	*Sgt. Joseph E. Muller*	1962	16 September 1969

Builders: *Valdez*: Walter Butler Shipbuilders, Duluth, Minnesota
Muller: Southeastern Shipbuilding, Savannah, Georgia
Displacement: 7,450 tons full load
Length: 338 ft 6 in (103.15 m) overall
Beam: 50 ft 4 in (15.3 m)

Draft: 21 ft (6.4 m)
Propulsion: diesel; 1,700 horsepower; 1 shaft
Speed: 11.5 knots
Complement: 155
Guns: none

These ships were built in World War II as coastal cargo ships. The Army operated the *Pvt. Jose J. Valdez* until 1947, when she was placed in reserve; the Navy acquired her on 2 September 1950 as the T-APC 119. The *Valdez* was again placed in reserve on 22 December 1959. She subsequently was reactivated and converted in August through November 1961 for the intelligence collection role. The ship was laid up in reserve in 1970 and subsequently scrapped.

The Army operated the *Muller* until 1950, when she was transferred to the Navy and operated as the T-APC 118. She was placed in reserve from 1957 to 1962. In 1962 the *Muller* was reactivated and converted to the intelligence collection role. After being taken out of service in 1969, the ship was scrapped.

Design: Built as C1-M-AV1 type cargo ships.

Designation: Upon conversion for intelligence collection, these ships were designated T-AG, indicating they were civilian manned by the Military Sea Transportation Service.

Names: The *Valdez* was launched as the *Round Splice* and renamed *Joe J. Martinez*.

1 Ship: Converted Aircraft Cargo Ship

Number	Name	Converted	Deactivated
T-AK 274/ T-AG 170	*Lt. James E. Robinson* (ex–*Czechoslovakia Victory*)	1962	June 1964

Builders: Oregon Shipbuilding, Portland
Displacement: 15,589 tons full load
Length: 455 ft (138.7 m) overall
Beam: 62 ft (18.9 m)
Draft: 29 ft 2 in (8.9 m)
Propulsion: steam turbine; 8,500 horsepower; 1 shaft
Boilers: 2
Speed: 16.5 knots
Complement: 100
Guns: none

The *Robinson* was completed in 1944 as an aircraft cargo ship (AKV 3). After World War II, the ship was operated by a commercial firm for the government in 1946–47. Acquired by the Army in 1947 and named *Lt. James E. Robinson*, the ship was transferred to the Navy's MSTS in May 1950 as the AKV 3. She was changed to AK 274 in May 1959.

The *Robinson* was converted into an intelligence collection ship in January 1962 and designated as a miscellaneous auxiliary (T-AG) in December 1962. The ship served in that role for 29 months. With the termination of her intelligence-related service, the *Robinson* was reclassified T-AK 274 on 1 July 1964 and resumed cargo operations.

The *Robinson* was placed in reserve on 17 March 1976, stricken from the Navy List on 16 January 1981, and subsequently scrapped.

Design: Built as a VC2-S-AP3 type Victory ship.

2 Ships: Converted Light Cargo Ships

Number	Name	Commissioned	Converted	Decommissioned
T-AKL 25/ AGER 1	*Banner*	24 November 1952	1965	14 November 1969
T-AKL 44/ AGER 2	*Pueblo*	13 May 1967	1966–67	See notes

Builders: Kewaunee Shipbuilding and Engineering, Kewaunee, Wisconsin
Displacement: 895 tons full load
Length: 176 ft 6 in (53.8 m) overall
Beam: 32 ft (9.8 m)
Draft: 9 ft 3 in (2.8 m)
Propulsion: 2 diesels; 1,000 horsepower; 2 shafts
Speed: 12 knots
Complement: 83
Guns: 2 .50-cal. machine guns (single)

Operated by the Army Transport Service from 1944 to 1950 as the FS 345. The Navy acquired the ship on 1 July 1950 and placed her in MSTS service as the T-AKL 25. Then she was placed in commission and named *Banner* in 1952.

The *Pueblo* was laid up in 1954 after Army service. She was transferred to the Navy on 12 April 1966, named *Pueblo*, and designated T-AKL 44.

Design: These ships were built for the Army as small freight and supply (FS) ships.

Designation: They were designated by Navy as light cargo ships (AKL) until their conversion to intelligence collection ships, with the *Banner* redesignated as an environmental research ship (AGER) on 1 June 1967 and the *Pueblo* on 14 May 1967.

Operational: Although North Korea seized the *Pueblo* on 23 January 1968, she remains listed as a commissioned U.S. Navy ship on the Naval Vessel Register.

1 Ship: Converted Light Cargo Ship

Number	Name	Commissioned	Converted	Decommissioned
AKL 45/ AGER 3	*Palm Beach*	13 May 1967	1966–67	1 December 1969

Builders: Higgins Industries, New Orleans
Displacement: 938 tons full load
Length: 179 ft 10 in (54.8 m) overall
Beam: 32 ft (9.75 m)
Draft: 9 ft 3 in (2.8 m)
Propulsion: 2 diesels; 1,000 horsepower; 2 shafts
Speed: 12 knots
Complement: 83
Guns: 4 20-mm (2 twin) cannon

This ship was delivered to the Army in December 1944, converted to a repair ship, and named the *Col. Armond Peterson*. The ship was placed in reserve in 1956. The Navy acquired her on 18 May 1966 and commissioned her as the *Palm Beach* (AKL 45).

Design: The ship was built for the Army as a small coastal freight and supply ship.

Designation: Designated by the Navy as light cargo ship, she was changed to AGER on 2 May 1967 upon her conversion to an intelligence collection ship.

Operational: After her decommissioning and being stricken on 1 December 1969, the ex–*Palm Beach* was sold to a private owner. She then was resold to a Panamanian company and renamed *Oro Verde*. The *Oro Verde* was involved in drug smuggling and ran aground in the Cayman Islands.

1 Ship: Landing Craft Repair Ship

Number	Name	Commissioned	Status
LST 963/ARL 24	*Sphinx*	10 May 1945	stricken 2 December 2002

Builders: Bethlehem-Hingham Shipyard, Hingham, Massachusetts
Displacement: 1,781 tons light; 3,960 tons full load
Length: 328 ft (100.0 m) overall
Beam: 50 ft (15.3 m)
Draft: 11 ft 2 in (3.4 m)
Propulsion: 2 diesels; 1,800 horsepower; 2 shafts
Speed: 11.6 knots
Complement: 250 (as ARL)
Guns: 8 40-mm guns (4 twin); 6 .50-cal. machine guns (single)

The *LST 963* was launched in November 1944. She was immediately converted to a landing craft repair ship named *Sphinx* and commissioned as the ARL 24 in 1945.

Armament: As built, one 3-inch/50-caliber anti-aircraft gun was fitted in addition to the 40-mm weapons.

Design: This ship was built as an *LST 542*–class tank landing ship.

Operational: She was placed in reserve on 26 May 1947, recalled for the Korean War on 3 November 1950, and returned to reserve on 31 January 1956. The ship again was reactivated on 16 December 1967 for the Vietnam War. She was returned to reserve on 30 September 1971 and was stricken from the Navy List on 16 April 1977.

The *Sphinx* was reactivated and placed in the Puget Sound Naval Shipyard for conversion to an intelligence collection ship in 1984 and recommissioned on 26 July 1985. She was again laid up in the reserve fleet on 15 June 1990. She was stricken from the Navy List in 2002 and subsequently scrapped.

6 Ships: Tank Landing Ships

Number	Name	Commissioned	Decommissioned	Status
LST 1179	*Newport*	7 June 1969	1 October 1992	to Mexico in 2001; stricken 13 July 2001
LST 1181	*Sumter*	20 June 1970	30 September 1993	to Taiwan in 1995; stricken 23 July 2002

Photo 36. The *Barnstable County* (LST 1197) shown during her 1982 Smokey Topaz cruise into Arctic waters on an intelligence collection operation. Her bow "horns" held a ramp to provide a hull configuration that enabled the LST to reach a speed of 20 knots. / U.S. Navy.

LST 1193	*Fairfax County*	16 October 1971	17 August 1994	to Australia in 1994; stricken 17 August 1994
LST 1194	*La Moure County*	18 December 1971	17 November 2000	stricken 17 November 2000
LST 1196	*Harlan County*	8 April 1972	14 April 1995	to Spain in 1995; stricken 23 July 2002
LST 1197	*Barnstable County*	27 May 1972	29 June 1944	to Spain in 1994; stricken 23 July 2002

Builders: LST 1179, LST 1181: Philadelphia Naval Shipyard; others: National Steel & Shipbuilding, San Diego
Displacement: 4,793 tons light; 8,450 tons full load
Length: 522 ft 2 in (159.2 m) overall
Beam: 69 ft 6 in (21.2 m)
Draft: 17 ft 6 in (5.3 m)
Propulsion: diesels; 16,500 horsepower; 2 shafts
Speed: 22 knots
Complement: 250
Guns: 4 3-inch (76-mm) anti-aircraft (2 twin); 1 20-mm Mark 15 Phalanx (multibarrel) in some ships

During the 1970s and 1980s, the United States employed at least six tank landing ships of the *Newport* class as intelligence collectors in the Barents Sea area. The ships' large tank decks and open main decks provided excellent space for the additional personnel and equipment (see chapter 9).

Armament: These ships were built with four 3-inch/50-caliber guns in twin mounts. Several ships had one mount replaced by the Phalanx close-in gun system, with two guns planned to replace the 3-inch mounts.

Class: Twenty ships of this design were completed from 1969 to 1972. The U.S. Navy discarded the last ships in 2008, with several having gone to other navies.

Design: This design departed from the traditional LST bow-door configuration to a hull design that could achieve a sustained speed of 20 knots. Fitted with bow and stern ramps for loading and unloading tanks and other vehicles, the ships had 17,300 square feet of vehicle storage space and accommodations for approximately 400 troops.

A helicopter landing space was provided on the main deck.

APPENDIX C

Other Spy Ships

Several other countries have employed spy ships. China, Japan, and Norway—all bordering on Soviet/Russian territory—have operated several ships in the intelligence collection role, while other states have employed mostly "ones or twos" in that role.

Only one of those ships is known to have been engaged in combat—the Argentine trawler *Narwal*, sunk by British forces during the Falklands conflict of 1982.

Argentina

Argentine forces invaded the British-owned Falkland Islands in the South Atlantic in April 1982. Britain's response was to dispatch a naval task force to recapture the islands.[1] That force included an aircraft carrier, surface warships, and nuclear-propelled submarines.[2] During the ten-week conflict, the Argentines dispatched aircraft and a spy ship—the fishing trawler *Narwal*—to reconnoiter the British forces.

When the British task force arrived off the Falklands, the *Narwal* was in the area. The British declared a "total exclusion zone," advising that any ships found in that area could be attacked. As the British warships operated off the Falklands, Admiral Sandy Woodward, commanding the British forces, recalled one of his action officers uttering, "It's that bloody fishing trawler again, sir. They just identified it. The *Narwal*, the same one we warned off ten days ago, the night before we arrived in the Zone."[3] The trawler had first encountered the British task force on 29 April and had been "scared off."[4] The trawler persisted in sailing close to the British ships.

Admiral Woodward declared, "Damn it. The last thing I need

is that little toad reporting our *exact* position, night and day, back to his bloody air force." To his action officer, he said, "This boat is full of fisherman—civilians. Be sure of your ground before you blot them out."

The British task force monitored the *Narwal*'s radio transmissions. Having fully established that the *Narwal* was a spy ship, on 9 May, Woodward ordered two carrier-based Harrier aircraft to attack. They had 30-mm cannon and carried 1,000-pound bombs. Fused for high-level bombing, as a Harrier released a 1,000-pounder at low level, it smashed into the ship but failed to detonate. One Argentine crewman was killed. The second Harrier peppered the trawler with cannon fire.

Damaged and immobilized, the trawler was boarded by British special forces who found 12 fishermen and Lieutenant Commander Juan Gonzales Llanos of the Argentine Navy on the ship. The British also found codebooks, charts, military radios, and so forth, and took the crew off the craft. The *Narwal* sank the following day while under tow.

The British had a spy ship—of sorts—the *Endurance*, an ice patrol ship, in the South Atlantic when Argentina seized the Falklands. The ship carried two small Wasp helicopters and was armed with two 20-mm Oerlikon cannon. According to her commanding officer, Captain Nicholas Barker, "HMS *Endurance*'s real weapon was her sigint and electronic listening suite."[5] Her intelligence collection successes—if any—have never been publicly disclosed.

Early in the Falklands conflict, the *Endurance* transmitted on "fake" communications to give the Argentines the impression that British nuclear-propelled submarines had already arrived in the area. Subsequently, the *Endurance* landed Marines on South Georgia Island, which had been captured earlier by a small number of Argentine troops.

Bulgaria

The Bulgarian Navy commissioned the hydrographic ship *401* on 29 March 1976 for intelligence collection. The ship had been converted from a Moma-class hydrographic ship built in Poland. The

401 operated under the direction of Bulgarian State Security until 1986, primarily in the Black Sea. On at least one occasion, the *401* deployed into the Mediterranean for intelligence purposes. In 1986 the *401* was renamed *Admiral Branimir Ormanov*, probably marking the end of the ship's covert employment.

The ship had a crew of 66 and could accommodate about 20 technicians. With the fall of the Soviet Union and the Bulgarian transition away from a communist government, the *Ormanov* reverted to hydrographic, research, and training roles until being decommissioned in 2008.

China

Probably the first dedicated Chinese spy ship was the Type 812, an electronic surveillance ship based on the design of a survey ship. The 1,700-ton ship was launched in 1982 but did not become operational because of severe problems with machinery vibration. (The heavy weight of the propeller positioned at the end of a cantilevered propeller shaft caused that problem.)

Two one-of-a-kind ships followed: First, the Type 841 *Bei-Diao*—a 2,000-ton, 309½-foot ship—was completed in 1986. (The ship was assigned the NATO class name Dadie.) Four such ships were planned, but only the one was delivered because of newer designs in the offing.

Next came the Type 856 *Xing Fengshan*, displacing 5,500 tons with a length of 377⅙ feet, that entered service in 1987. She was based on the design of a submarine rescue ship. Both the *Xing Fengshan* and *Bei-Diao* were armed with machine guns.

After an apparent hiatus of several years in developing SIGINT ships, the Type 815 *Beijixing* (North Star) joined the fleet in 1999. (She originally was named *Dong-Diao* [East Investigate], and her name changed when the Navy adopted planet and star names for electronic reconnaissance ships.) The ship displaces 6,000 tons full load with a length of 426½ feet. The ship has helicopter facilities—a hangar and flight deck—and is armed with one twin 37-mm and two twin 25-mm guns. (Later ships of the 815 series have advanced 30-mm cannon.)

The *Beijixing* was the lead ship for a series of Chinese AGIS.

Photo 37. The Chinese intelligence ship *Tianwangxing* at sea in 2021 displaying the design 815G's fine, attractive lines. Note the large radomes and the adjacent, twin funnels for her diesel engines. China and Norway both have produced significant numbers of intelligence collection ships. / Royal Australian Navy.

Photo 38. A Type 927 sound detection ship is similar in several respects to the AGOS-type ships operated by the United States and Japan. Those ships have SWATH configurations that provide stability and ease of handling their long towed acoustic arrays. / Courtesy *Ships of the World*.

Improvements have led to modified type designations, with changes in antennas, radomes, and other features. Those ships have operated throughout the Western Pacific. The Type 815A *Kaiyangxing* operated in international waters off the coast of Alaska in July 2017, apparently to monitor the tests of the U.S. ballistic missile defense system. The Type 815G *Tianwangxing* and other ships have operated off the coast of Australia to monitor U.S.-Australian naval exercises.

More recently the Chinese Navy has deployed several acoustic surveillance ships of the SWATH design, akin to the U.S. Navy's T-AGOS program. While the published information on the program is sparse, two designs of SWATH towed-array ships had been identified when this volume went to press: five Type 639A ships and three Type 927 ships.

Chinese Intelligence Ships

Type	Pennant	Name	In service
815	851	*Beijixing* (North Star)	1999
815G	852	*Haiwangxing* (Neptune)	2015
815G	853	*Tianwangxing* (Uranus)	2010
815G	854	*Tianlangxing* (Sirius)	2015
815G	855	*Tianshuxing* (Dubhe)	2015
815A	856	*Kaiyangxing* (Mizar)	2017
815A	857	*Tianquanxing* (Megrez)	2017
815A	858	*Yuhengxing* (Alioth)	2018
815A	859	*Jinxing* (Venus)	2018

The first Type 639 ship, completed in 2009, was an oceanographic research ship. She was followed by five Type 639A acoustic surveillance ships, completed from 2013 to 2015. They displace some 5,000 tons and are fitted with towed arrays. The follow-on Type 927 SWATH design consisted of three ships of about the same size. They appear to have significantly less acoustic detection and tracking capabilities than their U.S. counterparts.

China's seaborne intelligence collection efforts also include warships and submarines, as well as the nation's large, militarized fishing fleet.

Finland

The converted buoy tender *Kustaanmiekka* was employed as an intelligence collection ship in the Baltic Sea. Completed in 1963, she was converted to an AGI in 1993. The ship displaced 340 tons with a length of 120⅓ feet, and her crew numbered about a dozen men. The *Kustaanmiekka* served into the twenty-first century.

France

The French Navy has employed several specialized ships in the intelligence collection role. The first was the small stores ship *Berry*, completed in 1964. The ship had a full-load displacement of 2,700 tons with a length of 284½ feet. In 1976–77 she was converted to an electronic trials ship and operated primarily in the Mediterranean in the AGI role.

The *Berry* was replaced by the *Bougainville*, which was built as a specialized transport to support French nuclear tests in the Pacific. Completed in 1988, she was configured as a dock landing ship, with a floodable docking well for carrying small craft. Her displacement was 5,200 tons full load with a length of 370 feet. The *Bougainville* was converted to the intelligence collection role in 1998–99 to replace the *Berry*. In turn, in 2005, the *Bougainville* was converted to a mine countermeasures support ship.

The subsequent French intelligence ship is the purpose-built *Dupuy de Lôme*, built in the Netherlands and commissioned in the French Navy in 2006. With a full-load displacement of 3,600 tons and a length of 333¾ feet, the ship has a helicopter deck but no hangar. Her limited self-defense is provided by two 20-mm single guns and two Simbad short-range, surface-to-air missile systems. The *Dupuy de Lôme* has some 30 crewmen plus approximately 80 technical personnel.

The *Dupuy de Lôme* has deployed into the Black Sea on numerous occasions as part of NATO demonstrations in support of Ukraine.

East Germany

The German Democratic Republic (East Germany) operated a Soviet-built, Okean-type trawler in the intelligence collection role.[6] Named *Hydrograph*, she was completed in 1958 and displaced 700 tons with a length of 166⅔ feet. She entered service as an East Ger-

Photo 39. The *Bougainville* was a French multipurpose ship that demonstrated the versatility of her docking well configuration. Her career as an intelligence collection ship was brief. / Courtesy Bernard Prézelin.

Photo 40. The *Dupuy de Lôme* is a large, purpose-built intelligence ship. She has operated in the Mediterranean and Black Seas, and in 2021 sailed through the Taiwan Strait to demonstrate freedom of navigation in waters that China declared are its territory. / Courtesy Bernard Prézelin.

man AGI in November 1961 and sailed until 1983, when she was taken out of service and scrapped.

The *Hydrograph*'s replacement was the *Jasmund*. Built in Rostock, East Germany, she served as an intelligence ship from her completion in 1985 until Spain purchased the ship in 1992. She displaced 2,290 tons with a length of 251 feet and was fitted with machine guns. Her German crew numbered about 60.

In addition to those two medium reconnaissance ships, East Germany outfitted two patrol ships as small reconnaissance ships: the *Komet* and *Meteor*. Both were built in Wolgast and commissioned in 1972 as small patrol craft. They were converted into small reconnaissance ships in October 1990. They served in that role until the end of 1994, when both were decommissioned and sold to Estonia as the patrol ships *Sulev* (ex-*Komet*) and *Vambola* (ex-*Meteor*).

West Germany

The Federal Republic of Germany operated several intelligence collection ships, primarily in the Baltic area. The earliest ships included the *Alster* and *Oker*, two former side trawlers of 1,500 tons and 238¾ feet long. The *Oste* (ex-*Puddefjord*), a former World War II–era tug, was first converted into a tender, and in 1960 she joined the *Alster* and *Oker* in the SIGINT role.

The *Oker* was decommissioned in 1988 and transferred to Greece, where she continued intelligence work, primarily in the Aegean. In 1989 the *Alster* was transferred to Turkey for intelligence work in the Black Sea. The *Oste* was scrapped.

Three purpose-built AGIs followed, all taking their names and pennant numbers from their predecessors: The *Oste II* (A52) and *Oker II* (A53) were completed in 1988 and the *Alster II* (A50) in 1989. They are Type 423 *Oste*-class ships of 3,200 tons and 274 feet in length. Their crews number about 40 with about the same number of technical personnel. The ships have provisions for light guns, and no helicopter facilities are provided.

The *Alster II* was the focus of an international incident when on 26 October 2006, Israeli aircraft flew over the ship as she was operating off the coast of Lebanon in support of United Nations peacekeeping forces. German authorities charged that the aircraft had fired at the ship. While the Israeli government denied that an attack had occurred, it acknowledged the incident and declared that no aggression was intended. A second incident of Israeli aircraft buzzing the *Alster* was reported on 30 October 2006.

The German government signed a contract with the Lürssen shipyard in June 2021 for the design and construction of three Type 424 intelligence collection ships. The first of those ships are scheduled to enter service in 2027; they will "seamlessly" replace the *Oker*, *Alster*, and *Oste*, which will have been in service for more than 30 years. To ensure the most economical procurement possible, the new ships will be based on civilian design standards.

Great Britain

Britain employed the refitted fishing craft *Arctic Viking* and *Lord Essengen* off the Soviet Arctic coast in 1953 as SIGINT collectors. Later, the British ships *Romola* and *Magnolia* were similarly observed operating off the coast of Murmansk while flying the markings of "fishing protection," but employing extensive high-frequency radio communications indicative of an intelligence collection role.

During the 1960s and 1970s, the Royal Navy deployed destroyers with SIGINT vans on their helicopter decks into the waters north of Murmansk on nearly an annual basis. During the 1982 conflict in the Falklands, the ice patrol ship *Endurance* served as an intelligence collection ship (see Argentina entry).

Soviet sources also listed the British hydrographic research ships *Enterprise* and *Echo* as having occasionally been employed for SIGINT missions. For example, the *Echo* jointed a fleet of NATO and Baltic Sea nations' surveillance ships and aircraft monitoring a large-scale Russian naval exercise in the Barents Sea in September 2021.

Greece

The West German electronic surveillance ship *Oker* was decommissioned in 1988 and transferred to Greece. She was renamed *Hermes* and served in the Aegean from 1988 to 2002 as an AGI.

India

India commissioned the massive naval auxiliary *Dhruv* on 10 September 2021 *as a multi*-role support ship: intelligence, command, and missile range tracking.

Built by the Hindustan Shipyard in Visakhapatnam, the *Dhruv* displaces 15,000 tons with a length of 574 feet. Reportedly she carries a team of sigint operators as well as a normal crew of about 300. The ship embarks a helicopter.

Italy

The Italian *Elettra*, completed in 2003, is a purpose-built intelligence ship. She displaces 3,180 tons full load with a length of 306⅔ feet. A helicopter flight deck is provided but no hangar. A remotely operated submersible vehicle carried on board can work at depths to 1,000 feet. The ship has an armament of two single 25-mm guns plus machine guns. Her crew numbers about 90, including technical personnel.

Japan

Japan has undertaken the construction of SWATH-configured ships for acoustic detection and tracking on both the strategic and tactical levels. Significantly, the Japanese program has relied on the United States for the electronic systems for these ships.

The Japanese Navy completed the *Hibiki* in 1991, *Harima* in 1992, and *Aki* in 2020. The ships displace 3,048 tons and are 219¾ feet long, with an elongated helicopter deck; no hangar is provided. The ships have U.S. Surveillance Towed Array Sensor Systems (SURTASS) with the WQT-2 passive towed array and UQQ-2 active sonar installed in the United States. In May 2018, a Japanese defense spokesman said that the surveillance ships were intended to "further enhance Japan's capability to gather acoustic information in the seas amid increasing and expanding submarine activities by neighbouring countries."[7]

North Korea

The Korean People's Navy maintains a small number of intelligence-gathering ships. Little is known about their number, characteristics, or capabilities.

Photo 41. The *Aki* (AOS 5203) was the third SWATH-configured ocean surveillance ship of the Japan Maritime Self-Defense Force. The lower portion of each of the twin hulls has a torpedo-like shape. These ships and the U.S. Navy's T-AGOS ships tow long acoustic arrays. / Courtesy *Ships of the World*.

New Zealand

The Government Communications Security Bureau deployed the New Zealand Navy's hydrographic ship *Monowai* to monitor Chinese ballistic missile tests in South Pacific impact areas.[8] The ship also was employed to intercept Fijian military radio communications during the country's coups d'état in 1987. Displacing 3,900 tons full load and with a length of 298 feet, the *Monowai* was commissioned in 1977 and served until 1997. She had a crew of 126 and was fitted with two 20-mm cannon.

In 1986 the Security Bureau trained and employed naval SIGINT operators and equipped four frigates between 1986 and 1990 for periodic intelligence operations.

Norway

Bordering the Soviet Union/Russia and with direct access to the Northern Fleet operating area, Norway has been a vital component of the U.S.-NATO intelligence collection efforts.[9] In that context, Norway has deployed a succession of spy ships—most with the name *Marjata*.

Norwegian Intelligence Ships

Name	In service	Displacement	Notes
Marjata I	1966–75	691 tons	later to the Navy as *Vadsø*
Marjata II	1976–81	982 tons	
	1983–95	1,420 tons	rebuilt
Marjata III	1995–2016	7,560 tons	renamed *Eger*
Eger	2017–	8,008 tons	active
Marjata IV	2016–	10,000+ tons	active

As early as 1951, Norway chartered civilian ships and placed technicians on board to conduct SIGINT operations against Soviet naval activities in the Norwegian and Barents Seas. Among these ships was the small trawler *Eger*, which Soviet sources reported in the mid-1950s as "stuffed with electronics" and operating near the Kola Peninsula.

In 1966 the Norwegian Ministry of Defense acquired the small whaler *Global 14* and, partially funded by the United States, converted the ship into the SIGINT collection ship *Marjata*. (The word "Marjata" has no meaning in Norwegian. The sea story is that "Marjata" is an acronym constructed from the first letters of the names of the family of the then-head of Norwegian naval intelligence, Captain Alf Martens Meyer. However, a more likely origination of the use of *Marjata* as the Norwegians' primary SIGINT ship is that one of the first chartered ships used by the Norwegian Intelligence Service may have been the Glasgow, Scotland–built ship *Marjata*, completed in October 1946 and active in the North Sea from 1946 to 1963.)

The country's intelligence ships are operated by the Norwegian Intelligence Service (also called the E-Service) and not by the Navy. The first *Marjata* displaced 691 tons with a length of 167 feet. The ship was limited by her sea-keeping abilities in the Barents Sea and operated only from May to September. On her forays into northern waters, the ship was the object of intense interest from Soviet aircraft and ships, and some incidents were reported. Given the codename "Carmen," the ship captured important electronic intelligence on Soviet cruise missiles, radars, and anti-submarine warfare activities.

Following a decision by the Norwegian government to maintain an "unbroken" watch on Soviet naval activities in the Northern Fleet area, the *Marjata II* was domestically designed and constructed as a dedicated intelligence collector. She replaced the outdated *Marjata I* in 1976.

The *Marjata II* originally displaced 940 tons with a length of 151 feet. In 1981 she underwent conversion; a 50-foot section was added that increased her displacement to 1,430 tons and provided additional space for equipment and operators. The *Marjata II*'s seakeeping abilities enabled operations from March to November in the Barents Sea.

The *Marjata II* was replaced in 1995 by the radical-design *Marjata III*. She has a Ramform hull design—essentially a wedge shape with a sharp bow, a sinusoidal waterline, and a descending rear body that ends in a straight, cut-off stern where the ship has her greatest width. That design provides a very stable sensor platform and a wide fantail to facilitate the towing of sundry acoustic sensors. The ship has a very low noise signature and was specifically designed to collect acoustic intelligence as well as electronic signals intelligence. The *Marjata III* is highly automated with a crew of only 14 and carries 30 or more intelligence operators. She displaces 7,560 tons and is 267 feet in length. The *Marjata III* can generate intelligence analyses on board as well as collection in the Barents Sea area almost year-round.[10]

The *Marjata* program had its most highly publicized moment on 11 August 2000, when the *Marjata III* was monitoring a major Russian Navy weapon's firing exercise just northeast of Polyarny/Severomorsk. The ship was some 12 n.miles from the Russian Oscar-class missile submarine *Kursk* (Project 949A) when, at 1031, the *Marjata III*'s passive acoustic systems detected a "muffled explosion" that was thought to be a depth charge. However, two minutes, 11 seconds later came a detonation so energetic that it was detected by the USNS *Loyal* (AGOS 22), then located more than 200 n.miles to the west, just off the North Cape.[11] That second blast represented an estimated 2,000 pounds of high explosives and probably marked the destruction of the entire weapon's load in the *Kursk*'s forward torpedo room, causing the loss of the submarine and her 118-man crew.[12]

The *Marjata III*, in company with the Norwegian research/survey ship *H.U. Sverdrup II*, then closely monitored the Russian rescue attempts. The *Sverdup II* was a 1,387-ton ship that occasionally engaged in intelligence-related activities. (She was operated by the Norwegian Defense Research Establishment, not by the Intelligence Service.)

Although programmed for deactivation upon the arrival of the fourth-generation Norwegian spy ship in 2016, the *Marjata III*'s excellent condition indicated that she could continue to serve. In 2016 she was renamed the *Eger* and operated under the Intelligence Service, primarily in the Norwegian Sea.

The *Marjata IV*—Norway's fourth-generation dedicated intelligence ship—was designed for year-around reconnaissance and surveillance of Russian naval activity in the Barents Sea and above the Arctic Circle. At more than 10,000 tons displacement and 413 feet long, the ship is equipped for both signal and acoustic intelligence collection. While the previous *Marjata*s were officially designated as research ships, the *Marjata IV* is the first of the series to be designated as an intelligence ship and bears the symbol of the Norwegian Intelligence Service on her exhaust stack.

The ship's electronics equipment was developed and manufactured in the United States. Both the *Marjata IV* and the *Eger* could deploy the equivalent of the U.S. UQQ-2 SURTASS, which is employed by the U.S. and Japanese AGOS-series ocean-surveillance ships. Like her predecessors, the *Marjata IV* has no armament.

Poland

The Polish Navy's auxiliary *Baltyk* was a B10-type trawler, one of 89 units built from 1951 to 1957 at Gdansk for the Soviet and Polish fishing industries. The trawlers were 194½ feet in length and grossed 658 tons. Originally outfitted for the Polish Navy as a survey ship, the *Baltyk* operated in that role during the latter 1950s. In the early 1960s, she was refitted as an intelligence collector and employed until the mid-1970s.

The *Baltyk* was replaced by the *Hydrograf* and *Nawigator*, two Polish-built, Moma-class ships that were operated as AGIs. Completed in 1975, those ships displaced 1,675 tons full load with a length of 240⁵⁄₁₂ feet. Their details differed with respect to their configurations and antennas. Their crews numbered about 90, and there were provisions for four twin 25-mm gun mounts. The *Hydrograf* was active as late as 2009; the *Nawigator*, as late as 2018.

Romania

The Romanian Navy operated two AGIs during the 1980s and 1990s: the intelligence ship *Emil Racovita* and the rescue ship *Grigore Antipa*.

The *Racovita* was built in 1976, with a length of 230 feet, a gross tonnage of 1,900, and a crew of about 80. The *Antipa* is a 1,450-ton, 259-foot "Corsair"-type ship built in 1980. The *Antipa* could accommodate 75 crew and SIGINT operators. The ship also carried a submersible to assist in rescue operations and possibly for underwater intelligence.

Spain

From her completion in 1985, the *Alerta* (ex-*Jasmund*) served as an intelligence ship for East Germany until Spain purchased her in 1992. The Germans stripped her electronic equipment prior to the ship's transfer, and Spain refitted her for the AGI role. She displaces 2,290 tons with a length of 251 feet. Machine guns are fitted. The *Alerta* has a crew of about 60.

Sweden

The Swedish ship *Orion* was constructed for the intelligence collection role in a Polish shipyard and entered Swedish service in 1984. The ship displaces 1,400 tons with a length of 200¾ feet and has a helicopter platform fitted. Her crew numbers 35. The *Orion* also has U.S.-provided electronics.

On 29 October 1985, a Soviet Sonya-class minesweeper collided with the *Orion* while the Swedish AGI was monitoring the activities of a Soviet submarine off Sweden's Gotland Island. There were no injuries.[13]

In 2019 the replacement for the *Orion* was being outfitted at a Polish shipyard, with plans for her to be commissioned as the *Artemis*. Due to the Polish shipyard's financial condition, the contract was terminated, and the unfinished ship was towed to Sweden. There has been no work on the ship reported into 2021. When completed, the *Artemis* reportedly will have a gross tonnage of 2,200 and a length of 242¾ feet. Until her completion, the *Orion*'s service was extended. Two new SIGINT ships are planned.

Taiwan

Taiwan has operated at least one specialized intelligence collection ship—the *Yung Kang*. Like the U.S. Navy's AGERS, she was built originally as a light cargo ship for the U.S. Army in 1944 (the *FS-214*); then the Navy acquired her in 1947 as the USS *Mark* (AG 143) and later redesignated AKL 12. The ship was transferred to Taiwan in 1971 and renamed *Yung Kang* (hull 514). She served in the AGI role until placed on limited duty in 1993 and was retired in 1997.

Turkey

The Turkish Navy operated the former German electronic surveillance ship *Alster*, which was renamed *Yunus*, from 1989 until 2000 in the Black Sea in the SIGINT role. She was replaced in the AGI role by the *Ufuk*, which was delivered in late 2021.

Constructed at the Istanbul naval shipyard, the *Ufuk* is the first Turkish domestic-built intelligence ship. Based on the Ada-class anti-submarine corvette design, she displaces 2,400 tons with a length of 326⅓ feet. A helicopter platform and hangar are provided.

Yugoslavia

The Yugoslav Navy's *Andrija Mohorovičić* was a Moma-class hydrographic ship that was modified in 1971 to an AGI. Since the breakup of Yugoslavia, she has become a training ship for Croatia.

Ukraine

Upon the dissolution of the Soviet Union in December 1991 and the establishment of the non-communist Ukraine nation, there was a division of Soviet naval units in the Black Sea area. The Ukrainian Navy acquired an AGI from Russia and has employed at least one additional ship in that role.

The *Pereyaslav*, formerly the Soviet/Russian AGI *GS-13*, was built in a Lithuanian shipyard. Entering Russian hydrographic service in 1990, her displacement was 688 tons with a length of 177⅚ feet. The ship received the new designation of CCB-400 (reconnaissance ship, or AGI) in 1990. The *GS-13*, with the other three ships of the Muna class, were not equipped as signals intelligence ships; rather, they were equipped and crewed to covertly deploy and recover combat swimmers and their powered underwater sleds from lockout tubes beneath the waterline. Prior to 1996, the *GS-13/SSV-400* served in the Caspian Sea and then in the Black Sea. She was transferred to Ukraine in 1996. Her crew numbers 22 plus up to 15 combat swimmers.

In August 2019, the *Pereyaslav* was sailing across the Black Sea en route to Georgia to participate in the exercise Agile Spirit 2019. While in international waters, the *Pereyaslav* received a radio warning from a Russian Navy ship to turn back. Soon thereafter a Russian Grisha V-class anti-submarine corvette approached the *Pereyaslav* and engaged in aggressive maneuvering, which only ceased when a Turkish reconnaissance plane arrived overhead.

The *Simferopol'* (ex-*Jupiter*) was an AGI of the Moma series, built in Gdansk, Poland, and subsequently modified into a reconnaissance ship (AGI) in 1977. With the dissolution of the Soviet Union and the subsequent distribution of the Black Sea Fleet ships, the *Jupiter* was transferred to Ukraine in 1996 and operated as an intelligence collector. The *Simferopol'* displaced 1,600 tons full load with a length of 240 5/12 feet and had a complement of 85. She was decommissioned in 2012.

On 30 January 2020, the Ukrainian Navy announced that it is completing a modification to a refrigerated trawler hull at an Odessa shipyard, based on an unfinished hull of the Project 502EM series. The modifications are designed to produce a medium sig-

Photo 42. Polish shipyards have constructed large numbers of naval auxiliary ships and merchant ships for the Soviet/Russian navies, including some 40 Moma-class ships with several units operated as AGIs. The Polish Navy had two Moma spy ships, including the *Nawigator*, shown here in 1978. / *German Democratic Republic Navy*.

nals intelligence/reconnaissance ship of new construction. The name of the new ship is not assigned. At 179¾ feet long, the ship will displace 1,220 tons, have a maximum speed of 11.6 knots or higher, and have a cruising range of 7,200 n.miles, with autonomy of 28 days. The status of the ship is not known following the Russian invasion of Ukraine in February 2022.

NOTES

Perspective

1. Maffeo, *Most Secret and Confidential*, 96.

2. The French signal towers and their destruction are described in Maffeo, *Most Secret and Confidential*, 71–73.

3. An excellent discussion of wireless intelligence is found in Keegan, *Intelligence in War*, 99–143.

4. "Report from HMS Diana on Russian Signals intercepted at Suez," 28 January 1904, Naval Library, Ministry of Defence, London. At the time, there was a protected cruiser named *Diana* in the Russian Navy; she fought in the Russo-Japanese conflict in the Far East (1904–5).

5. Although sister ships, the *Kasuga*'s main battery was one 10-inch and two 8-inch guns, while the *Nisshin* mounted four 8-inch guns. Both cruisers were built in Italy for Argentina. Japan purchased them while still under construction; they were completed early in 1904.

6. Details of radio communications in the Russo-Japanese War are in Hezlet, *Electron and Sea Power*; and Hezlet, *Electronics and Sea Power*, 43–49. Hezlet provides an excellent overview of the subject. Also see Sergeev, *Russian Military Intelligence*.

7. See Carnes, "Soviet Naval Intelligence," in Watson and Watson, *Soviet Navy*, 168–74. Also, Nekrasov, *North of Gallipoli*.

8. Cited in Price, *History of US Electronic Warfare*, 1:5. The two German ships subsequently were transferred to the Turkish Navy with Admiral Souchen remaining in command.

9. Grant, *U-Boat Intelligence 1914–1918*, 10–11.

10. James, *Eyes of the Navy*, 29.

11. See Beesly, *Room 40*; and Beesly, *Very Special Intelligence*, 1–8. Historian David Kahn devotes a chapter to the *Magdeburg* in his excellent *Seizing the Enigma*. He also details the British obtaining codes from German weather ships and the submarine *U-110* during World War II.

12. A comprehensive account of HF/DF is in Williams, *Secret Weapon*.

13. Macintyre, *U-Boat Killer*, 70–71; and revised edition, 78–79. Macintyre, when in command of the destroyers *Walker* and then *Hesperus*, sank five U-boats. See Norman Polmar, "My Friend, the Hunter-Killer," Naval Historical Foundation, May 29, 2013, https://www.navyhistory.org/2013/05/normans-corner-my-friend-the-hunter-killer/.

14. Palmer, *Command at Sea*, 294. This is an outstanding discussion of the subject. At the end of World War II, George Orwell (Eric Arthur Blair), a noted British author, first used the term "cold war" in his essay "You and the Atomic Bomb," published on 19 October 1945 in the British newspaper *Tribune*. Contemplating a world living in the shadow of the threat of nuclear war, he warned of a "peace that is no peace," which he called a permanent "cold war."

15. For the Crabb story and myths, see Pugh, *Frogman*; and Hutton, *Frogman Spy*.

16. GRAB = galactic radiation and background.

1. The Dawn of Spy Ships

1. The U.S. Navy established the position of chief of naval operations as the senior serving naval officer in 1915.

2. Later Admiral Sir William Reginald Hall. See Safford, "Brief History," 3–4. See also [Author name redacted], "Origination and Evaluation," 22n3.

3. Parker, "Pearl Harbor Revisited."

4. Matt Zullo email to Lee Mathers, 10 March 2021. Five of the radiomen in the Asiatic Fleet became very proficient in katakana Wabun code. The graceful yacht *Isabel* was built as a private motor yacht. The U.S. Navy acquired and converted her to a destroyer in 1917. From 1921 to 1928, she served on the Yangtze River.

5. The *Huron* originally was named *South Dakota* at her launching in 1904. She was renamed on 7 June 1920 to make that state's name available for a new-construction battleship (BB 49).

6. The *Monocacy* was reclassified from patrol gunboat to river gunboat (PR 2) on 15 June 1928.

7. [Author name redacted], "Origination and Evaluation," 24. Also see Zacharias, *Secret Missions*.

8. [Author name redacted], "Origination and Evaluation," 24.

9. U.S. Naval Cryptologic Veterans Association, "Birth of Cryptologic Direct Support."

10. Gustafson, "Shanghai, China (Station A)."

11. Havern, "*Isabel* (S. P. 521)."

12. Hezlet, *Electron and Sea Power*, 176–77.

13. Within the Dollar Steamship Lines, the agreement with the Navy was known only by the president of the company, and that was made during the Great Depression when the firm's ocean liners were sailing at half capacity with enormous operating losses. Dollar Steamship Lines was declared "unsound" in 1938, reorganized, and renamed the American President Lines.

14. Pearson and Gustafson, "Shipboard COMINT Mission."

15. This section is based on Drea, "Reading Each Other's Mail," 185–205. See also Deacon, *Kempei Tai*. The Drea article contains a wealth of Japanese-language references.

16. Deacon, *Kempei Tai*, 129.

17. Deacon, *Kempei Tai*, 188.

18. Sanematsu, *Nichi-Bei johosenki*, 66–67.

19. Havern, "*Isabel* (S. P. 521)."

20. Murray and Millett, *Military Innovation*, 358.

21. Rear Admiral Joseph N. Wenger rotated between OP-20-G and fleet communications/intelligence positions throughout his career. "More than anyone else, he was responsible for establishing a Navy-wide cryptographic organization." Wenger served as the deputy director of the Armed Forces Security Agency in 1952 and later as the vice director of the National Security Agency. See Cryptologic Heritage Hall of Honor, "2005 Hall of Honor Inductee."

22. Havern, "*Isabel* (S. P. 521)."

23. [Author name redacted], "Origination and Evaluation," 31.

24. Parker, "Pearl Harbor Revisited," 10.

25. [Author name redacted], "Origination and Evaluation," 27.

26. National Security Agency, "COMINT Stations Overseas."

27. An excellent published account of the *Panay* incident is in Tolley, *Yangtze Patrol*, 245–52. The *Panay* was built in Shanghai for the U.S. Navy and entered service in 1927.

28. *Citizendium: Citizens Compendium*, "Signals Intelligence before the Second World War," last modified 3 September 2010, https://en.citizendium.org/wiki/Signals_intelligence_before_the_Second_World_War.

29. Station Hypo, "Sense of Urgency!"

30. Station Hypo, "Sense of Urgency!"

31. Packard, *Century of U.S. Naval Intelligence*, 20. Also see Dorwart, *Conflict of Duty*, 108.

32. Hezlet, *Electron and Sea Power*, 184.

33. National Security Agency, "'B-Dienst' aboard U-boats."

34. Tolley, "Strange Mission."

35. Breaking the Japanese machine-based diplomatic code—Purple—was accomplished by the U.S. Army. The high level of U.S. interest in the diplomatic decrypts led to U.S. Navy analysts and translators being tasked to assist the short-handed army. Thus, they were diverted from their primary focus on Japanese naval codes, especially the Japanese Navy's main operational code (JN-25), which did not become readable to any meaningful extent until the spring of 1942. Some claim a November 1941 JN-25 message that was not decrypted until 1946 could have provided advance warning of the Japanese attack on Pearl Harbor. But even had that message been available in real time, its meaning would have been obscure: Pearl Harbor was never mentioned in the message, and only with imagination and the advantage of hindsight could that message be taken to indicate the intended target of the Japanese attack.

36. Zullo email to Mathers. According to Zullo's research, Safford sent a war warning out to all commands holding U.S. Navy codes to destroy codes prior to surrender or capture. The Navy took over the *Gold Star* in 1921 and commissioned her as the *Arcturus* (AK 12) in 1922. Then it immediately renamed the ship *Gold Star* and reclassified her as AG 12.

37. Tolley, "Strange Mission." Tolley explained, "Had the Japanese fired on any of these small vessels, it would have constituted an overt act on the part of Japan."

38. Havern, "Isabel (S. P. 521)."

39. Tolley, "Strange Mission."

40. Tolley, "Strange Mission."

41. Japanese Research Section, Military History Division, General Headquarters, Far East Command, Monograph No. 118, *Operational History of Naval Communications: 1941 December–August 1985, Japanese Studies in World War II*, 7.

42. The *I-55* was renamed *I-155* on 20 May 1942.

43. The *Isabel* returned to the United States in October 1945, was decommissioned on 11 February 1946, and sold for scrap.

44. Tolley, "Strange Mission."

45. The *Lanikai* was returned to her previous, commercial owner at Manila in 1946, but the owner refused to accept her in such poor condition. While undergoing repairs at Subic Bay in 1947, the *Lanikai* sank during a typhoon.

46. Pike, "History of the Naval Security Group."

2. Western Spy Submarines

1. Major published sources on this subject are Sontag and Drew, *Blind Man's Bluff*; Ring, *We Come Unseen*; and Hennessy and Jinks, *Silent Deep*. Also see Brian Fung and Andrea Peterson, "America Uses Stealthy Submarines to Hack Other Countries' Systems," *Washington Post*, 29 July 2016, https://www.washingtonpost.com/news/the-switch/wp/2016/07/29/america-is-hacking-other-countries-with-stealthy-submarines/.

2. Comprehensive accounts of submarine operations in World War II are Roscoe, *United States Submarine Operations*; and Holmes, *Undersea Victory*. Also see Packard, *Century of U.S. Naval Intelligence*, 120–23.

3. The principal instigator of the operation was Ewen Montagu, a lawyer who served in British naval intelligence during the war and afterward became the judge advocate of the fleet. He received the Military Order of the British Empire for conceiving Operation Mincemeat. Montagu's book about the operation, *The Man Who Never Was*, later was made into a movie. Also see Macintyre, *Operation Mincemeat*; and Smyth, *Deadly Deception*. The latter books add details to the story that still were classified when Montagu wrote *Man Who Never Was*.

4. Fifty-two U.S. war-built fleet submarines were modernized under the GUPPY program after the war, incorporating features from the German Type XXI U-boat to enhance their underwater performance.

5. The *Cochino*'s ordeal is described in Sontag and Drew, *Blind Man's Bluff*, 12–24.

6. McLaren, *Silent and Unseen*, 28.

7. McLaren, *Silent and Unseen*, 47.

8. John Connally, Memorandum for the Secretary of Defense, Subject: Briefing Items of Current Navy Interest (12 May 1961), enclosing briefing paper "The Role of the Submarine in Cold, Limited and General War," Op-311e (24 April 1961), file 5050 at the Naval History and Heritage Command, Washington DC.

9. MacLean, *Ice Station Zebra*. The film *Ice Station Zebra* (1968) starred Rock Hudson, Patrick McGoohan, Ernest Borgnine, and James Brown.

10. See "*Ronquil* (SS-396)," Naval History and Heritage Command, 20 October 2005, https://www.history.navy.mil/research/histories/ship-histories/danfs/r/ronquil.html.

11. Woodward, *Veil*, 57–58.

12. On 18 June 1961, the *K-19* suffered a failed seal on one of her two reactors, causing radiation leakage and a severe emergency for the submarine; several of her crew died from radiation poisoning. On 24 February 1972, the *K-19* suffered a fire while operating submerged some 600 n.miles northeast of Newfoundland. Although the submarine was able to surface, the fire spread; 28 crewmen died. Left without propulsion, the submarine was towed across the Atlantic to the Kola Peninsula, a 23-day effort. The film *K-19: The Widowmaker* (2002) was based on Captain Peter A. Huchthausen's book *K-19*.

13. "U.S. Submarines, 'Hostile Vessels' Collided 9 Times," *Washington Star*, 16 February 1970, 1.

14. Admiral Arleigh Burke, USN, Chief of Naval Operations, Memorandum for Admiral [Arthur] Radford, "Submarine Patrols," 7 November 1956, reproduced in "Transcript of 2017 NSL History Seminar," 40.

15. Laurence Stern, "U.S. Subs Spying in Soviet Waters," *Washington Post*, 4 January 1974, A1, A8. Also see Seymour M. Hersh, "Submarines of U.S. Stage Spy Missions inside Soviet Waters," *New York Times*, 25 May 1975; and George Lardner Jr., "Earlier Spy Reports Went Unprosecuted," *Washington Post*, 23 May 1986, A8.

16. Stern, "U.S. Subs."

17. Hennessy and Jinks, *Silent Deep*, 98. Coote's executive officer, Lt. John Fieldhouse, was a future chief of Defence Staff.

18. The *Tabard*'s commanding officer at that time was Lt. Cdr. Peter Samborne, later the first commanding officer of Britain's first nuclear-propelled submarine, HMS *Dreadnought*.

19. Hennessy and Jinks, *Silent Deep*, 111.

20. The *Dreadnought* went to sea eight years after the first U.S. nuclear submarine, the *Nautilus* (SSN 571), was completed. The British submarine had an American-provided S5W nuclear reactor and related machinery.

21. Hennessy and Jinks, *Silent Deep*, 281.

22. Ring, *We Come Unseen*, 109.

23. Ring, *We Come Unseen*, 178.

24. Ring, *We Come Unseen*, 170–71.

25. Ring, *We Come Unseen*, 172.

26. Prebble, *Secrets of the Conqueror*, 48.

27. Prebble, *Secrets of the Conqueror*, 56.

28. The *General Belgrano* was the former USS *Phoenix* (CL 46), commissioned in 1938. She was transferred to Argentina in 1951.

29. Prebble, *Secrets of the Conqueror*, 228–29.

30. Prebble, *Secrets of the Conqueror*, 242.

31. Karremann, *In Deepest Secrecy*, 162–63.

32. Karremann, *In Deepest Secrecy*, 219.

33. The incident is described in Aleksin, "Incidents in the Barents Sea," 21–22; and Miasnikov, "Submarine Collision off Murmansk," 6–15.

34. The United States and the Soviet Union/Russia both recognize the 12-n.mile limit, but the two nations have different methods of applying the limit. Russia measures from a line marked 12 n.miles beyond the line between two pieces of land that extend farthest into the sea on either side of a bay or a gulf—in this case, Tsypnavolok Cape, on Rybachi Peninsula, and the northern shore of Kildin Island.

35. Maryukha, "American Submarines," 3.

36. Bill Gertz, "Soviet Minisubs Spying on West, Experts Say," *Washington Times*, 3 April 1986, 3, 19.

37. Gertz, "Soviet Minisubs."

38. Academician Sergey N. Kovalev discussion with N. Polmar in St. Petersburg, 6 May 1997. Kovalev was the chief designer of the Project 667A/Yankee SSBN, its several Delta-series variants, and the Project 945/Typhoon SSBN, the world's largest submarine.

39. Commanding Officer, USS *Batfish* (SSN 681), to Chief of Naval Operations (OP-095), Report of Mission LS-26, 2 March 1978–17 May 1978, LS-26-D-0006-T-78 (17 May 1978).

40. Chief Warrant Officer John A. Walker Jr., USN, was a communications specialist who provided the Soviets with massive amounts of information from about 1967 until his arrest in 1985. He operated a spy ring that included his son, his brother, and a close friend—all of whom were naval personnel. Walker died in prison in 2014.

41. Commanding Officer, USS *Pickerel* (SS 524), to Chief of Naval Operations, "Report of Reconnaissance Patrol off Amoy and Foochow Areas of China Coast to Report Any CHICOM Movement to Invade Taiwan," 2 August 1950. From 16 March to 5 April 1950, the *Pickerel* completed a 5,200-mile voyage from Hong Kong to Pearl Harbor in 21 days while completely submerged, probably the longest distance ever traveled underwater by a diesel-electric submarine (with snorkeling).

42. Schratz, *Submarine Commander*, 372.

43. Vyborny and Davis, *Dark Waters*, 7–11.

44. Commanding Officer, USS *Guardfish* (SSN 612), to Commander-in-Chief U.S. Pacific Fleet, "Trail of Soviet ECHO II Nuclear Submarine," SSN 612:LGV:sq 3840 Ser 00015–72, 10 June 1972. See also Minton and Berzin, *From Opposite Sides*. Minton was the commanding officer of the *Guardfish*, and Berzin was the commanding officer of the *K-184*.

45. "300th Peking 'Warning' to U.S.," *New York Times*, 30 June 1964, 3.

46. The *Halibut*, completed in 1960 as a Regulus cruise missile submarine, was designated SSGN 587; upon conversion to a "special mission" submarine, she was redesignated SSN 587 on 15 August 1965. See Polmar and White, *Project Azorian*, 29–30, 51–60, 197–99. The *Halibut*'s conversion also is addressed in Sontag and Drew, *Blind Man's Bluff*, 60–62. Dunham's *Spy Sub* is a thinly veiled fictional account of the *Halibut* (i.e., the USS *Viperfish*); the book tells of life aboard the submarine but

is otherwise disappointing with respect to her operations. Dunham had served on the *Halibut*.

47. Craven, *Silent War*, 141. Dr. Craven was the acting director and the chief scientist of the U.S. Navy's Deep Submergence Systems Project. Unfortunately, *Silent War* is riddled with factual errors.

48. The United States operated an intelligence listening site in Iran until early 1979. See Charles W. Corddry, "U.S. Intelligence Is Set back by Loss of Last Iran Spy Site," *Baltimore Sun*, 2 March 1979, 1.

49. The missile range instrumentation ships were the *General H. H. Arnold* (T-AGM 9) and the *General Hoyt S. Vandenberg* (T-AGM 10). The destroyer escort (DE) ships were the *Claud Jones* (DE 1033), *John R. Perry* (DE 1034), *Charles Berry* (DE 1035), and *McMorris* (DE 1036). All four DEs were sold to Indonesia in 1973–74.

50. Some conspiracy theorists claimed that a few "renegade" personnel were attempting to launch the missiles against U.S. bases on Oahu. That theory has been completely discounted by facts, including the range of the R-21 being 755 n.miles.

51. The acoustic data related to the sinking of the *K-129* is detailed in Rule, "Russian SSBNs," 98–106. Rule was the longtime senior analyst for the Sound Surveillance System (SOSUS) program.

52. See Polmar and White, *Project Azorian*.

53. Saturation diving involves remaining under ambient pressure for long periods. This process enables divers to enter and leave the (ocean) environment with a reduced risk of decompression sickness (known as the "bends"). Divers have worked and lived in this situation for weeks (e.g., U.S. Navy SEALAB projects) and have demonstrated the technique to depths of at least 600 feet. See Craven, *Silent War*, 137, 154; and Siiteri, *Papa Topside*.

54. As a missile submarine, the *Halibut* (SSGN 587) had a hangar that could accommodate five Regulus I or four Regulus II cruise missiles. See Polmar and O'Connell, *Strike from the Sea*, 41–42, 59–70.

55. Lehman, *Oceans Ventured*, 41.

56. The first comprehensive account of Ivy Bells was published by Sontag and Drew, *Blind Man's Bluff*, 158–63.

57. Sontag and Drew, *Blind Man's Bluff*, 180–81.

58. The *Seawolf* was unique among U.S. nuclear-propelled submarines, being built with a liquid sodium–cooled reactor plant; that later was replaced with a standard pressurized-water plant. All other U.S. nuclear submarines have had pressurized-water reactors.

59. Details of the *Seawolf*'s ordeal are in Sontag and Drew, *Blind Man's Bluff*, 226–30.

60. Sontag and Drew, *Blind Man's Bluff*, 218–19.

61. The admiral was Edmund P. Giambastiani Jr., who served as the vice chairman of the U.S. Joint Chiefs of Staff from 2005 to 2007.

62. Brusnitsin, *Openness and Espionage*, 14. At the time, the author was the deputy chairman of the State Technical Commission of the USSR.

63. Brusnitsin, *Openness and Espionage*, 29–30.

64. One of the recovered recording devices is now on display in the Federal Security Service Museum in Moscow; the building is the former KGB headquarters. One of the authors of this book viewed the device at the museum in 1992.

65. About 30 submarines of the *Seawolf* class were planned. With the end of the Cold War, the program was truncated to three units.

66. The submarine was built as the Royal Navy's *Upholder*, commissioned in 1990; she was transferred and entered Canadian service in 2015. David Common, "Canadian Sub on Mission to Bolster North Korea Surveillance," CBC News, 6 February 2018, https://web.archive.org/web/20180206222701/http://www.cbc.ca/news/canada/hmcs-chicoutimi-submarine-canada-pacific-north-korea-1.4511238.

67. Kurdin and Grasdock, "Loss of a Yankee SSBN," pt. 1, 57. The second part of the article appeared in the magazine's January 2001 issue.

68. See Polmar and Mathers, *Opening the Great Depths*.

69. Polmar and Mathers, *Opening the Great Depths*, 232–44.

70. Polmar and Mathers, *Opening the Great Depths*, 244.

71. The *Mystic* (DSRV-1) was originally certified to 3,500 feet and the *Avalon* (DSRV-2) to 5,000 feet. Subsequently, the *Mystic* was certified to the greater depth.

72. The surface mother ships for the DSRVs were the submarine rescue ships *Pigeon* (ASR 21) and *Ortolan* (ASR 22). Those ships had a unique, catamaran (twin-hull) design.

73. Craven, *Silent War*, 117. The Deep Submergence Systems Project (DSSP) was established in 1965 after the 1963 loss of the submarine *Thresher*. The DSSP was responsible for the development of submarine location, escape, and rescue systems; deep-ocean salvage capabilities; and the *NR-1* nuclear-propelled submersible.

74. The institute's facility was established in 1930 in Woods Hole, Massachusetts. It is the largest independent oceanographic research institution in the United States with about 1,000 staff and students.

75. NR stands for nuclear reactor. The development and operations of the *NR-1* are well described in Vyborny and Davis, *Dark Waters*. Vyborny was a member of the original crew of the *NR-1*. Unfortunately, the book contains numerous factual errors. Also see Polmar and Allen, *Rickover*, 435–45.

76. Rickover, "Naval Nuclear Propulsion Program," 30.

77. Untitled White House press release (Austin, Texas), 18 April 1965. Part of Admiral Rickover's secrecy probably was based on the *NR-1*'s cost: The original (March 1965) estimate was $30 million; with full systems, as the submarine was completed, the estimated cost was $94.9 million. See "Deep Submergence Vehicle Gets Rave Trials Notice," *Navy Times*, 24 September 1969.

78. Vyborny and Davis, *Dark Waters*, 78. Also, Polmar, "Search the Oceans," 103–4.

79. The proposed *NR-2* also was known as a Hull Test Vehicle (HTV). See George C. Wilson, "Rickover Requests $130 Million to Build 2nd Nuclear Minisub," *Washington Post*, 5 November 1976, A2.

80. The DSRV-2 was taken out of service in 2000, and the DSRV-1 and *NR-1* were taken out of service in 2008.

81. William Arkin, "Phase Zero: Spying on the U.S. Submarine That Spies for the NSA and CIA," William M. Arkin Online: Secret No More, 7 April 2015, https://williamaarkin.wordpress.com/2015/04/07/phase-zero-spying-on-the-u-s-submarine-that-spies-for-the-nsa-and-cia/.

82. Adam Weinstein and William Arkin, "Spying on the U.S. Submarine That Spies for the NSA and CIA," gawker.com, 7 April 2015, http://phasezero.gawker.com/spying-on-the-u-s-submarine-that-spies-for-the-nsa-and-1693109418. Emphasis in original.

83. Edward Snowden, an employee of a contractor to the National Security Agency, exposed the Radiant Gemstone program and other intelligence operations in June 2013. After his revelations to the press were published, Snowden fled to the Soviet Union, where he was granted asylum.

84. Fung and Peterson, "America Uses Stealthy Submarines."

3. The Cold War: The Red Side

Epigraph: Kuzin and Nikol'skiy, *Voyenno-morskoy Flot SSSR*, 380. This volume provides excellent coverage of the Soviet Navy at the end of the Soviet regime.

1. An excellent overview of this subject is Richelson, "Soviet Ocean," in Wise, *International Countermeasures Handbook*, 36–44.

2. Stuart and Taylor, "Soviet Naval Auxiliary Force," in Watson and Watson, *Soviet Navy*, 109.

3. A brief but valuable description of Soviet naval intelligence is Brooks, "Intelligence Collection," 47–49. Brooks, as a rear admiral, served as the director of the Office of Naval Intelligence from July 1988 to August 1991.

4. An interesting history of the GRU and its organization is Suvorov (pseud.), *Inside Soviet Military Intelligence*.

5. The Spetsnaz are similar to the U.S. Navy's seals and other special forces. The Soviet/Russian forces conduct sabotage, assassination, reconnaissance, and other covert missions.

6. GS stands for *gidrograficheskoye sudno* (hydrographic ship), and SSV represents *svyazi sudno* (communications vessel).

7. West, *SIGINT Secrets*, 277.

8. Central Intelligence Agency, "Photographic Interpretation Notice No. 37–74" (Washington DC: 15 November 1974).

9. Sen. Robert Paul Griffin, remarks in *Congressional Record*, 90th Congress, 2nd Session, vol. 114, part 2, *30 January 1968—7 February 1968* (Washington DC: Government Printing Office, 1968), 1176.

10. CIA, "Communist Bloc," i.

11. Russian president Vladimir Putin had visited the Lourdes facility in December 2000 and met with Cuban president Fidel Castro. See Bill Gertz, "Soviets Said to Operate Spy Base in Cuba Able to Monitor U.S. Phones," *New York City Tribune*, 25 March 1985, 1; and Kevin Sullivan, "Cuba Upset by Closure of Russian Spy Base," *Washington Post*, 9 October 2001, A26.

12. Drew Middleton, "Soviet Sea Spying on Britain Grows: Officials Declare Trawlers and Submarines Intensify Electronic Espionage," *New York Times*, 22 July 1960, 6.

13. See Cdr. John Murphy, USN (Ret.), "Cold War Warriors: Spy Ships—Theirs and Ours," *Emmitsburg (MD) News Journal* (online), 2011, https://www.emmitsburg.net/archive_list/articles/misc/cww/2011/spy_ships.htm.

14. Murphy, "Cold War Warriors."

15. Murphy, "Cold War Warriors."

16. Winkler, *Cold War at Sea*, 31.

17. Admiral Thomas Hayward letter to Dr. David Winkler, 10 July 1992. Hayward was the chief of naval operations from 1 July 1978 to 30 June 1982.

18. Hayward letter to Winkler, 10 July 1992.

19. Rear Admiral V. A. Karev, Russian Navy, "Unknown Reconnaissance Pages of the Pacific Fleet," *Serve the Fatherland* (*Primorskaya* newspaper), October–November 2010.

20. Several of those Soviet destroyers mounted four aft-firing SS-N-2 Styx antiship missiles in addition to their standard armament.

21. A comprehensive account of the confrontation is Goldstein and Zhukov, "Tale of Two Fleets," 27–63.

22. Goldstein and Zhukov, "Tale of Two Fleets," 54.

23. Goldstein and Zhukov, "Tale of Two Fleets," 46.

24. Robert C. Brewster (Department of State), memorandum to Henry A. Kissinger (White House), subject: Response to National Security Memorandum 119, 16 April 1971. See also Winkler, *Cold War at Sea*, 68, 168; and Allen, "Incidents at Sea," 40–45.

25. Drew Middleton, "2 Soviet Subs Reported in Crisis Area," *New York Times*, 14 April 1982, 14. In reality, no Soviet submarines were in the area at that time.

26. Kuzin and Nikol'skiy, *Voyenno-morskoy Flot SSSR*, 381.

27. Stuart and Taylor, "Soviet Naval Auxiliary Force," in Watson and Watson, *Soviet Navy*, 112.

28. A class of three nuclear-propelled space event support ships was planned: the *Marshal Nedelin*, completed in 1983; *Marshal Krylov*, completed in 1990; and *Marshal Biriuzov*, not completed and broken up.

29. Stuart and Taylor, "Soviet Naval Auxiliary Force," in Watson and Watson, *Soviet Navy*, 380.

30. The United States built one nuclear-propelled cruiser, the *Long Beach* (CGN 9) of 15,540 tons, completed in 1961. Seven smaller U.S. nuclear-propelled, guided missile frigates (DLGN) were reclassified as cruisers (CGN) in 1975.

31. Central Intelligence Agency, *Moscow's Fisheries Development Program.*

32. See, for example, Ackley, "Fishing Fleet and Soviet Strategy," 30–38; and Central Intelligence Agency, *Soviet Fishing.*

33. Smith, *Polar Star*; and Smith, *Gorky Park.*

34. Central Intelligence Agency, *Soviet Fishing*, 1.

35. Bussert, "Soviet Naval Electronic Technology," 105.

36. James Foley, "Soviets Deploy Spy Ships off U.S.," *Christian Science Monitor*, 1 August 1977, 17.

37. Central Intelligence Agency, *Soviet Pacific Fishing Fleet*, iii.

38. "Soviet Defector Tells of Fishing Spies," *Baltimore Sun*, 13 April 1984, A13.

39. "U.S. Boards Soviet Ship to Check on Cable Break," *Washington Daily News*, 27 February 1959, 4; and Department of Defense, press release, "Navy Ship Investigates Undersea Cable Damage," No. 217–59, 26 February 1959.

40. Gross tonnage is a nonlinear measure of a ship's overall internal volume; deadweight tonnage is a measure of how much weight a ship can carry (the total weight of cargo, fuel, fresh water, ballast water, provisions, passengers, and crew).

41. At the time, the United States ranked seventh in number of merchant ships with 424 privately owned and 251 government owned.

42. McKeown, "Their Merchant Fleet," 164.

43. U.S. oceanographic/hydrographic ships were operated by the Navy, National Oceanic and Atmospheric Administration, National Science Foundation, and other government agencies, as well as selected universities and oceanographic institutions.

44. See Central Intelligence Agency, *Soviet Oceanographic Research Program*.

45. Central Intelligence Agency, *Soviet Oceanographic Research Program*, iii.

46. Central Intelligence Agency, memorandum for the director, "Soviet Naval Presence in the Indian Ocean," 14 December 1970, 1.

47. Kuzin and Nikol'skiy, *Voyenno-morskoy Flot SSSR*, 382.

48. Yuri Alekseyevich Gagarin, a Soviet military pilot, became the first human to journey into outer space, completing one orbit around the earth on 12 April 1961 (Beverly Polmar's birthday).

49. The *Gagarin*, built at the Baltic Shipyard in Leningrad as Project 1589, was based on the *Sofia* supertanker design.

4. The Cold War: Red Submarines

1. An interesting legal overview is in Kraska, "Putting Your Head," 164–48.

2. Bobkov and Khurs, "Reconnaissance at Sea." The article was reprinted in a memorandum for the director of Central Intelligence. Admiral Bobkov was the head of Soviet naval intelligence from 1960 to 1965, and Captain Khurs was the head from 1979 to 1987.

3. Korenevskiy, "Over the Side," 3.

4. When World War II erupted in Europe in September 1939, the German Navy had 57 operational submarines, and at that time the Soviet Navy had the world's largest submarine force with 168 undersea craft in service.

5. See Polmar and Moore, *Cold War Submarines*, 1–9.

6. "No Curb on Submarines: Foreign Craft Free to Roam outside 3-Mile Limit, Say Navy Men," *New York Times*, 27 March 1948, 2.

7. R. Bruce Rule email to Lee Mathers, 21 April 2021.

8. See, for example, Tyler, *Running Critical*, 34–35, 38–45; that was reprinted in part in "The Rise and Fall of the SSN 688," *Washington Post*, 11 October 1986, A1, A18.

9. Hennessy and Jinks, *Silent Deep*, 142–44.

10. See Submarine Defence Commission, "Countering the Submarine Threat"; Ellis, "Sweden's Ghosts?," 94–106; Given and Cashman, "'Whiskey' on the Rocks,"

112–15; Wicklund, "Whiskey on the Rocks," 26–31; Kocherov and Mozgovoy, "'Swedish Komsomolets' Syndrome," pt. 1, 7; and Kocherov and Mozgovoy, "'Swedish Komsomolets' Syndrome," pt. 2, 8.

11. Submarine Defence Commission, "Countering the Submarine Threat," 25–26. The report states that "submarine 137 had shown itself, on investigation, to be carrying nuclear weapons with a degree of probability bordering on certainty." Also see Frank J. Prial, "Sweden to Release Soviet Sub: Finds Signs of Nuclear Arms," *New York Times*, 6 November 1981, 1; and McCormick, *Stranger than Fiction*.

12. Frank J. Prial, "Soviet Captain Is Interrogated in Sub Incident," *New York Times*, 3 November 1981, A1.

13. Zubko, "Order Was to Blow Up," 6.

14. "Swedish Navy Still Hunting a Submarine," *New York Times*, 7 October 1982.

15. Peter Osnos, "Sweden Charges Six Soviet Subs Violated Waters," *Washington Post*, 27 April 1983, A1, A15.

16. Gertz, "Soviet Minisubs."

17. McCormick, *Stranger than Fiction*, 3–4.

18. See Tunander, *Secret War against Sweden*.

19. Rear Admiral John L. Butts, USN, director of Naval Intelligence, "Statement before Senate Armed Services Committee," 26 February 1985.

20. Butts, "Statement."

21. Central Intelligence Agency, *Soviet Naval Activity*, 13.

22. Bill Gertz, "Russian Submarine Is Spotted off Coast," *Washington Times*, 23 June 1995, A7.

23. Central Intelligence Agency, *Soviet Naval Activity*, 13.

24. "Losharik" is the name of a children's animated horse composed of wooden spheres, the name being a combination of the Russian words for horse (*loshad*) and small ball (*sharik*). The horse is the hero of a well-known Russian cartoon film.

25. The official government casualty report listed seven captains 1st rank, three captains 2nd rank, two captains 3rd rank, one captain-lieutenant, and one lieutenant colonel of medical services.

5. American Spy Ships: Part 1

1. The communists took control of mainland China in 1949. The surviving Nationalist leadership fled to Taiwan, which the Japanese had occupied as Formosa during World War II.

2. Winkler, *Cold War at Sea*, 35.

3. Upon completion the *Staten Island* (AG 278) was commissioned in the U.S. Navy on 26 February 1944 and immediately was transferred to the Soviet Union, being renamed *Severny Veter* (North Wind). She was returned to the U.S. Navy in 1951 as the AGB 5, briefly named *Northwind*, and then changed to *Staten Island* in 1952. The ship was transferred to the U.S. Coast Guard as the *Staten Island* (WAGB 278) in 1966 and served until 1974 when she was decommissioned and scrapped.

4. The term "DeSoto" is a contraction of DeHaven Special Operations off Tsingtao (China) and was derived from the first patrol being carried out by the USS *DeHaven*.

5. Watson and Watson, *Soviet Navy*, 112, 259.

6. Karniol, "Russia Seeks," 27.

7. Alger, "Review," 1.

8. Wigglesworth, "Cuban Missile Crisis," 73–83.

9. Alger, "Review," 7.

10. See Gribkov and Smith, *Operation Anadyr*; and Polmar and Gresham, *DEFCON-2*.

11. Dobbs, *One Minute to Midnight*.

12. Major Anderson was killed. Previously on 1 May 1960, the Soviet Union shot down a U-2 spy plane piloted by Francis Gary Powers, who was able to parachute to safety. Four Nationalist Chinese (Taiwanese) U-2s also were shot down over China.

13. Dobbs, *One Minute to Midnight*.

14. This discussion is based on Grulich, comment on "Submarine Intelligence Gathering Operations," 224.

15. Howe, "Technical Research Ships," 20.

16. Alger, "Review," 19, 22.

17. Alger, "Review," 22.

18. Hooper, *Mobility, Support, Endurance*, 217.

19. COMSTSLANT message 031818Z February 1969, "Scuttle and Destruct Report on Interim Installation."

20. Alger, "Review," 129.

21. CINCLANT 022304Z February 1968, CINCLANT OPORD 2130, "USNS Muller Protective Operations."

22. The *Robinson* was built as a cargo ship. The Navy acquired and classified her as a cargo ship and aircraft ferry (AKV 3), and later reclassified her as a cargo ship (AK 274) in May 1959.

23. See Polmar and White, *Project Azorian*. The Navy acquired the lift ship, after conversion to a drill ship, on 30 September 1976 and designated her AG 193. She was stricken from the Navy List on 19 November 2007 and scrapped.

24. Sherman Wetmore interview with Michael White, 8 June 2007. Wetmore was the heavy lift operations manager on board the *Hughes Glomar Explorer*.

25. The *Chazhma* was converted to a missile tracking ship in 1963, shortly after her completion as a bulk ore/coal carrier. She displaced 14,065 tons full load with a length of 459 feet.

26. Shtyrov quoted in Burbyga, "Submarine from 'Grave Bay,'" 6.

27. Central Intelligence Agency, "Project Azorian," 39. The CIA article and related materials are on the website of the National Security Archives, George Washington University, Washington DC, https://nsarchive2.gwu.edu/nukevault/ebb305/index.htm.

28. Central Intelligence Agency, "Project Azorian," 46.

29. Rear Admiral Edward D. Sheafer Jr., USN (Ret), discussion with N. Polmar, 13 September 2010. Sheafer was the director of Naval Intelligence from August 1991 to September 1994. The Soviet naval officer's comment to Sheafer occurred in Bethesda MD in December 1974.

6. The Attack on the USS *Liberty*

1. An important source for material on the *Liberty* attack is Schwar, *Arab-Israeli Crisis and War*.

2. Smithsonian National Air and Space Museum, "Operation Moon Bounce."

3. Gerhard and Millington, "Attack on a SIGINT Collector," 63.

4. McGonagle was a "black shoe" officer—that is, a surface warfare specialist. He previously had served mostly in small ships—minesweepers and tugs—and had command of the fleet tug *Mataco* (ATF 86) in 1957–58 and the salvage ship *Reclaimer* (ARS 42) in 1961–63.

5. Bregman, *Israel's Wars*, 71.

6. Ennes, *Assault on the* Liberty, 38–39. Ennes makes many unfounded and incorrect statements, including that McGonagle requested a warship escort from the Sixth Fleet and that the *Liberty* passed the spy ship *Valdez* off the North Africa coast the night of 4–5 June. At the time the *Valdez* was docked in New York City.

7. National Security Agency, "Fact Sheet for Director, NSA," 1, question 2.

8. USS *Liberty* message 080742Z JUN 67; and Gerhard and Millington, "Attack on a SIGINT Collector," 25.

9. Gerhard and Millington, "Attack on a SIGINT Collector," 37.

10. Commander in Chief, U.S. Naval Forces Europe, "Liberty Chronology Eight June (U)," message 151003Z, June 1967, https://www.nsa.gov/Portals/70/documents/news-features/declassified-documents/uss-liberty/navy-messages/uss_liberty_atgr_5_research_electronics.pdf.

11. On 7 June, both Egyptian and Israeli sources reported shelling of the area by possible Egyptian warships. However, on the eighth an investigation determined that the explosions—so large they were seen by the *Liberty* bridge crew and by Kursa flight leader Captain Spector—probably were from ammunition dump explosions.

12. The *Liberty* crewmen reported numerous overflights by Israeli aircraft, which they felt should have provided adequate identification of the *Liberty* as a nonhostile ship. Beyond the maritime surveillance aircraft searching for Egyptian submarines, the vast majority of the planes were Israeli combat aircraft at high altitudes transiting to and from Egyptian targets.

13. The torpedo boats were wood-hull, diesel-powered, French-built craft of the Israeli *Ayah* class, each with two torpedo tubes and one 40-mm and four 20-mm guns and some .50-caliber machine guns. The boats were capable of 42 knots.

14. Gerhard and Millington, "Attack on a SIGINT Collector," 37.

15. Greenberg, "Attack on the *Liberty* Incident," 11.

16. Commander in chief, U.S. Naval Forces Europe, "Liberty Chronology Eight June (U)."

17. Arieh O'Sullivan, "Liberty Attack Tapes Revealed," *Jerusalem Post*, 6 June 2004, https://freerepublic.com/focus/f-news/1148399/posts?page=33. The *Liberty*'s profile is mast-(funnel/mast)-mast. That the flight leader reported one mast and one funnel reveals the limits of a pilot's visual acuity from 3,000 feet at attack speed, makes moot claims by the *Liberty*'s crew that the flag was flying, and falsifies theories that the pilots were criminal in attacking a properly marked and identifiable U.S. ship.

18. The two "guns" reported by Spector apparently were misidentifications of a trainable radio dish antenna mounted on the bow and other equipment. His observation reveals the limitations on a jet aircraft pilot's visual acuity at 2,000 feet or higher altitude while making a high-speed pass over a naval ship. See Wikimedia Commons, *USS Liberty (AGTR-5) underway in Chesapeake Bay on 29 July 1967 (K-39927)*, 29 July 1967, https://commons.wikimedia.org/wiki/File:USS_Liberty_(AGTR-5)_underway_in_Chesapeake_Bay_on_29_July_1967_(K-39927).jpg.

19. Bregman, *Israel's Wars*, 88–90; Commander in chief, U.S. Naval Forces Europe, "Liberty Chronology Eight June (U)"; and Gerhard and Millington, "Attack on a SIGINT Collector," 37.

20. The *Liberty*'s doctor reported treating no napalm cases. Israel released transcripts including conversations with the second pair of attacking aircraft that show an aircraft attacking with napalm dropped his canisters early, and they fell into the water. The second pilot adjusted his aim, and at least one of the napalm canisters hit the ship (one *Liberty* crewman recovered a gelatinous residue after the attack for analysis).

21. The *Liberty*'s logs are as much as five to ten minutes out of sync with the times reported by the Israeli Air Force and Navy; the MTB (Motor Torpedo Boat) War Log is out of sync with the Navy headquarters (HQ); and the Navy HQ is out of sync with the Air Force HQ. These problems occur because hand entries into a logbook may be made several minutes after the event, and clocks are not calibrated against each other. The only precise times are to be found on transcripts taken from Israeli Air Force circuits with automatic time tics recorded on the original. According to the *Liberty*'s logs, the second pair of aircraft commenced attack at 1411.

22. U.S. Navy auxiliary ships had their hull numbers painted on their bows, usually with the letter "A" deleted; thus, the *Liberty* was marked as "GTR 5."

23. Quotations are from the report of the Israeli examining judge, Lt. Col. Yeshayahu (Isaiah) Yerushalmi, the former judge advocate general of the Israeli Navy and Air Force. See Yerushalmi, "Preliminary Inquiry File 1/67."

24. Bregman, *Israel's Wars*, 88–90. Also see Arieh O'Sullivan, "Liberty Revisited: The Attack," *Jerusalem Post*, 4 June 2004, 20.

25. Personnel on board the *Liberty* reported that Israeli attacking aircraft jammed all of the *Liberty*'s communications, including emergency frequencies, and they have emotionally and falsely characterized that action as "a violation of international law." The first U.S. airborne jamming equipment for the Israeli Air Force was transferred during the Yom Kipper War of 1973. It is probable that the reported jamming was unrecognized damage to the ship's electronic systems. See Doyle, "Yom Kippur War," 62.

26. Some documents concerning the *Liberty* incident refer to Rear Admiral Shlomo Erell as "Commodore Shlomo Arel" in English-language translations.

27. Gerhard and Millington, "Attack on a SIGINT Collector," 41.

28. Gerhard and Millington, "Attack on a SIGINT Collector," 39.

29. Commander in Chief, U.S. Naval Forces Europe, "Liberty Chronology Eight June (U)."

30. Naval Communications Unit, Naples message 061222Z 6 JUL 67; Commander in Chief, U.S. Naval Forces Europe, 192026Z 19 JUN 67; and Gerhard and Millington, "Attack on a SIGINT Collector," 30.

31. Much derision and sarcasm has been levied upon this misidentification as being grossly unbelievable. Greenberg, "Attack on the *Liberty* Incident," 23, shows photos of both ships from identification guides, and lacking size correlation, there are similarities that make the misidentification believable, especially with the *Liberty* largely shrouded in black smoke. However, Lieutenant Commander Oren reported that the target "resembled" the Egyptian ship *El-Quesir*, then immediately requested authorization for a torpedo attack. Deadly force in a non-imminent situation at sea is not appropriate if based upon *resemblance* rather than positive *identification*. See "Arab Navies Identification Ships," translated by Major Chana, Tel Aviv, 16 January 1990, http://www.libertyincident.com/docs/arab-navies.pdf.

32. "War Log—Division 914," Navy Headquarters, Sea Section 3, excerpt 8 June 1967, time: 1120–1750 local, http://www.libertyincident.com/docs/israellog914e.pdf.

33. Division 914, "War Log," Navy Headquarters, Sea Section 3, excerpt 8 June 1967, time: 0550–1615 local, http://www.libertyincident.com/docs/israellogopse.pdf.

34. Gerhard and Millington, "Attack on a SIGINT Collector," 38. The National Security Agency's summary of events has Oren's attack commencing at 1436. See National Security Agency, "USS *Liberty* (USN-855) (AGTR-5)."

35. Rabin, *Rabin Memoirs*, 197.

36. Greenberg, "Attack on a SIGINT Collector," 19. This event is logged by the *Liberty* as one torpedo boat approached and inquired in English by megaphone, "Do you need help?" Followed by the question, "Do you want us to stand by?" Commander McGonagle replied with a handheld signal lamp, "No thank you. We do not need help." Oren wished the ship "a safe journey."

37. Ennes, *Assault on the* Liberty, 77. Ennes resorted to speculation and manufactured drama to mask the limited documentation and unclassified data then available to him. The book is inundated with factual errors and unfounded accusations.

38. Vice Admiral Donald D. Engen, USN (Ret.), discussion with Norman Polmar, Washington DC, 17 June 1998. Also see Engen, *Wings and Warriors*, 320–22. British FGR2 Phantoms based in West Germany did carry U.S. nuclear bombs from 1972 to 1976.

39. Wells, "*Liberty* Victims," 89. Also see responding by Cristol, Comment on "*Liberty* Victims," 28.

40. Quoted in Cristol, Liberty *Incident*, 100. Cristol was a sitting federal judge when he wrote that volume.

41. Halliwell, "Sixth Fleet's Attempt."

42. Gerhard and Millington, "Attack on a SIGINT Collector," 12. The EC-121M Warning Star aircraft were based at Rota, Spain; for the Middle East missions they were staged through Athens, Greece.

43. National Security Agency, "Aftermath of Israeli Attack."

44. Lee Mathers interview with Chief Petty Officer Marvin E. Nowicki, USN (Ret.), 20 November 2020. Nowicki affirmed the accuracy of the transcript of the intercepts, published as National Security Agency, "Aftermath of Israeli Attack."

45. Note that the flight time of the two helicopters launched from Hatsor airfield northeast of Ashkelon was 42 minutes to the *Liberty*. With the 15 minutes of preparation required for their launch, it took the Israeli Air Force almost one hour to confirm the suspicions that it had attacked a U.S. Navy ship.

46. "USS Liberty Incident," U.S. Defense Attaché Office, Tel Aviv, message 151615Z JUN 67.

47. Central Intelligence Agency, "Intelligence Memorandum," SC 08384-67.

48. Gerhard and Millington, "Attack on a SIGINT Collector," 32.

49. U.S. Defense Attaché Office, Tel Aviv, message 081414Z 8 JUN 1967.

50. Gerhard and Millington, "Attack on a SIGINT Collector," 3, question 4.

51. Cristol, Liberty *Incident Revealed*, 8. This volume is an updated edition of his earlier book.

52. The first two were unfortunate blue-on-blue incidents, and the case of the Tartus raid was an inadvertent civilian casualty during warfare. See Goldstein and Zhukov, "Tale of Two Fleets," 46.

53. Farley, "Oral History Interview," 113–15. Carter died in 1993.

54. The National Security Agency failed to officially request safer standoff distances for the *Liberty* on the fifth or sixth. Pressure from the chief of naval operations to move the *Liberty* out of danger finally pushed the Joint Chiefs of Staff into action on the seventh. National Security Agency, "USS *Liberty* (USN-855) (AGTR-5)."

55. Central Intelligence Agency, "Intelligence Memorandum," SC 08384-67.

56. Central Intelligence Agency, "Intelligence Memorandum," SC 08384-67.

57. Joseph C. Lentini, "I Was On Board the *Liberty*" (letter), *Washington Post*, 4 October 1977, was reprinted in USNI *Proceedings*, December 1977, 108–9.

58. Scott, *Attack on the* Liberty, 47, 53. The author's father, John Scott, was on board the *Liberty* at the time of the Israeli attack.

59. See Moorer, Davis, Staring, and Akins, "Findings."

60. Rusk, "Telegram from Department of State."

61. Rusk, "Telegram from Department of State."

62. Brooks, Review of *The* Liberty *Incident*, 23.

63. Cristol, Liberty *Incident Revealed*, 244–45.

7. American Spy Ships: Part 2

1. Johnson, "Book II: Centralization Wins," 395.

2. Johnson, "Book II: Centralization Wins."

3. Evans, "Eugene G. Fubini," in National Academy of Engineering, *Memorial Tributes*.

4. Johnson, "Book II: Centralization Wins," 359.

5. Johnson, "Book II: Centralization Wins," 396.

6. Johnson, "Book II: Centralization Wins."

7. Pfister, "USS *Banner* (AGER-1)." Unless otherwise noted, data on the *Banner* originates from this *Banner* letter 5720, dated 19 May 1969.

8. CNO msg 141603Z, October 1965, found in the command history, Pfister, "USS *Banner* (AGER-1)," enclosure 2, 1.

9. Lieutenant Durocher was a seminarian from age 14 to 22, and then he joined the Navy. After retiring from naval service after 20 years, in a life-changing decision at age 53, he was ordained a priest at St. Peter's Cathedral in Wilmington, Delaware.

10. Packard, *Century of U.S. Naval Intelligence*, 116–17.

11. Pfister, "USS *Banner* (AGER-1)," enclosure 2, 6.

12. Tooma, "Five Short Tales," tale #5.

13. Department of State Telegram to American Embassy Moscow 1298, 18 November 1965, Subject: *Banner* Incident; telegram from American Embassy Moscow 14873, 18 December 1965: MFA Note No. 53/USA; and Department of State telegram to American Embassy Moscow 1549, 23 December 1965: Memorandum of Conversation, Subject: Collision of Soviet Vessel with USS *Banner* between Llewellyn E. Thompson and Anatolily F. Dobrynin, 25 June 1966.

14. The U.S. destroyer *Walker* was "scraped" twice by Soviet destroyers while operating in the Sea of Japan on 10–11 May 1967.

15. "U.S.-Soviet Naval Incident: U.S. Ship Bumped Twice," 17 May 1967, https://web.stanford.edu/group/tomzgroup/pmwiki/uploads/2930-1967-05-17-FoF-a-EYJ.pdf; and John W. Finney, "A U.S. Destroyer in Far East Bumped by Soviet Warship," *New York Times*, 11 May 1967, 5.

16. Burtenshaw, Fulgham, and Walls, "Pueblo Incident."

17. Rex Catron, "Guests' Comments: January–December 2002," USS *Pueblo* (AGER-2), dated Tuesday, 30 April 2002, 10:59:28, http://www.usspueblo.org/guest_comments/Guests_2002.htm.

18. BRIGAND stands for Bistatic Radar Intelligence Gathering and Detection.

19. Cheevers, *Act of War*, chap. 2.

20. Cheevers, *Act of War*.

21. Robert Fredlund email to Lee Mathers, June 2021.

22. Burtenshaw, Fulgham, and Walls, "Pueblo Incident," fig. 2-1, and p. 14.

23. See Ralph [no surname provided], "Guests' Comments: January–December 2001," USS *Pueblo* (AGER-2), dated Saturday, 14 April 2001, 09:44:47 -0600 (MDT), http://www.usspueblo.org/guest_comments/Guests_2001.htm. See also Cheevers, *Act of War*.

24. Vulcano, "SIGINT Collection Ships."

25. Huchthausen and Sheldon-Duplaix, *Hide and Seek*, 193–94.

26. Howe, "Technical Research Ships," 37–45.

27. See Lyndon B. Johnson, "Annual Budget Message to the Congress, Fiscal Year 1970," 15 January 1969, American Presidency Project, https://www.presidency.ucsb.edu/documents/annual-budget-message-the-congress-fiscal-year-1970; and Richard Nixon, "Annual Budget Message to the Congress, Fiscal Year 1971," 2 February 1970, American Presidency Project, https://www.presidency.ucsb.edu/documents/annual-budget-message-the-congress-fiscal-year-1971.

8. The Seizure of the USS *Pueblo*

1. Lt. Cdr. John Arnold, USN (Ret.), "Guest Comments: January–December 2002," USS *Pueblo* (AGER-2), dated Saturday, 4 May 2002, 19:54:57, http://www.usspueblo.org/guest_comments/Guests_2002.htm.

2. Arnold, "Guest Comments."

3. Bucher, *Bucher: My Story*, 112.

4. Bucher, *Bucher: My Story*, 112.

5. Bucher, *Bucher: My Story*, 112.

6. Bucher, *Bucher: My Story*, 125.

7. Bucher, *Bucher: My Story*, 139–40.

8. Bucher, *Bucher: My Story*, 153.

9. COMNAVFORJAPAN confidential message 180752Z DEC 1967, "Pinkroot Operation One."

10. NSA message 29 December 1968 to JCS, *Pinkroot Operation 1*, found in Newton, "Capture of the USS *Pueblo*," 177.

11. Message from Commander Task Force 96 (another title for the Commander, Naval Forces, Japan), 050512Z JAN 1968, "Ichthyic One Formerly Pinkroot One."

12. Commander Task Force 96, 050512Z JAN 1968.

13. Bucher, *Bucher: My Story*, 137.

14. Calling the two Marines "linguists" was probably an overstatement; they had undergone a 16-week course in the Korean language two and a half years earlier.

15. Burtenshaw, Fulgham, and Walls, "Pueblo Incident," 14.

16. Bucher, *Bucher: My Story*, 162–80.

17. Murphy, *Second in Command*, 116.

18. Newton, "Capture of the USS *Pueblo*," 54.

19. Bucher, *Bucher: My Story*, 178.

20. Cdr. Douglas M. Hackett, USN (Ret.), "Analysis of North Korean Evidence," Office of Naval Intelligence, briefing classified Secret, created by the Department of State, Office of the Assistant Secretary for East Asian and Pacific Affairs. Hackett gave the presentation at the 2015 Naval Intelligence Professionals conference at the International Spy Museum, Washington DC.

21. Murphy, *Second in Command*, 126.

22. Newton, "Capture of the USS *Pueblo*," 56. The report refers to intercept 3/00/KCJ/R13–68 072040Z 1968 (TSC/ISHTAR). Ishtar indicates that the intercept originated from a Japanese COMINT source.

23. Newton, "Capture of the USS *Pueblo*," 56–59. One of the derelictions of duty for which Harris was recommended for court-martial by the Court of Inquiry was that he did not notify Bucher that the two temporary Korean "linguists" provided by the Naval Security Agency Activity at Kami Seya lacked language proficiency.

24. The P-4 torpedo boats were aluminum-hull craft built in China. Each had two 17-inch (430-mm) torpedoes and several machine guns of varying caliber; they were capable of 55 knots.

25. Schumacher, *Bridge of No Return*. Schumacher placed that event at about 1315.

26. Burtenshaw, Fulgham, and Walls, "Pueblo Incident," 18.

27. Newton, "Capture of the USS *Pueblo*," 63, 65, 171.

28. For Commander Bucher's full "confession," see "Prisoners: Excerpts from Bucher's Final Confession," recorded 1995, USS *Pueblo* (AGER-2), http://www.usspueblo.org/Prisoners/Pete_Final_Confession.html.

29. Captain John R. Brock, USN, Navy Judge Advocate General's Office, testimony before the U.S. Navy's *Pueblo* Court of Inquiry, as reported by Robert Crabbe, "*Pueblo* Nab Illegal, Says Navy Lawyer," *Atlanta Constitution*, 6 March 1969, 27.

30. Kobke, "U.S.S. *Pueblo* Incident," 67–69.

31. Central Intelligence Agency, "North Korea Provokes," 6–7.

32. Newton, "Capture of the USS *Pueblo*," p.163.

33. Vice Admiral Harold G. Bowen Jr., USN, "Findings of Fact, Opinions and Recommendations of a Court of Inquiry Relating to the Seizure of USS *Pueblo* (AGER 2)," 9 April 1969.

34. First Endorsement to Vice Adm. Harold G. Bowen Jr., "Findings of Fact, Opinions and Recommendations of a Court of Inquiry Relating to the Seizure of USS *Pueblo* (AGER-2)," by the Commander in Chief, U.S. Pacific Fleet, letter dated 2 May 1969.

35. First Endorsement to Vice Admiral Harold G. Bowen Jr.

36. Secretary of the Navy John H. Chafee, "Chafee Statement after Court of Inquiry, 6 May 1969," USS *Pueblo* (AGER-2), http://www.usspueblo.org/Court_of_Inquiry/SecNav_Chafee.html.

37. See "USS PUEBLO (AGER 2)," Naval Vessel Register, 13 September 2011, https://www.nvr.navy.mil/SHIPDETAILS/SHIPSDETAIL_AGER_2.HTML. The only older U.S. Navy ship that remains in commission is the sailing frigate *Constitution*. Also known as "Old Ironsides," she was completed in 1797 and is preserved in Boston as a museum ship.

38. See Mobley, "Lessons from the Capture," 1–10; and Streifer and Sabitov, "'Improbable Allies,'" 104–40. The latter is a unique and detailed analysis of the EC-121 shootdown.

39. Streifer and Sabitov, "'Improbable Allies,'" 119.

40. Mobley, "EC-121 Down!," 62–66. Also see Kissinger, *White House Years*, 312–21.

9. Unusual Spy Ships

1. The LST "carrier" operations are described in Polmar, *Aircraft Carriers*, 1:338–39, 341–42, 344, 468–69.

2. See O'Neil, "Journey to a Far Sea," 93–96.

3. O'Neil, "Journey to a Far Sea," 93–94.

4. "*Brink of Apocalypse* 2/5: Interview with Admiral Vladen Smirnoff, USSR Northern Fleet, Deputy Chief," [2007], Television Documentary Archive, Kings College London, https://kingscollections.org/catalogues/lhcma/collection/b/brink-of-apocalypse/brink-of-apocalypse-2.

5. Previously the U.S. Navy had operated the range support ship *Kaimalino*, which had a SWATH configuration.

10. Some Bottom Lines

1. See Richard Halloran, "U.S. Navy Surveillance Ship Is Stationed off Central America," *New York Times*, 25 February 1982, A1.

2. An excellent discussion of this subject is in Flakus, "Use of Large Unmanned Vehicles." The article is based on his award-winning paper submitted to the Naval War College, Newport RI.

Appendix C. Other Spy Ships

1. The best accounts of the British recapture of the Falklands—Operation Corporate—are Woodward, *One Hundred Days;* and West, *Secret War for the Falklands.* Also see the official government reports from the British and U.S. governments: Secretary of State for Defence, *Falkland Campaign;* and Secretary of the Navy, *Lessons of the Falklands.*

2. The carrier was HMS *Hermes*, embarking Harrier vertical/short takeoff and landing aircraft and helicopters.

3. Woodward, *One Hundred Days*, 191.

4. West, *Secret War for the Falklands*, 22.

5. Hughes-Wilson, *Military Intelligence Blunders*, 284.

6. East and West Germany were united in 1990.

7. See Gabriel Dominguez, "Japan Launches Third Hibiki-Class Ocean Surveillance Ship," *Jane's Defence News*, 3 February 2020, https://www.janes.com/defence-news/news-detail/japan-launches-third-hibiki-class-ocean-surveillance-ship.

8. The Government Communications Security Bureau is the equivalent of the U.S. National Security Agency.

9. See Riste, *Norwegian Intelligence Service.*

10. Nilsen, "Spy Ship Changes Name."

11. Bruce Rule email to Lee Mathers, 16 August 2021.

12. "A Blast, a Deluge, Then Death in a Metal Tomb," *Guardian*, 20 August 2000.

13. Rolf Soderlind, "Soviet Vessel Rams Swedish Spy Ship," United Press International, 1 November 1985, https://www.upi.com/Archives/1985/11/01/Soviet-vessel-rams-Swedish-spy-ship/3972499669200/.

BIBLIOGRAPHY

Books in English

Armbrister, Trevor. *A Matter of Accountability: The True Story of the* Pueblo *Affair.* New York: Coward McCann, 1970.

Baker, A. D. *Combat Fleets of the World.* Annapolis MD: Naval Institute (various editions).

Ball, Desmond. *Soviet Signals Intelligence (SIGINT).* Canberra: Australian National University, 1989.

Beesly, Patrick. *Room 40: British Naval Intelligence 1914–1918.* New York: Harcourt Brace Jovanovich, 1982.

———. *Very Special Intelligence: The Story of the Admiralty's Operational Intelligence Centre 1939–1945.* London: Greenhill, 2000; original edition, Hamish Hamilton, 1977.

Bregman, Ahron, *Israel's Wars: A History since 1947.* New York: Routledge, 2000.

Brusnitsin, Nikolay. *Openness and Espionage.* Moscow: Military Publishing House, 1990.

Bucher, Lloyd M. *Bucher: My Story.* New York: Doubleday, 1970.

Burrows, William L. *Deep Black: Space Espionage and National Security.* New York: Random House, 1986.

Cheevers, Jack. *Act of War: Lyndon Johnson, North Korea, and the Capture of the Spy Ship* Pueblo. New York: New American Library, 2013.

Craven, John Piña. *The Silent War: The Cold War Battle Beneath the Sea.* New York: Simon & Schuster, 2001.

Cristol, A. Jay. *The* Liberty *Incident: The 1967 Israeli Attack on the U.S. Navy Spy Ship.* Washington DC: Brassey's, 2002; rev. ed. 2013.

———. *The* Liberty *Incident Revealed: The Definitive Account of the 1967 Israeli Attack on the U.S. Navy Spy Ship.* Annapolis MD: Naval Institute, 2013.

Deacon, Richard. *Kempei Tai: A History of the Japanese Secret Service.* New York: Beaufort, 1983.

Dobbs, Michael. *One Minute to Midnight: Kennedy, Khrushchev, and Castro on the Brink of Nuclear War.* New York: Alfred A. Knopf, 2008.

Dorwart, Jeffrey M. *Conflict of Duty: The U.S. Navy's Intelligence Dilemma, 1919–1945.* Annapolis MD: Naval Institute, 1983.

Dunham, Roger C. *Spy Sub: Top Secret Mission to the Bottom of the Pacific*. Annapolis MD: Naval Institute, 1996.

Dutton, Peter. *Scouting, Signaling, and Gatekeeping: Chinese Naval Operations in Japanese Waters and the International Law Implications*. China Maritime Study No. 2. Newport RI: Naval War College, 2009. https://web.archive.org/web/20120720004430/http://www.usnwc.edu/Research-Gaming/China-Maritime-Studies-Institute/Publications/documents/CMS2_Dutton.aspx.

Engen, Donald D. *Wings and Warriors: My Life as a Naval Aviator*. Washington DC: Smithsonian, 2004.

Ennes, James N., Jr. *Assault on the* Liberty*: The True Story of the Israeli Attack on an American Intelligence Ship*. New York: Random House, 1987.

Ford, Christopher, and David Rosenberg. *The Admirals' Advantage: U.S. Navy Operational Intelligence in World War II and the Cold War*. Annapolis MD: Naval Institute, 2005; rev. ed., 2014.

Gallery, Daniel V. *The* Pueblo *Incident*. New York: Doubleday, 1970.

Grant, Robert M. *U-Boat Intelligence 1914–1918*. London: Putnam, 1969.

Greenway, Ambrose. *Soviet Merchant Ships*. Hampshire: Kenneth Mason, 1969, 1985, 1989.

Gribkov, Anatoli I., and William Y. Smith. *Operation Anadyr: U.S. and Soviet Generals Recount the Cuban Missile Crisis*. Chicago: Edition q, 1994.

Harris, Stephen R. *My Anchor Held*. New York: F. H. Revell, 1970.

Hennessy, Peter, and James Jinks. *The Silent Deep: The Royal Navy Submarine Service since 1945*. London: Allen Lane/Penguin, 2015.

Hezlet, Arthur. *The Electron and Sea Power*. London: Peter Davies, 1975. Published in the United States as *Electronics and Sea Power*. New York: Stein and Day, 1975.

Holmes, W. J. *Double-Edged Secrets: U.S. Naval Intelligence Operations in the Pacific during World War II*. Annapolis MD: Naval Institute, 1979.

———. *Undersea Victory: The Influence of Submarine Operations on the War in the Pacific*. New York: Doubleday, 1966.

Hooper, Edward B. *Mobility, Support, Endurance: A Story of Naval Operational Logistics in the Vietnam War, 1965–1968*. Washington DC: Department of the Navy, 1972.

Huchthausen, Peter A. *K-19: The Widowmaker: The Secret Story of the Soviet Nuclear Submarine*. Washington DC: National Geographic, 2002.

Huchthausen, Peter A., and Alexandre Sheldon-Duplaix. *Hide and Seek: The Untold Story of Cold War Naval Espionage*. New York: John Wiley & Sons, 2009.

Hughes-Wilson, John. *Military Intelligence Blunders*. New York: Carroll & Graf, 1999.

Hutton, J. Bernard. *Frogman Spy: The Incredible Case of Commander Crabb*. New York: McDowell, Obolensky, 1960.

James, William. *The Eyes of the Navy: A Biographical Study of Admiral Sir Reginald Hall*. London: Methuen, 1955.

Kahn, David. *Seizing the Enigma: The Race to Break the German U-Boat Codes, 1939–1943*. Boston: Houghton Mifflin, 1991.

Karremann, Jaime. *In Deepest Secrecy: Dutch Submarine Espionage Operations from 1968 to 1991*. Amsterdam: Marineschepen, 2018.

Keegan, John. *Intelligence in War: Knowledge of the Enemy from Napoleon to Al-Qaeda*. New York: Alfred A. Knopf, 2003.

Kissinger, Henry A. *The White House Years*. Boston: Little, Brown, 1979.

Lehman, John. *Oceans Ventured: Winning the Cold War at Sea*. New York: W. W. Norton, 2018.

Lerner, Mitchell B. *The* Pueblo *Incident: A Spy Ship and the Failure of American Foreign Policy*. Lawrence: University Press of Kansas, 2002.

Macintyre, Ben. *Operation Mincemeat*. New York: Harmony, 2010.

Macintyre, Donald. *U-Boat Killer*. London: Weidenfeld & Nicholson, 1956. Rev. ed.: Annapolis MD: Naval Institute, 1956.

MacLean, Alistair. *Ice Station Zebra*. New York: Random House, 1963.

Maffeo, Steven E. *Most Secret and Confidential: Intelligence in the Age of Nelson*. Annapolis MD: Naval Institute, 2000.

McCormick, Gordon H. *Stranger than Fiction: Soviet Submarine Operations in Swedish Waters*. Santa Monica CA: Rand, 1990.

McLaren, Alfred Scott. *Silent and Unseen: On Patrol in Three Cold War Attack Submarines*. Annapolis MD: Naval Institute, 2015.

Minton, David C., and Alfred S. Berzin. *From Opposite Sides of the Periscope: The Trail Is On*. New York: Archway, 2018.

Mobley, Richard A. *Flash Point North Korea: The* Pueblo *and the EC-121 Crises*. Annapolis MD: Naval Institute, 2003.

Montagu, Ewen. *The Man Who Never Was*. Philadelphia: J. P. Lippincott, 1953.

Murphy, Edward R., Jr. *Second in Command: The Uncensored Account of the Capture of the Spy Ship* Pueblo. New York: Holt, Rinehart and Winston, 1971.

Murray, Williamson, and Allan R. Millett. *Military Innovation in the Interwar Period*. Cambridge: Cambridge University Press, 1996.

Nekrasov, George. *North of Gallipoli: The Black Sea Fleet at War 1914–1917*. New York: Columbia University Press, 1992.

Oren, Michael B. *Six Days of War: June 1967 and the Making of the Modern Middle East*. New York: Random House Ballantine, 2002.

Packard, Wyman H. *A Century of U.S. Naval Intelligence*. Washington DC: Department of the Navy, 1996.

Palmer, Michael A. *Command at Sea: Naval Command and Control since the Sixteenth Century*. Cambridge MA: Harvard University Press, 2005.

Pavlov, A. S. *Warships of the USSR and Russia 1945–1995*. Annapolis MD: Naval Institute, 1997.

Perry, Hamilton Darby. *The* Panay *Incident: Prelude to Pearl Harbor*. New York: Macmillan, 1969.

Polmar, Norman. *Aircraft Carriers: A History of Carrier Aviation and Its Influence on World Events*. Vol. I, *1909–1945*. Dulles VA: Potomac Books, 2006.

———. *Guide to the Soviet Navy*. 5th ed. Annapolis MD: Naval Institute, 1991.

———. *Ships and Aircraft of the U.S. Fleet*. Annapolis MD: Naval Institute (various editions).

Polmar, Norman, and Thomas B. Allen. *Rickover: Genius and Controversy*. New York: Simon & Schuster, 1982.

Polmar, Norman, and John D. Gresham. *DEFCON-2: Standing on the Brink of Nuclear War during the Cuban Missile Crisis*. Hoboken NJ: John Wiley & Sons, 2006.

Polmar, Norman, and Lee J. Mathers. *Opening the Great Depths: The Bathyscaph* Trieste *and Pioneers of Undersea Exploration*. Annapolis MD: Naval Institute, 2021.

Polmar, Norman, and K. J. Moore. *Cold War Submarines: The Design and Construction of U.S. and Soviet Submarines*. Washington DC: Brassey's, 2004.

Polmar, Norman, and John O'Connell. *Strike from the Sea: The Development and Deployment of Strategic Cruise Missiles since 1934*. Annapolis MD: Naval Institute, 2020.

Polmar, Norman, and Michael White. *Project Azorian: The Raising of the K-129*. Annapolis MD: Naval Institute, 2010.

Prebble, Stuart. *Secrets of the Conqueror: The Untold Story of Britain's Most Famous Submarine*. London: Farber & Farber, 2012.

Price, Alfred. *The History of US Electronic Warfare*. Vol. 1. Alexandria VA: Association of Old Crows, 1984.

Pugh, Marshall. *Frogman: Commander Crabb's Story*. New York: Charles Scribner's Sons, 1956.

Rabin, Yitzhak. *The Rabin Memoirs*. London: Weidenfeld & Nicolson, 1979.

Ring, Jim. *We Come Unseen: The Untold Story of Britain's Cold War Submariners*. London: John Murray, 2001.

Riste, Olav. *The Norwegian Intelligence Service 1945–1970*. London: Frank Cass, 1999.

Roscoe, Theodore. *United States Submarine Operations in World War II*. Annapolis MD: Naval Institute, 1958.

Sayers, Ken W. *Uncommon Warriors: 200 Years of the Most Unusual American Naval Vessels*. Annapolis MD: Naval Institute, 2012.

Schratz, Paul R. *Submarine Commander: A Story of World War II and Korea*. Lawrence: University Press of Kansas, 1989.

Schumacher, Frederick C. *Bridge of No Return: The Ordeal of the USS* Pueblo. New York: Harcourt Brace Jovanovich, 1970.

Schwar, Harriet Dashiell, ed. *Arab-Israeli Crisis and War, 1967*. Vol. 19 of *Foreign Relations of the United States, 1964–1968*, edited by Edward C. Keefer. Washington DC: Department of State, 2004.

Scott, James. *The Attack on the* Liberty*: The Untold Story of Israel's Deadly 1967 Assault on a U.S. Spy Ship*. New York: Simon & Schuster, 2009.

Sergeev, Evgeny. *Russian Military Intelligence in the War with Japan, 1904–05: Secret Operations on Land and at Sea*. New York: Routledge, 2008.

Siiteri, Helen A. ed. *Papa Topside: The Sealab Chronicles of Captain George F. Bond, USN*. Annapolis MD: Naval Institute, 1993.

Smith, Martin Cruz. *Gorky Park*. New York: Random House, 1981.

———. *Polar Star*. New York: Random House, 1989.

Smith, Peyton. *Assault on the USS* Liberty: *Deliberate Action or Tragic Accident?* Carlisle PA: Army War College, 2007.

Smyth, Denis. *Deathly Deception: The Real Story of Operation Mincemeat*. New York: Oxford University Press, 2010.

Sontag, Sherry, and Christopher Drew. *Blind Man's Bluff: The Untold Story of American Submarine Espionage*. New York: PublicAffairs, 1998.

Suvorov, Viktor (pseud.). *Inside Soviet Military Intelligence*. New York: Macmillan, 1984.

Tolley, Kemp. *Cruise of the* Lanikai: *Incitement to War*. Annapolis MD: Naval Institute, 1973.

———. *Yangtze Patrol: The U.S. Navy in China*. Annapolis MD: Naval Institute, 1971.

Tunander, Ola. *The Secret War against Sweden: US and British Submarine Deception in the 1980s*. London: Frank Cass, 2004.

Tyler, Patrick. *Running Critical: The Silent War, Rickover, and General Dynamics*. New York: Harper & Row, 1986.

Vego, Milan. *Soviet Naval Tactics*. Annapolis MD: Naval Institute, 1992.

Vyborny, Lee, and Don Davis. *Dark Waters: An Insider's Account of the NR-1, the Cold War's Undercover Nuclear Sub*. New York: New American Library, 2003.

Watson, Bruce W., and Susan M. Watson, eds. *The Soviet Navy: Strengths and Liabilities*. Boulder CO: Westview, 1986.

West, Nigel. *The Secret War for the Falklands: The SAS, MI6, and the War Whitehall Nearly Lost*. London: Little, Brown, 1997.

———. *The SIGINT Secrets: The Signals Intelligence War, 1900 to Today*. New York: William Morrow, 1986.

Williams, Kathleen Broome. *Secret Weapon: U.S. High-Frequency Direction Finding in the Battle of the Atlantic*. Annapolis MD: Naval Institute, 1996.

Winkler, David F. *Cold War at Sea: High-Seas Confrontation between the United States and the Soviet Union*. Annapolis MD: Naval Institute, 2000.

Woodward, Bob. *Veil: The Secret Wars of the CIA, 1981–1987*. New York: Simon & Schuster, 1987.

Woodward, Sandy. *One Hundred Days: The Memoirs of the Falklands Battle Group Commander*. London: HarperCollins, 1992.

Zacharias, Ellis M. *Secret Missions: The Story of an Intelligence Officer*. New York: G. P. Putnam's Sons, 1946.

Zullo, Matt. *The U.S. Navy's On-the-Roof Gang, Vol. 1, Prelude to War*. Laurel MD: Matt Zullo, 2020.

———. *The U.S. Navy's On-the-Roof Gang, Vol. 2, War in the Pacific*. Laurel MD: Matt Zullo, 2020.

Book in German

Breyer, Siegfried. *Handbuch der Warschauer-Pakt-Flotten* (Manual of Warsaw Pact Navies). Munich: Bernard & Graefe, 1994.

Books in Japanese

Nakamuda Ken'ichi. *Johoshikan no kaiso* (Reminiscences of an intelligence officer). Tokyo: Sonorama, 1985.

Sanematsu Yuzuru, *Nichi-Bei johosenki* (Record of Japanese-American intelligence war). Tokyo: Tosho, 1980.

Books in Russian

Bubnov, Andrei S. *V tsarskoy* (In the Tsar's Headquarters). New York: Chekhov, 1955. *Note*: Bubnov was a rear admiral in the Tsarist navy and was closely involved with Black Sea operations during World War I.

Kuzin, V. P., and V. I. Nikol'skiy. *Voyenno-morskoy Flot SSSR, 1945–1991* (The Navy of the USSR, 1945–1991). St. Petersburg: Historical Oceanic Society, 1996.

Articles in English

Note: Citations to newspaper articles appear in endnotes only. USNI = U.S. Naval Institute.

(Author excised.) "The Origination and Evaluation of Radio Traffic Analysis—Part 2: The Period between the Wars." Doc ID 3362395. *Cryptologic Quarterly*, 1988. https://www.nsa.gov/portals/75/documents/news-features/declassified-documents/cryptologic-quarterly/the_period_between_wars.pdf.

Ackley, Richard T. "The Fishing Fleet and Soviet Strategy." USNI *Proceedings*, July 1975.

Allen, Thomas B. "Incidents at Sea." USNI *Proceedings*, September 1990.

Bigelow, Robert P. "Wireless in Warfare, 1885–1914." USNI *Proceedings*, February 1951.

Bilyeu, Braden. "NR-1: Exploring Naval History on the Ocean Floor." *Undersea Warfare* (Winter-Spring 2002).

Breyer, Siegfried. "Soviet EW Vessel in the Baltic." *International Defense Review* 12 (1987).

Brooks, Thomas A. "Intelligence Collection." USNI *Proceedings*, December 1985.

———. Review of *The* Liberty *Incident* by A. Jay Cristol. *Naval Intelligence Professionals Quarterly*, October 2002.

Bussert, Jim. "Soviet Naval Electronic Technology." USNI *Proceedings*, February 1978.

Carnes, Calland F. "Inside Soviet Naval Intelligence." *Naval Intelligence Professionals Quarterly*, Spring 1990.

———. "Soviet Naval Intelligence." In *The Soviet Navy: Strengths and Liabilities*, edited by Bruce W. Watson and Susan M. Watson, 168–74. Boulder CO: Westview, 1986.

Central Intelligence Agency. "Project Azorian: The Story of the Hughes Glomar Explorer." *Studies in Intelligence*, Fall 1985.

Cristol, A. Jay. Comment on "*Liberty* Victims Did Not Die in Vain." USNI *Proceedings*, March 2005.

Drea, Edward J. "Reading Each Other's Mail: Japanese Communications Intelligence, 1920–1941." *Journal of Military History*, April 1991.

Ellis, M. G. M. W. "Sweden's Ghosts?" USNI *Proceedings*, March 1986.

Evans, Bob O. "Eugene G. Fubini 1913–1997." *National Academy of Engineering. Memorial Tributes: National Academy of Engineering*, vol. 10. Washington DC: National Academies, 2002. https://www.nae.edu/188030/EUGENE-GFUBINI-19131997.

Flakus, Joshua, and Michael Flakus. "Use of Large Unmanned Vehicles in Joint Intelligence, Surveillance, and Reconnaissance." *Submarine Review*, September 2022.

Given, Deam W., and William Cashman. "'Whiskey' on the Rocks." USNI *Proceedings*, April 1982.

Goldstein, Lyle J., and Yuri M. Zhukov. "A Tale of Two Fleets: A Russian Perspective on the 1973 Naval Standoff in the Mediterranean." *Naval War College Review*, Spring 2004.

Gregory, William H. "Their Tattletales (Our Problems)." *USNI Proceedings*, February 1984.

Grulich, Fred. Comment on "Submarine Intelligence Gathering Operations." *Warship International*, no. 3 (2002).

Hollins, Hunter. "Cold War, North Korea, and United States Naval Intelligence." *War in History*, no. 3 (2018).

Karniol, Robert. "Russia Seeks to Keep SIGINT Link." *Jane's Defence Weekly*, 12 September 1992.

Kraska, James. "Putting Your Head in the Tiger's Mouth: Submarine Espionage in Territorial Waters." *Columbia Journal of Transnational Law*, no. 16 (2015).

Kurdin, Igor, and Wayne Grasdock. "Loss of a Yankee SSBN." *Submarine Review* pt. 1, October 2000; pt. 2, January 2001.

Mathers, Lee J., and Beauford E. Myers. "The Navy's Deep Ocean Grab." *Naval History*, February 2013.

McKeown, Robert E. "Their Merchant Fleet." USNI *Proceedings*, October 1982.

Miasnikov, Eugene. "Submarine Collision off Murmansk: A Look from Afar." *Submarine Review*, April 1993.

Mobley, Richard A. "EC-121 Down!" USNI *Proceedings*, August 2001.

———. "Lessons from the Capture of the USS *Pueblo* and the Shootdown of a US Navy EC-121—1968 and 1969." *Studies in Intelligence*, March 2015.

Nicholson, W. M. "Commentary: Truth Is in the Eye of the Beholder." USNI *Proceedings*, June 1995.

Nilsen, Thomas. "Spy Ship Changes Name and Continues Intelligence Mission." *Barents Observer*, 30 March 2016.

O'Neil, William D. "Journey to a Far Sea." USNI *Proceedings*, February 1982.

Plante, Trevor K. "'Two Japans': Japanese Expressions of Sympathy and Regret in the Wake of the *Panay* Incident." (National Archives) *Prologue Magazine*, Summer 2001.

Polmar, Norman. "American Spy Ships." USNI *Proceedings*, October 2003.

———. "How Many Spy Subs . . . ?" USNI *Proceedings*, December 1996.

———. "In the Wake of a Sunken Soviet Submarine." USNI *Proceedings*, December 2010.

———. "The Passing of Passive Intelligence Ships." *Navy* (England), November 1969.

———. "Search the Oceans." *USNI Proceedings*, January 1998.

———. “Space Ships.” USNI *Proceedings*, April 1988.

Richelson, Jeffery. “Soviet Ocean and Space Surveillance Activities.” In *The International Countermeasures Handbook*, 15th ed., edited by David Wise, 36–44. Englewood, Colo.: Cardiff, 1990.

Rule, R. Bruce. “Russian SSBNs—A ‘Dead Man’ Launch Capability?” *Submarine Review*, April 2012.

Streifer, Bill, and Irek Sabitov. “‘Improbable Allies’: The North Korean Downing of a U.S. Navy EC-121 and U.S.-Soviet Cooperation during the Cold War.” *Naval War College Review*, Spring 2020.

Stuart, George, and Linda Taylor. “The Soviet Naval Auxiliary Force.” In *The Soviet Navy: Strengths and Liabilities*, edited by Bruce Watson and Susan M. Watson, chap. 8. Boulder, Colo.: Westview, 1986.

Tolley, Kemp. “The Strange Mission of the *Lanikai*.” *American Heritage Magazine*, October 1973.

“Transcript of 2017 NSL History Seminar: The Hunt for Red October—Fact and Fiction.” *Submarine Review*, December 2017.

Wells, Anthony R. “*Liberty* Victims Did Not Die in Vain.” USNI *Proceedings*, March 2005.

Wicklund, Walter. “Whiskey on the Rocks.” *Naval Forces*, 1983.

Article in Japanese

The Japanese magazine *Ships of the World* (monthly) regularly publishes excellent photography and information on a variety of the world’s intelligence ships.

Articles in Russian

Aleksin, V. “Incidents in the Barents Sea.” *Morsky Sbornik* 5 (1992).

Bobkov, Boris, and Ivan Khurs. “Reconnaissance at Sea.” *Voyennaya mysl’*, no. 2 (1964). Translated and reprinted in a memorandum for the director of Central Intelligence. Subject: “Military Thought (USSR): Reconnaissance at Sea.” Washington DC: CIA, 17 June 1964.

Burbyga, Nikolay. “The Submarine from ‘Grave Bay.’” *Izvestiya*, 7 July 1992.

Kocherov, Vyacheslav, and Alexandr Mozgovoy. “The ‘Swedish Komsomolets’ Syndrome.” *Rossiyskaya Gazeta* pt. 1, 28 November 1992; pt. 2, 1 December 1992.

Korenevskiy, M. “Over the Side of the *Shch-211*.” *Krasnaya Zvezda*, 8 January 1966.

Maryukha, V. “American Submarines off Russia’s Northern Coasts.” *Krasnaya Zvezda*, 20 February 1992.

Zubko, Marat. “The Order Was to Blow Up the Submarine.” *Izvestiya*, 29 January 1992.

Published Government Reports

[Author name redacted]. “The Origination and Evaluation of Radio Traffic Analysis—Part 2: The Period between the Wars.” Doc ID 3362395. Fort George G. Meade MD: National Security Agency, 1986. https://webcache.googleusercontent.com/search?q=cache:YOBvLOJnY70J: https://www.nsa.gov/Portals/70/documents/news

-features/declassified-documents/cryptologic-quarterly/the_period_between_wars.pdf+&cd=2&hl=en&ct=clnk&gl=ca.

Alger, Julie. "A Review of the Technical Research Ship Program 1961–1969." Fort George G. Meade MD: National Security Agency, 1 May 1970. https://www.governmentattic.org/5docs/ReviewTechResearchShipPgm_1961-1969u.pdf.

Burtenshaw, Edward C., Dan D. Fulgham, and James W. Walls. "The Pueblo Incident." PACAF 68-DTE-00004. Hickam AFB HI: Headquarters Pacific Air Force, 15 April 1968. https://www.readcube.com/articles/10.21236%2Fada586301.

Central Intelligence Agency. "The Communist Bloc." CIA Daily Brief, 28 April 1960.

———. "Intelligence Memorandum Prepared in the Central Intelligence Agency, SC 08384–67, Washington DC, 21 June 1967." Central Intelligence Agency Files: Job 85–01007R, Box 5, Folder 50. Top Secret; Trine. Prepared in the Central Intelligence Agency's Directorate of Intelligence, Washington DC. Reprinted in Schwar, *Arab-Israeli Crisis and War*, memo 317. https://history.state.gov/historicaldocuments/frus1964-68v19/d317.

———. *Moscow's Fisheries Development Program in the Non-Communist Third World: The New Offensive*, GI 86-10039S. Washington DC: August 1986.

———. "North Korea Provokes New Confrontation," CIA Weekly Summary. Washington DC: 26 January 1968.

———. *Soviet Fishing in Third World Waters: Continued Gains Unlikely*, SOV 84-10170-X. Washington DC: October 1984.

———. *Soviet Naval Activity outside Home Waters during 1983*, SOV 84-10133CX. Washington DC: 1 August 1984.

———. *Soviet Naval Presence in the Indian Ocean*. Memorandum for Director. Washington DC: 14 December 1970.

———. *The Soviet Oceanographic Research Program*, SW 84–10007. Washington DC: February 1984.

———. *The Soviet Pacific Fishing Fleet: After More than Fish*, GI 82-10065. Washington DC: March 1982.

Committee on Armed Services, U.S. House of Representatives. "Inquiry into the USS *Pueblo* and EC-121 Plane Incidents." 91st Cong., 1st sess. Washington DC: 28 July 1969.

Evans, Thomas W., Commanding Officer, USS *Batfish* (SSN 681). "Report of Mission LS-26, March 2–May 17, 1978." Letter ser LS-26-D-0006-T-78, 17 May 1978.

Farley, Robert D. "Oral History Interview NSA OH-15–88 with LGEN Marshall S. Carter, 3 October 1988, Colorado Springs." Fort Meade MD: National Security Agency, 3 October 1988. https://www.nsa.gov/Portals/70/documents/news-features/declassified-documents/oral-history-interviews/NSA-OH-15-88-Carter.pdf.

Gerhard, William D., and Henry W. Millington. "Attack on a SIGINT Collector, the U.S.S. *Liberty* (S-CCO)." Special Research History SRH-256. Fort George G. Meade MD: National Security Agency, 1980. https://nsarchive2.gwu.edu/NSAEBB/NSAEBB24/nsa10.pdf.

Greenberg, Matti. "The Attack on the *Liberty* Incident." Tel Aviv: Israel Defense Forces History Department, ca. 1981.

Howe, George F. "Technical Research Ships, 1956–1969: An Historical Summary." Special series number 2. Doc ID 6586522. Fort George G. Meade MD: National Security Agency, Cryptographic History Program, 1965. https://archive.org/stream/TechnicalResearchShips/Technical%20research%20ships_djvu.txt.

Johnson, Thomas R. "Book II: Centralization Wins, 1960–1972." Of *American Cryptology during the Cold War, 1945–1989*, 289–611. Doc ID 523682. Fort George G. Meade MD: Cryptographic History Program, National Security Agency, 1995. https://www.scribd.com/document/171706327/American-Cryptology-During-the-Cold-War-2013-Release.

Minton, David C., III, Commanding Officer, USS *Guardfish* (SSN 612). "Trail of Soviet ECHO II Nuclear Submarine." Letter 612:LGV:sq 3840 Ser 00015–72. 10 June 1972.

National Photographic Interpretation Center. "Soviet Primorye-Class Intelligence Collection Ships," Z-14096/84. Washington DC: December 1984.

National Security Agency. "Aftermath of Israeli Attack on USS *Liberty*: Compiled Transcripts of Intercepted Israeli Helicopter Communications." SIGNIT Readiness Bravo "Crayon" Report NR. 2149, four sections. Fort George G. Meade MD: National Security Agency, 22 June 1967. https://fas.org/irp/nsa/liberty.pdf.

———. "Fact Sheet for Director, NSA—USS *Liberty* (AGTR)." Fort George G. Meade, Md.: National Security Agency, 12 June 1967. http://www.nsa.gov/liberty/51671/3086539.pdf.

———. "USS *Liberty* (USN-855) (AGTR-5): Chronology of Events." Fort George G. Meade MD: National Security Agency, 8 June 1967. https://www.nsa.gov/Portals/70/documents/news-features/declassified-documents/uss-liberty/chronology-events/chronology-events.pdf.

Naval Security Group. "Naval Security Group around the World 1986." https://navycthistory.com/images4/dirsup_1986big.jpg.

Newton, Robert E. "The Capture of the USS *Pueblo* and Its Effect on SIGINT Operations." Doc ID 3997429. Fort George G. Meade MD: Center for Cryptologic History, National Security Agency, 1992. https://nsarchive2.gwu.edu/NSAEBB/NSAEBB278/US_Cryptologic_History-The_Capture_of_the_USS_Pueblo.pdf.

Parker, Frederick D. "Pearl Harbor Revisited: United States Navy Communications Intelligence 1924–1941." Fort George G. Meade MD: National Security Agency, 1994. https://www.history.navy.mil/research/library/online-reading-room/title-list-alphabetically/p/pearl-harbor-revisited-usn-communications-intelligence/part-1.html.

Pfister, Donald Lee. "USS *Banner* (AGER 1): History for the Period September 1965 through December 1968." *Banner* Command History, letter 5720, 19 May 1969.

Rickover, H. G. "Naval Nuclear Propulsion Program, 1967–68." Hearings before the Joint Committee on Atomic Energy, Congress of the United States. Washington DC: Joint Committee on Atomic Energy, U.S. Congress, 1968.

Safford, Laurance F. "A Brief History of Communications Intelligence in the United States." Special Research History SRH 149. Washington DC: Department of the Navy, 1952. https://irp.fas.org/nsa/safford-2009.pdf.

Schratz, Paul R., Commanding Officer, USS *Pickerel* (SS 524). "Report of Reconnaissance Patrol off Amoy and Foochow Areas of China Coast to Report Any CHICOM Movement to Invade Taiwan." 2 August 1950.

Secretary of State for Defence (United Kingdom). *The Falklands Campaign: The Lessons.* London: Her Majesty's Stationery Office, December 1982.

Secretary of the Navy. *Lessons of the Falklands: Summary Report.* Washington DC: Department of the Navy, February 1983. https://apps.dtic.mil/sti/pdfs/ADA133333.pdf.

Smithsonian National Air and Space Museum. "Operation Moon Bounce." Indian Head MD: Naval Surface Warfare Center, 24 July 2016. https://airandspace.si.edu/stories/editorial/operation-moon-bounce.

Submarine Defence Commission. "Countering the Submarine Threat: Submarine Violations and Swedish Security Policy." Official Report Series 13. Stockholm: Ministry of Defence, 1983.

Wigglesworth, Donald C. "The Cuban Missile Crisis: A SIGINT Perspective [1984–85]." Doc ID: 3875445. Fort George G. Meade MD: National Security Agency, released 23 June 2011. https://www.nsa.gov/Portals/70/documents/news-features/declassified-documents/cryptologic-quarterly/Cuban_Missile_Crisis.pdf.

Yerushalmi, Yeshayahu. "Preliminary Inquiry File 1/67." Tel Aviv: Israel Court of Military Justice, 21 July 1967. http://gtr5.org/evidence/yerushalmi.html.

Commercially and Privately Published Reports

Global Marine Development Inc. *The Glomar Explorer: Deep Ocean Working Vessel, Technical Description and Specification.* Newport Beach CA: 1975.

Naval Cryptologic Veterans Association. *A History of Communications Intelligence in the United States with Emphasis on the United States Navy.* Denver CO: 1982.

Miscellaneous Documents Online

Cryptologic Heritage Hall of Honor. "2005 Hall of Honor Inductee: Rear Admiral Joseph N. Wenger, USN." National Security Agency, 2005. https://www.nsa.gov/History/Cryptologic-History/Historical-Figures/Historical-Figures-View/Article/1622379/rear-admiral-joseph-n-wenger-usn/.

Doyle, Joseph S. "The Yom Kippur War and the Shaping of the United States Air Force." Thesis, School of Advanced Air and Space Studies, Air University, Maxwell Air Force Base AL, June 2016. https://apps.dtic.mil/sti/pdfs/AD1030385.pdf.

Gustafson, John. "Shanghai, China (Station A) Moved to USS *Monocacy* (PG-20)—the Beginning." Station Hypo, 26 March 2016. https://stationhypo.com/2016/03/26/shanghai-china-station-a-moved-to-uss-monocacy-pg-20-the-beginning/.

Halliwell, K. J. "Sixth Fleet's Attempt to Defend *Liberty*." 6 August 2016. https://sites.google.com/site/usslibertyinquiry/essay30.

Havern, Christopher B., Sr. "Isabel (S. P. 521), 1917–1946." Washington DC: Naval History and Heritage Command, 10 August 2017. https://www.history.navy.mil/research/histories/ship-histories/danfs/i/isabel.html.

Kobke, Kent D. "The U.S.S. *Pueblo* Incident: Warning Cycle." Thesis, Defense Intelligence College, 1984.

Moorer, Thomas H., Raymond G. Davis, Merlin Staring, and James E. Akins. "Findings of the Independent Commission of Inquiry into the Israeli Attack on USS 'Liberty,' the Recall of Military Support Aircraft while the Ship Was under Attack, and the Subsequent Cover-up by the United States Government." 22 October 2003, Washington DC. https://en.wikisource.org/wiki/The_Moorer_Report.

National Security Agency/Central Security Service. "'B-Dienst' aboard U-boats." *German Naval Communications Intelligence*. Vol. 3 of *Battle of the Atlantic*. SRH-024. Washington DC: National Security Agency, chap. 5., n.d. https://www.ibiblio.org/hyperwar/ETO/Ultra/SRH-024/index.html#index.

———. "COMINT Stations Overseas." 20 August 2021. https://www.nsa.gov/History/Cryptologic-History/Historical-Events/Article-View/Article/2740660/comint-stations-overseas/.

Pearson, James W., and John Gustafson. "A Shipboard COMINT Mission: May 1933–June 1934." Station Hypo, 20 December 2019. https://stationhypo.com/2019/12/20/a-shipboard-comint-mission-may-1933-june-1934/.

Pike, John. "History of the Naval Security Group." Washington DC: Federation of American Scientists, updated 3 May 1997. https://fas.org/irp/agency/navsecgru/history.htm.

Rusk, [Dean]. "Telegram from Department of State to the Embassy in Israel," Washington, 8 June 1967, 2 p.m. National Archives and Records Administration, RG 59, Central Files 1967–69, POL 27 ARAB-ISR. Johnson Administration: State Department Documents from 1967 War (June 8–10, 1967), Item 215. https://www.jewishvirtuallibrary.org/state-department-documents-from-the-1967-war-june-1967-2.

Station Hypo. "A Sense of Urgency (1914–1941)!" 18 August 2018. https://stationhypo.com/2018/08/18/pre-wwii-comint-time-line-a-sense-of-urgency/.

Tooma, Sam. "Five Short Tales." USS *Banner* Anecdotes, tale #5. USS *Pueblo* (AGER 2). http://www.usspueblo.org/Background/BANNER_Tales.html.

U.S. Naval Cryptologic Veterans Association. "The Birth of Cryptologic Direct Support." 21 April 2021. https://www.usncva.org/ct-rating-history.html.

Vulcano, Mario. "SIGINT Collection Ships, Part 5 of 8—Soviet Exercise off Norway." Station Hypo, 6 August 2020. https://stationhypo.com/2020/08/06/sigint-collection-ships-part-5-of-8-soviet-fleet-exercise-off-norway/.

GENERAL INDEX

SHIP AND SUBMARINE INDEX

U.S. Navy and Coast Guard ships are identified by hull number.